THE AGE OF EQUALITY

THE AGE OF EQUALITY

The Twentieth Century in Economic Perspective

✦

RICHARD POMFRET

The Belknap Press of
Harvard University Press
Cambridge, Massachusetts
London, England
2011

Library of Congress Cataloging-in-Publication Data

Pomfret, Richard W. T.
The age of equality : the twentieth century in economic perspective / Richard Pomfret.
p.   cm.
Includes bibliographical references and index.
ISBN 978-0-674-06217-7 (alk. paper)
1. Economic history—20th century.   2. Equality—History—20th century.
3. Free enterprise—History—20th century.   4. Globalization—History—
20th century.   I. Title.
HC54.P638   2011
330.9'04—dc22   2011014351

Contents

Preface

This is a book about the recent past. It is based on the premise that we can better understand the present by examining the past, which is the only data source we have about how the world works. It is also based on the premise that the most important developments take time to unfold. When asked two centuries after the event whether the French Revolution was a good thing, Chinese prime minister Zhou Enlai replied that it was too soon to tell.

This book starts with the French Revolution of 1789 and the roughly contemporary industrial revolution in Britain, and examines how a global economy emerged and how it has affected our lives. As a unifying theme it takes the French revolutionary mantra *Liberté, Egalité, Fraternité,* arguing that the century after peace was established in Europe in 1815 was the age when liberty was central, both in politics and in economics. The nineteenth century illustrated how levels of economic prosperity could be multiplied at unprecedented rates by a combination of technical change and capital formation driven by market signals in an appropriate institutional setting. The twentieth century was dominated by alternative visions of how to share the fruits of economic prosperity within and between countries, and this book centers on the Age of Equality. Whether the twenty-first century will be the age of fraternity is an open question, but in a world with weapons of mass destruction the alternative is likely to be grim.

Attaching three simple concepts to three centuries is, of course, a gross simplification of the complexity of history, but some organization is essential. Others have different organizing principles. A popular approach, used for example by Broadberry and O'Rourke (2010), breaks the twentieth century into a sequence of globalization to 1914, deglobalization between 1914 and 1950, and reglobalization after 1950. The transitions in this sequence, however, are best explained by systemic responses—whether communism or fascism or the ultimate winner, open, market-based economies with welfare states—to the challenge posed by unprecedented productive potential and the unacceptable degree of associated inequality.

Characterizing the twentieth century as the Age of Equality is intended to capture the main driving force behind long-term economic evolution in the 1900s. I am definitely not claiming that it was a century of equality. Indeed, apart from the 1917 revolution in Russia, actual steps toward reducing inequality within and across nations only gathered serious momentum in the second half of the century. Even in the final decades of the century, there were diverging patterns. Rapid growth in China, India, and other emerging market economies was reducing inequality of outcomes globally. At the same time, in some of the richest countries incomes were becoming more unequal as the global economy provided massive rewards to some innovators and financiers and the income gap between more highly educated and less-skilled workers widened; education is available to all, but not all citizens benefit equally.

At the end of the Age of Equality we live in a world in which the distribution of wealth is far from equal. In 2010, 3 billion individuals, more than two-thirds of the world's adult population, had net assets worth under $10,000, while the 24 million dollar millionaires accounted for less than 1 percent of the global adult population but owned more than a third of the world's household wealth (Credit Suisse, 2010); of these millionaires 41 percent lived in the United States, 32 percent in Europe, 10 percent in Japan, 4 percent in Canada, 3 percent in China, 3 percent in Australia, and 7 percent in the rest of the world. Capgemini (2010), with a narrower definition, that is, a million dollars of investable assets excluding the home, estimated about 10 million millionaires, of whom 3.1 million lived in the United States, 3.0 million in Europe, and 3.0 million in the Asia-Pacific region. In the United States, books titled *Richistan* (Frank, 2007) and *Superclass* (Rothkopf, 2008) became best sellers.

The new rich in the United States are very rich; for example, in the early twenty-first century each of Sam Walton's five children has greater net wealth in real terms than the first U.S. billionaire, John D. Rockefeller, had a hundred years earlier. Another striking feature is that although old money is still around, the new rich are mostly there by their own efforts; in the United States about two-fifths made their wealth as entrepreneurs and about two-fifths by rising up the management ladder in major companies—sports and entertainment millionaires are a highly visible, but small number. To a substantial degree the rich in the early twenty-first century are products of more equal opportunity, although there may be fears that the new rich are skewing future equality of opportunity by giving their children a head start. Nevertheless, the extent to which governments are concerned about inequality, and intervene to promote it, is in striking contrast to a century earlier, as is the extent of the safety net for those at the other end of the wealth distribution in high-income countries.

Similarly, characterizing the twenty-first century as the age of fraternity may, a decade into that century, appear discordant. The current world situation has many examples of unfraternal behavior and failures of international cooperation. However, the final chapter argues that there are powerful forces pushing toward a more cooperative and less nationalistic global environment during the twenty-first century and that by 2100 the world will have entered an age of fraternity.

Economies and societies are complex and no two are the same, but in seeking to draw systemic characteristics it is useful to define identifying concepts. In this book "planning" and "market-based" are shorthand for the dominant resource allocation mechanism in an economy. In traditional, precapitalist economies much allocation is by custom underpinned by power, but in a market-based economy resources are allocated in response to price signals and in a planned economy resources are allocated by state officials. In the political sphere I use "liberal democracy" as shorthand for a system in which individual rights are valued and respected (as in nineteenth-century "liberalism") and people have a say in the choice of government, although there are many variants of how rights are protected (and which rights are valued) and of how governments are chosen. Finally, I use the term "welfare state" to describe a situation in which the government takes steps to promote equality of opportunity and outcome in a market-based economy; market outcomes may be modified by prohibitions (e.g., banning parents from keeping children out of school) or by incentives (e.g., tax breaks for retirement savings). I appreciate that words such as "liberal" and "welfare" can mean different things in British and American English and to people of differing beliefs, but hope that readers will accept the labels in this book as descriptive terms.

Many people read earlier drafts of the book and offered helpful comments. I am especially grateful to Ian McDonald, Ian McLean, and Tom Sheridan for providing detailed written comments on the entire manuscript. Several generations of international students at the University of Adelaide (and Steven Barrett as co-lecturer) helped to sharpen the arguments. My agent, Andrew Schuller, helped to guide the manuscript to Harvard University Press, where Mike Aronson was a critical but enthusiastic editor. Kathleen Drummy was a pleasure to work with as the editorial assistant in Cambridge, as was Barbara Goodhouse, the editor at Westchester Book Services responsible for seeing *The Age of Equality* through the production process. My thanks go to all of the above people, and to anonymous readers. I appreciated Elsevier's non-bureaucratic process for granting permission to use the figure from Jay L. Zagorsky, "Was Depression Era Unemployment Really Less in Canada Than the U.S.?" published in *Economics Letters*. Finally, I benefited from the use of facilities at my home institution, the University of Adelaide, at the Centre d'Economie de la Sorbonne in Paris (special thanks to Boris Najman and to Mathilde Maurel for arranging my status as visiting fellow in the Globalisation and Development Department), and at the Johns Hopkins University Bologna Center, where I spent the 2010–11 academic year (special thanks to Mike Plummer, Barb Wiza, Gail Martin, and John Williams).

I have aimed to write for the general reader. There is little formal exposition of economic theories, although growth and trade theory in particular underlie much of the analysis, and there is no rigorous discussion of data issues. Most of the quoted numbers on income levels and economic growth are from Maddison (2006); as Maddison himself stressed, no historical estimates are definitive and the point of any book such as his is to challenge revision, but for the moment his book remains the best single compendium of our quantitative knowledge. For the purpose of the present book, it seemed better to be consistent in citing from a common source than to enter into detailed data debates.

Where I am simply drawing on a published source, the reference is in parentheses; longer bibliographical details are in endnotes. I have also used the endnotes to provide entry points into controversies and to offer digressions or extensions to points in the text. The guiding principle was to keep the text as readable as possible without neglecting the need to justify statements or provide sources.

Introduction

✦

The twentieth century saw the transformation of our world from one where most people's lives were short and spent living at close to subsistence level to one where the majority enjoy unprecedented material well-being and greater longevity. In 1900 life expectancy at birth was in the mid-forties in Western Europe, North America, and Japan, in the thirties in Russia and Latin America, and a mere 24 in China and India; the world average was 31 years. By 2000 the average life expectancy at birth was 66 years, with life expectancy around 80 in the high-income countries, 71 in China, and 60 in India. The global average is pulled down by Africa's average of 52, but even there, life expectancy doubled over the twentieth century. The magnitude of the change, as with estimates of material well-being, is massive and unprecedented.[1]

This book tells the story of that transformation. The modern economy was shaped by economic and political events in Western Europe. The economic changes commonly known as the industrial revolution involved the use of new technologies to accelerate the division of labor and investment in machinery and equipment to increase the productivity of labor. The institutional counterpart was capitalism: remove restrictions on enterprise and the market mechanism would deliver economic growth through the invisible hand as described by Adam Smith in his 1776 *Inquiry into the Nature and Causes of the Wealth of Nations*. The moral component of Smith's theory is that pursuit of individual self-interest is compatible with desirable social outcomes, as long as it occurs within an appropriate institutional and legal framework.

The nineteenth century opened with just one major economic power, the United Kingdom, whose victory over Napoleon's France decisively illustrated that economic power was the basis for political power; in a long war, modern industry would prevail over numbers or military skill.[2] By 1900 most of northwestern and Central Europe as well as the European-settled lands of North America was industrializing, and a global economy dominated by those countries had been created. Despite two world wars and other traumatic upheavals, the twentieth century ultimately saw the economic benefits spread more widely within the rich countries and across the globe.

Dividing history into periods is always too simple. The industrial revolution that occurred in northwestern Europe and enabled that small and previously backward part of the globe to briefly rule over most of the world had its origins in the way that Western Europe emerged from the premodern economy based on land and regulated urban occupations.[3] The Renaissance with its questioning of faith and the scientific revolution were crucial prerequisites for the emergence of technical change as a driver of economic prosperity. The philosophers of the Enlightenment laid the intellectual basis for the replacement of kings by elected representatives and for rewarding achievement rather than by birthright.[4] The "age of discovery," when navigators from Portugal and Italy charted the globe, provided the geographical knowledge behind the later creation of the global economy and imperialism. Political fragmentation enabled competition and innovation in economic, financial, and social organization, such that the conservative weight of the great dynastic empires was undermined by upstarts such as Italian city-states, the Netherlands, and England. All of these preliminaries were essential, but they came together dramatically in the industrial revolution in Britain after the 1760s and in the political revolution in France in 1789.

The industrial revolution was quantitatively and qualitatively different from anything that had come before. The surge in global trade that began in the second half of the 1700s accelerated after the end of the Napoleonic wars in 1815. European wars largely sheltered the rest of the world from these changes until 1815, but after that the path to a global economy dominated by Europe and its offshoots was straightforward. The fact that it was led by the triangular trade of Britain exporting cotton textiles, importing raw cotton from the Caribbean and North America, and supplying labor for the plantations by exporting slaves from West Africa highlighted the intercontinental nature of trade in the 1700s. After the 1820s European long-run growth reached unprecedented rates, and sustained growth gradually spread east and south from the starting points in England, Scotland, Belgium, and northern France. The huge edge that the leaders had is apparent from the spread of the British and French empires (at a time when Spain's was shrinking) and from Belgium's ability to exploit the Congo, a resource-rich part of Africa larger than all of Western Europe.

Growth rates were not only high, but were also sustained, and the key to this was evidence-based technical and institutional change. In each country, after its initial industrial revolution, savings rates and investment rates increased. Financial systems emerged to increase the efficiency with which the savings were allocated among investment projects. Financial intermediation was also a potential source of instability (financial crises were severe and not infrequent in the 1800s) and led to the phenomenon of business cycles (as opposed to the natural disasters and bad harvests that caused economic downturns in preindustrial economies). Nevertheless, despite increased insecurity and instability, the post–industrial revolution economy delivered long-run rising living standards for the majority of the population. The Malthusian cycle had been definitively broken, for the first time in history, in Western Europe after the mid-1800s.[5] Over the next century and a half, this outcome would spread across the globe to country after country (Table I.1).[6]

The next chapter sets the scene by reviewing the century after 1815, which was a period of unprecedented economic expansion and the first time that economic growth became self-sustaining. Capitalism spread by settlement of sparsely populated areas (North America, Siberia, Australasia, temperate and subtropical South America, and southern Africa), by conquest, and by enforced opening of more densely populated parts of Asia. By the century's end there were several economic powers, although still concentrated in Europe and in lands settled by Europeans. In 1900 the globe was subdivided into these countries'

Table I.1 Per capita output by region at constant purchasing power, 1000–1998

	1000	1500	1820	1870	1913	1950	1973	1998
Western Europe	400	774	1,232	1,974	3,473	4,594	11,534	17,921
Western offshoots	400	400	1,201	2,431	5,257	9,288	16,172	26,146
East Europe & Russia	400	483	667	917	1,501	2,601	5,729	4,354
Latin America	400	416	665	698	1,511	2,554	4,531	5,795
Japan	425	500	669	737	1,387	1,926	11,439	20,413
Asia excluding Japan	450	572	575	543	640	635	1,231	2,936
Africa	416	400	418	444	585	852	1,365	1,368
World	*435*	*565*	*667*	*867*	*1,510*	*2,114*	*4,104*	*5,709*

Source: Maddison (2006, 126).

Notes: The units are 1990 international dollars (approximately what could be purchased for a U.S. dollar in 1990). "Western offshoots" are the United States, Canada, Australia, and New Zealand. The earlier estimates are based on conjecture (e.g., an assumed value of $400 for hunter-gatherer societies), but the order of magnitude of changes after 1820 is indisputable.

empires and spheres of influence, and the world economy was driven by market forces, reinforced by gunboats and a stable means of exchange.

Freedom in political and economic relations was associated with and given moral legitimacy by the philosophy of liberalism in the sense of Locke, Hume, and Kant: any individual should be free to act and think as they please, as long as nobody else is harmed. The French Revolution and the subsequent spread of republican ideas challenged absolute political power and privilege based on birth, and, even after the defeat of Napoleon and restoration of hereditary monarchs in 1815, the rights of individuals continued to gain ground across Europe over the next century. The economic counterpart to political liberty was the incursion of economic freedom into markets previously dominated by feudalism and guilds. The rise of market-based economies, with freely agreed prices and contracts, demanded individual freedom to respond to price signals and a rule of law to protect property rights, rather than having military power or traditional influence determine the division of spoils. The 1800s saw the spread of market relations and economic liberalism through Western Europe and across the globe.

The nineteenth century was the Age of Liberty as the concepts of individual rights and democracy, gradually and with many setbacks, triumphed over a stubborn *ancien régime*. The principle was spelled out by John Stuart Mill (1859, 22): "The only purpose for which power can be rightfully exercised over any member of a civilized community, against his will, is to prevent harm to others." The practice was, of course, far from the ideals, even in the most democratic states; for example, women did not have the right to vote.[7] The triumph of individual rights and democracy was most complete in the United States, where precapitalist forces were weak and immigrants from Europe were largely self-selected seekers after fortune or at least a comfortable economic situation freed from oppressive government and class divisions, but even in the United States people of African or Asian origin had limited civil rights. Nevertheless, the situation in Europe and areas settled by Europeans was by 1914 dramatically different from a century earlier. The last major despotic regimes were overthrown in China in 1911 and in Russia in February 1917, and the German, Austro-Hungarian, and Ottoman emperors were deposed in 1918.

From an economic perspective, the Age of Liberty peaked in the decade before 1914. Global output was higher than ever before. The economic success of capitalist economies swept away feudalism. In the industrializing economies, enlightened members of the aristocracy and the growing middle class pushed reforms to increase equality of opportunity in the economic sphere; restraints on trade and inherited privileges were reduced, and educational opportunities for disadvantaged children and urban working and living conditions were improved.[8] Capitalism was criticized by conservatives who valued the stability and ethos of the precapitalist world and worried about the disruption of the established order and threat to religion from the new emphasis on individual liberty. Yearning for a preindustrial past continues to this day, but in the long run such reactionary thinking was no match for the material plenty offered by a modern capitalist economy.

A different and more potent criticism focused on the inequality within the industrialized countries and between parts of the world, which could be blamed on capitalism. By its nature, the market mechanism relies on inequality of outcomes: the prospect of higher incomes encourages work, innovation, entrepreneurship, and so forth, and those who do not respond or who make the wrong decisions receive less income. Socialist critics of capitalism, demanding systemic change to ensure greater equality of outcomes, quickly appeared; Marx and Engels published the *Communist Manifesto* in 1848.

The crude nineteenth-century views of anarchists or socialists who saw capitalism as evil and opposed private property rights had little impact once it became clear that workers in the industrialized countries enjoyed having access to material comfort and convenience.[9] The urban working classes saw their living standards increase, and the attraction of earning wages that allowed discretionary spending beyond basic needs was a big factor behind the massive rural-urban migration. In the English industrial heartlands of Lancashire and the West Midlands, by the late 1800s sporting events attracted large crowds, diets could be improved and kitchen drudgery reduced by visiting the fish and chip shop, work could be forgotten at the pub, and mobility was increased by a tram trip or bike ride or even a train trip to the seaside.[10] The two-up two-down workers' housing without indoor plumbing seems primitive by today's perspective, but was superior to many farmworkers' living conditions. Nevertheless, the distribution of income and wealth became increasingly unequal. This trend peaked in the decade before 1914. Even in the most industrialized nation, Britain, "an army of well over a million domestic servants" (Mingay, 1986, 51) was in the late 1800s the second-largest occupational group after agricultural laborers.[11] Both of these occupations have now virtually disappeared in Britain.

Inequality between different parts of the world was massive. Various responses to inequality dominated world history in the twentieth century; the global conflict between established and rising powers between 1914 and 1945, decolonization and anti-imperialism after 1945, and the epic struggle between central planning and capitalism that began with the 1917 Russian Revolution and lasted until the end of the Cold War in 1989. The last of these highlights the connection between balancing economic prosperity and equality at the domestic level and systemic tensions in the global economy.

The Age of Liberty ended in 1914 with military conflict among the European powers, followed by three decades of war and disillusionment with the working of market-based systems. The global economy was fractured as elements of a restored pre-1914 economy coexisted with a malfunctioning financial system, generalized depression after 1928, and the creation of conflicting trade blocs. Emphasis on constitutional rights rather than social responsibilities seemed inappropriate to many in the post-1918 world, and the liberal democracies were slow to respond to the challenge of inequality. The Russian Empire withdrew from the global system after 1917 and established socialism in one country. Elsewhere in Europe, liberal democracies appeared weak, falling like dominoes from 1917 to 1940 as country after country turned to authoritarian leaders, some of whom embraced traditional bases of authority such as the established church or the monarchy, while others were more radical in their rejection of inherited privilege and claims to represent the national will. Most importantly for world history, in the 1930s Germany and Japan adopted fascist economic and political systems and pursued nationalist goals to gain *Lebensraum* in Eastern Europe or to create a Greater East Asia Co-Prosperity Sphere.

The period 1917–1940 appeared as an era of authoritarian governments; Chapter 2 analyzes the era in the noncommunist world, and Chapter 3 analyzes the Soviet economic model, which would after 1945 be the major competitor to market-based economies.

The nationalist expansionism of Germany and Japan was opposed by a grand alliance of the United Kingdom, the United States, and the Union of Soviet Socialist Republics. Both Germany and Japan were defeated, and fascism was discredited. A more or less clean sheet was opened in 1945 with the end of World War II and explicit attempts to create a better world order by the two main victors, the United States and the Soviet Union. The central economic controversy was over whether to modify market outcomes or to reject the market mechanism altogether with central planning and abolition of private property rights.

The conflict had been addressed in the 1800s on the ideological level by Marx and on a practical level by Bismarck's attempts to introduce a welfare state (e.g., state pensions for those too old to earn their keep) in Germany. However, the German experiment went down the dead-end street of fascism, a corporatist economic system in which individual rights are subordinated to the needs of the nation as represented by a charismatic leader. Marxist theory became the ideology of governments after Russia's October 1917 revolution, and Russia's victory in World War II gave legitimacy to central planning, which was exported to Eastern Europe after 1945 and copied in the 1950s by China, North Korea, and Cuba, as well as influencing many other new independent countries. Whereas the progressive movement in the nineteenth century had been toward market relationships and private property rights, the dominant feature of the twentieth century was a reaction against the inequalities associated with pure capitalism. The twentieth century was an Age of Equality.

The market economies of Western Europe, North America, and Australasia tried to address the equity issue by reducing the worst inequalities of capitalism, especially after the depression of the 1930s. In the quarter-century after 1945, governments implemented and extended unemployment insurance and other social security programs for the elderly and disabled, while free or heavily subsidized education and health care were extended to an increasing proportion of the population. The specifics of the welfare state varied from country to country, but the general principle was to soften the distributional consequences of capitalism through public intervention and social programs while retaining democratic governments and respect for individual liberty. Chapter 4 describes how these changes occurred in the context of a long economic boom from 1948 to 1973 that was accompanied by reestablishment of a global economy, monitored and guided by multilateral institutions that provided a framework for market-driven international economic relations while recognizing that governments would be active in addressing domestic issues such as unemployment.

The alternative visions of central planning and the welfare state set the major conflict of the twentieth century. The conflict between communism and capitalism became global in the third quarter of the twentieth century. As the old colonial empires disintegrated, many new independent states attempted to promote economic development with equity. Liberation movements in Asia, Africa, and Latin America largely accepted the view that capitalism had impoverished the periphery, and after gaining power they were attracted to socialism. China in 1949, Cuba after 1959, and Vietnam in the 1970s adopted the Soviet model, while influential new independent states like India or new modernizing regimes as in Egypt adopted planning with less extreme changes in the ownership of the means of production. Chapter 5 demonstrates that countries which sought to insulate themselves from the global economy by promoting import-substituting industrialization achieved short-term increases in growth as resources were mobilized, but in the long term the planned and semiplanned economies stagnated due to declining efficiency. By the 1970s an alternative model of outward-oriented development based on specialization in labor-intensive manufactured goods was being recognized as dramatically successful in a handful of East Asian new industrializing economies.[12]

During the 1960s there was much talk of systemic convergence: capitalist economies would have more intervention in the name of equality, while communist economies would admit a larger role to the market in the name of efficiency. Examples of such convergence were the wide-ranging welfare state in Scandinavia and indicative planning in France, as well as the Great Society in Johnson's America, or a middle way in the United Kingdom of Macmillan and Wilson and the policies of Trudeau in Canada, or the 1966–1969 Grand Coalition in Germany. Market-oriented reforms were actively debated in Eastern Europe at least until the Czech experiment of 1968, although actual reforms amounted to no more than minor tinkering. The hybrid system of workers' self-management in Yugoslavia seemed an interesting middle way, but, as in other economies with central allocation of capital, economic efficiency was compromised.

After 1968 there was a retreat from the middle way, and the division between planned economies and market economies became wider. In the market economies, Nixon in 1968, de Gaulle in 1969, and Heath in 1970 each won closely fought elections in the United States, France, and the United Kingdom, respectively, by arguing against the center and in favor of less-regulated market forces. Systemic reforms were forestalled in the 1970s by pressure to find short-term responses to major macroeconomic shocks such as the breakdown of the international monetary system based on fixed exchange rates, the 1973–1974 oil shock, and the uncharted macroeconomic landscape of slow growth plus high inflation. After 1979, however, the Thatcher government in Britain and the Reagan administration in the United States pursued ideological attacks on the modification of capitalism by government regulation, public ownership, and the welfare state. The lasting legacy of this conservative reaction was to demonstrate the merits of the market in allocating resources and the potential costs of distorting the process through excessive regulations or state ownership. However, attacks on the welfare state were not sustained, and were even reversed in the 1990s. Chapter 6 analyzes this episode, emphasizing the consensus position around which most political debates in high-income countries now revolve; despite the rhetoric of some right-wing politicians, nobody seriously advocates untrammelled capitalism with no public support for the disadvantaged. The closest to a pure capitalist model was the British colony of Hong Kong between 1945 and 1997, but even there the government provided public housing and subsidized education and health care.

After the mid-1960s the USSR under Brezhnev closed down reform in Czechoslovakia and became increasingly hostile toward reform anywhere in the communist world. Even the reform leader in Eastern Europe, Hungary, did not progress far in the 1970s.[13] After the death of Tito in 1980 and Brezhnev in 1982, there was pressure for economic change in Yugoslavia, the USSR and Eastern Europe, but it was resisted by, for example, the imposition of martial law in Poland in December 1981. When convergence did eventually occur in Europe after 1989, it was a one-way street as formerly centrally planned economies and the workers' self-managed Yugoslav economy all embraced market-oriented systems—in some cases more enthusiastically than Western Europe. The collapse of the centrally planned economies, dissolution of the Soviet Union, and transition to more market-based economies are analyzed in Chapter 7.

The final quarter of the twentieth century saw a universal movement away from state control over resource allocation, primarily because of its proven failure in achieving higher material welfare. The trend to liberalization in poor countries accelerated after the 1982 debt crisis, whose impact was especially strong in Latin America. China's shift away from central planning after 1978, with the dissolution of the large collective farms and opening up of the economy to foreign trade and investment, was a major signal, but even that was overshadowed by the collapse of communism in Eastern Europe in the second half of 1989 and then in 1991 the dissolution of the USSR. Reforms in South Asia in the early 1990s followed by the awakening of the Indian Tiger reinforced the pattern. By the end of the 1990s there had been a global rejection of central planning apart from a few minor holdouts (Cuba and North Korea) and a positive embracing of market mechanisms.

In the half-century before 1945, there were two successful transformations from economic backwardness: the USSR and Japan. When after 1945 dozens of countries became independent or came under the rule of new modernizing regimes, they were strongly influenced by the economic success of the USSR and neglected Japan whose economy lay in ruins after military defeat. Yet the economic miracles of the second half of the twentieth century were Japan and a succession of East Asian countries that began to follow Japan's model of outward-oriented capitalism after the early 1960s. After the success of these new industrialized economies was recognized in the late 1970s, a long and inconclusive debate took place over the role of governments in their success, but there is no question that they are market-based economies in which people respond to price signals and that have benefited from integration into the global economy. The new industrialized economies of South Korea, Taiwan, Singapore, Malaysia, and Thailand combine individual liberty and a welfare state, but in cultural contexts that differ from Europe or countries settled by Europeans. Chapter 8 analyzes the systems of these new industrialized economies as well as the transformation of Latin America since 1982 and asks why some countries still do not benefit from the prosperity offered by the economic developments of the last two centuries.

The great economic experiment of the twentieth century—central planning to promote the greater economic good—has been decisively abandoned, and by the end of the century market economies ruled, but there was no wish to return to the unbridled capitalism and gross inequality of the early twentieth century. All market economies, even nakedly capitalist Hong Kong and newly capitalist Russia where some people have become very rich, have extensive government involvement intended to counter inequality of opportunity and of outcome in a market-based economy. The existence of inequality at the end of the Age of Equality reflects acceptance of a compromise between a market economy based on unequal returns and government intervention to modify that process; the welfare state funded by taxation made capitalism palatable, without necessitating the end of liberty.

In the twenty-first century the world is moving on to address issues related to life in a common space. Supranationality is increasing on a regional level, most notably in Europe where European Union law supersedes member states' national laws. At the same time communities are demanding more say over local affairs, whether by seceding from nation-states in which they feel uncomfortable or by resisting rules imposed by a distant government in Beijing or Washington or Moscow. The challenge will be to find a political system that can respond at many levels while retaining the achievements of the last two centuries in the form of a market-based global economy modified by effective measures to promote equality of opportunity (e.g., through accessible education) and equality of outcome (e.g., through targeted assistance to those unable to benefit from or unavoidably hurt by the market economy and through more equal health outcomes).

At the global level, the United Nations institutionalizes tolerance of national, racial, and other differences. Although racism and other forms of intolerance are far from being eliminated, it is a different world from 1919 when the Great Powers refused to accept a Japanese suggestion that the League of Nations Charter should include a phrase about racial equality. Global issues such as exploitation of the oceans or climate change are generating a cooperative response, even though individual countries may resist unwanted limitations on their autonomy. The responsibility to protect is invoked to justify outside intervention in "failed states" where citizens' rights are not respected. Rights of individuals, which were won in the Age of Liberty and curtailed by totalitarian regimes in the Age of Equality, will need to be balanced against the spirit of community in the Age of Fraternity.

CHAPTER 1

The Age of Liberty

.✳.

The complex of innovations and institutional changes that formed the industrial revolution of the late 1700s was crucial to the development of a global economy. Writing in 1776, Adam Smith already identified in the first chapter of *The Wealth of Nations* that the division of labor was crucial to economic progress. This was a truism that applied back in the days of hunters and gatherers or to the urban revolution of five millennia ago, but the distinctive feature of the late 1700s was the breakdown of tasks and the application of mechanical technology. The key application was in the textile industry, where spinning machines could produce many times more yarn than an individual operating a spinning wheel and weaving machines produced far more cloth than a handloom weaver and workers in the textile mills performed specialized tasks to ensure maximum use of and output from the machines.

The machines were initially driven by waterpower, which helps to explain the location of the first modern textile mills in Lancashire and especially in the valleys through which water rushed down from the Pennine Hills. Waterpower is, however, not always reliable, and a next step was to develop alternative sources of power, notably the steam engine. The steam engine could be fueled by wood or charcoal, but coal was more efficient, and by happy coincidence coal was plentiful in southern Lancashire. Manufacturing the textile machinery was first done by local blacksmiths, who were the people most skilled in metalworking, but as the industry expanded specialist machine-makers emerged and they in turn demanded high-quality iron. By the early 1800s the industrial revolution encompassed a complex of new technology in textiles, machinery, iron, and steam engines.

Why did the first industrial revolution occur in Britain? To a greater extent than in continental Europe, property rights were guaranteed by law, rather than being subject to the king's whim; the political revolution of the 1640s when King Charles I was beheaded and the restoration of the monarchy in the 1660s under strict control by parliament represented the defeat of absolute monarchy and the old economic system and led to establishment of institutions favorable to entrepreneurship. Geographical features may have also played a role in Britain's priority, such as the ready access to seaports and the lack of timber, which led to exploitation of coal, which turned out to have superior technical properties as a fuel. The industrial revolution was preceded by an agricultural revolution in which progressive farmers, embracing a scientific approach and controlled experiments, increased agricultural productivity, thus allowing the release of labor that moved to the new factories without loss of agricultural output, as well as the accumulation of capital that could be lent to industrial entrepreneurs. Domestic savings may have been augmented by capital from the British Empire, although the extent to which exploitation of the colonies funded the industrial revolution is controversial.[1] In sum, there are many possible explanations, but here the focus will be on the consequences rather than the causes of the industrial revolution.

An important example of good institutions was the development of a relatively sophisticated banking system. English banks outside London (the "country banks") formed a national financial network that traded loans through London intermediaries, collecting the savings of wealthy farmers in southern England and the east Midlands and lending them to entrepreneurs in northern England and the west Midlands. In 1750 there were virtually no country banks, by 1800 there were 300, and by 1815 there were 650. Some country banks were more like modern venture capital firms; Praed Co. of Truro, for example, was heavily engaged in financing the adoption of Watt steam engines, a risky new technology, in the period 1775–1800 (Brunt, 2006). Thus, the country banks not only intermediated between savers and borrowers to their mutual benefit, but some also made high-risk loans that accelerated the spread of new technologies but might sometimes lead to bank failures. The role of the financial sector in channeling resources into productivity-increasing investments is a key feature of a well-functioning market economy, but its presence adds to volatility. Financial intermediation underlay the emergence of business cycles, as changes in demand from entrepreneurs was more volatile than changes in the supply of savings, and inadequate aggregate demand had a multiplied impact on real output.[2] Financial intermediation also increased the probability and severity of crises, as people borrowed to fund what turned out to be speculative purchases and eventually led to large losses when the mania turned to panic.[3]

The rapid productivity increase due to the division of labor was limited by the size of the market. Initially the textiles produced in the new cotton and woolen mills were sold in southern England, but to take full advantage of the opportunities for specialization and mechanization the industry needed ever larger markets. Once the Napoleonic wars were ended and peace was established in 1815, British textiles were sold across the world. By 1820 cotton products accounted for 62 percent of British exports, from almost zero fifty years earlier (Maddison, 2006, 98). Trade was important for increasing the market, but also for inputs—cotton is not grown in the United Kingdom.[4]

The products of the industrial revolution conquered the world in the century after 1815. The huge increases in productivity ensured that factory-produced textiles could undercut the price of handmade textiles even after paying transport and other trade costs. Industrial goods also offered consistent quality and greater choice. In competitive markets, the most successful firms beat their rivals by supplying an attractive range of products. As early as the 1760s the English potter Josiah Wedgwood employed designers to create products targeted at various income levels, from the queen of England and the empress of Russia to the growing middle class. Even in small domestic markets, once the guild system of regulated production had broken down talented entrepreneurs, such as the Arabia pottery company in Finland after 1873, created attractive product lines ranging from luxury goods to simple tableware.

Beyond the improvement in necessities such as cloth or food utensils, the industrial revolution created an environment in which entirely new products were made available to a wide range of consumers. The adaptation of steam power to transport by railway and ship played a major part in creating a global economy, while invention and mass production of bicycles increased individual mobility over shorter distances. The use of gas and later electricity for lighting and power transformed people's lives. Other developments democratized what had been luxury goods; for example, cigarette factories spread tobacco consumption, and matches provided a simple method of lighting cigarettes. The sewing machine, perfected in the 1850s by Isaac Singer and others, not only revolutionized the commercial clothing industry but also allowed home production of fashionable clothing, based on cheap textiles and paper patterns, or of curtains and other household effects. The great expansion of household appliances would come in the twentieth century, but already by 1914 household interiors in the high-income countries would be recognizable to a time traveler from today in a way that most people's living conditions before 1750 would not be.

In the last half-century before 1914, a global economy was created, reflecting a search for materials and markets by the industrial countries. It featured large labor flows to settle "empty" countries, as well as to meet the needs of the global economy (e.g., migration within Asia brought workers and merchants to areas where they were lacking), and large capital flows, especially to provide infrastructure such as railways. The mechanism driving these movements of goods, people, and capital was differences in market-determined prices, albeit with often huge imbalances in market power and where outcomes were enforced unilaterally by the military power of rich countries.

Global incomes increased faster than ever before in history, but were unevenly distributed both across countries and within countries. From 1820 until the mid-1800s economic growth was highest in Britain and Belgium, and in economies settled by British migrants. Some of the spread effects worked through demand for food and raw materials, but as the century progressed, the new technologies and industrial organization spread across Europe and beyond. After 1870 industrial output grew especially rapidly in the United States, Germany, and Japan. Follower countries could benefit from using the technologies and institutions developed by trial and error in the leaders and perhaps making their own improvements to cut corners (Gerschenkron, 1962); Germany after 1870 industrialized much more rapidly than Britain or

France had done earlier, and this was also true of some of the smaller European countries.

The advantages of followers is an argument for expecting convergence of incomes as poorer countries catch up to the richer countries, but what we have observed since the industrial revolution is divergence "big time" (Pritchett, 1997). Globally the gap between rich and poor nations widened in the century and a half after 1820 because few countries actually began to catch up; countries starting to grow since the first industrial revolution have grown faster the later they start, but the gap between the high-income countries and the nonstarters widened (Lucas, 2009). In the twentieth century, there were signs of convergence among a subgroup of countries (roughly the members of the Organisation for Economic Co-operation and Development), which suggests that convergence only occurs if the setting is favorable, that is, convergence is conditional on good policies and institutions.[5] By the late 1900s there were signs that many countries (including some with very large populations) were catching up, but in the first half of the 1900s the global gap between rich and poor was at its widest.

Trade

Trade is a positive-sum game from which all participants can potentially benefit because specialization increases joint output. The principle of comparative advantage was spelled out by David Ricardo in 1817. It can be illustrated by a numerical example. Suppose that the hours needed for a worker to produce a bushel of wheat are two in France and three in Morocco, while the hours needed to produce a yard of cloth are one in France and four in Morocco. Thus, France is more efficient at producing both goods, but relatively more efficient at producing cloth. If France shifts a worker from wheat to cloth and Morocco shifts three workers from cloth to wheat, in each hour joint cloth output goes up by a quarter of a yard and joint wheat output goes up by half a bushel. As long as transport costs are low enough, both countries can gain from specializing and trading. With higher joint output, both high- and low-productivity countries benefit from trade if each specializes according to its comparative advantage. This is an important insight because differences in *relative* efficiencies are universal. There are gains from trade, and eras of prosperity have been characterized by expansion of trade. However, the gains may not be evenly shared between countries or within countries.

The industrial revolution created pressures for globalization by widening international productivity differences, and hence increasing potential gains from trade. Britain's exports were already experiencing historically rapid long-term growth rates in the century before 1820. In the next half-century exports from the leading industrializers, Britain and Belgium, grew at 5 percent a year (Table 1.1). By the 1870–1913 period virtually all of Western and Central Europe had export growth rates of 3 percent or more. Export growth was even faster from the lands settled by Europeans—Australia, Canada, and the United States—and especially (albeit from a low base) from Japan. Faster export growth was associated with greater increases in per capita output, as in 1820–1870 Belgium and the United Kingdom enjoyed the biggest gains among European countries and Italy lagged.

The industrial revolution also created pressures for globalization by reducing transport and communication costs as new technologies were applied to land and sea transport. Engineering projects, such as the Suez Canal, required technical expertise and financial development. There is an endogeneity issue, that is, did the transport innovations or recognition of the gains from trade come first? Innovations reduced the costs of trade, but recognition of potential gains from trade increased the incentive to reduce transport costs in order to realize further gains from trade. In any case, once begun, a virtuous circle of reducing the cost of trade and realizing gains from trade was set in motion. Improvements in the telegraph in the 1830s and 1840s initiated the biggest change in communication since the invention of writing; further inventions from the telephone to wireless radio transmission to Skype reduced the cost of real-time communication between any two points on the planet to almost zero.[6]

Recognition of the gains from trade led to reduction of barriers to trade. Britain, with the repeal of the Corn Laws in 1846 and adoption of free trade by 1860, did this unilaterally. Other European countries followed, usually through bilateral trade treaties with most-favored-nation

Table 1.1   Growth in the volume of exports, 1720–1913, and in per capita GDP, 1820–1913

	Volume of exports			Real GDP per capita	
	1720–1820	1820–1870	1870–1913	1820–1870	1870–1913
Australia			4.8	1.9	0.9
Austria		4.7	3.5	0.6	1.5
Belgium		5.4*	4.2	1.4	1.0
Canada			4.1		2.3
Denmark		1.9*	3.3	0.9	1.6
Finland			3.9	0.8	1.4
France	1.0*	4.0	2.8	0.8	1.3
Germany			4.1	0.7	1.6
Italy		3.4	2.2	0.4	1.3
Japan			8.5	0.1	1.4
Netherlands	−0.2		2.3*	0.9	1.0
Norway			3.2	0.7	1.3
Sweden			3.1	0.7	1.5
Switzerland		4.1	3.9		1.2
United Kingdom	2.0	4.9	2.8	1.2	1.0
United States		4.7	4.9	1.5	1.8
Arithmetic average		*4.2*	*3.9*	*0.9*	*1.4*

Source: Maddison (1995, tables 3.15 and 3.1).

Notes: Annual average compound growth rates in percentages.

* In column 1 France 1715–1820; in column 2 Belgium 1831–70, Denmark 1844–70; in column 3 Netherlands 1872–1913.

clauses that offered benefits to both exporters and importers; the unconditional most-favored-nation clause meant that when, say, Austria and Sardinia signed a commercial treaty, both benefited from the other country's past and future trade agreements (Pomfret, 2001, 16–20). Elsewhere, especially in Asia, markets were opened to trade by force. By 1870 a global economy existed; an important symptom was the 1873–1896 fall in wheat prices in Western Europe, which was driven not by local harvest conditions as in the past, but by imports from outside Western Europe.[7]

The global trend in the half-century after 1815 was toward free trade. However, forces for protection of domestic producers and for discrimination among trading partners remained powerful. Trade was an important element of Britain's growth between 1815 and 1860, and Britain remained committed to free trade until after the 1914–1918 war, but other countries did not all follow a free trade policy. Germany and the United States protected domestic industries, and both countries grew rapidly after the 1860s, overtaking Britain as industrial powers by 1914. Whether their economic success was because they protected their infant industries or despite these policies continues to be debated.[8]

The increase in grain exports from Russia after the end of the 1853–1856 Crimean War and from North America after the end of the 1861–1865 Civil War in the United States, combined with increased farm productivity and reduced transport costs, underpinned a fall in world grain prices that lasted until the mid-1890s.[9] Western European reactions to increased grain imports in the 1870s varied (Kindleberger, 1951; 1975). In the United Kingdom, where industrial interests dominated political decision-making, and in Denmark, where livestock farmers producing butter and bacon benefited from lower input prices, the outcome was a stronger commitment to free trade. In France, where farmers were dependent on grain and politically powerful since the 1789 revolution gave each man a vote, the response was a return to protectionist trade policies. In Germany, the farm lobby alone was insufficiently powerful to obtain protection against imported grain, but the large landowners of the east made an alliance with the capital-intensive industries of the west, for whom increased bread prices and higher wages were relatively unimportant; the rye-steel alliance succeeded in obtaining protection against imported grain and industrial products. In Italy and Austria-Hungary the governments responded slowly to economic pressures; there was no immediate change in trade policy, which led to large-scale emigration by uncompetitive grain farmers. This was an important episode because the policy decisions accelerated the decline of agriculture in Britain and slowed it down in France, the consequences of which would still be evident when the European Union was debating agricultural policy a century later, and in Germany the rye-steel alliance between the militaristic large land-owners and the producers of steel provided a setting favorable to war in 1914 and to fascism in the 1930s.[10]

As the Western European and North American countries industrialized, their trade with the rest of the world increased. Initially much of this was with colonies: Britain with India, France with Indochina, and the Netherlands with the Dutch East Indies. Other large Asian markets were opened up by force or the threat of force, but political dominance was informal as the foreigners were wary of a rival gaining a preferred position in China, Japan, or Thailand. The outcomes from the opening up of China after the 1839–1842 Opium War, Japan after American gunboats entered Tokyo Bay in 1853, and Thailand after the 1855 Bowring Treaty differed hugely, as China ineffectively tried to ignore Western influences while the Thai monarchy and the Japanese leadership sought to learn from Western technical and economic superiority. Thailand retained its independence by acting as a buffer between the French in Indochina and the British in Malaya and Burma, but in the absence of major political and institutional change, economic development was limited.[11] After the 1868 Meiji Restoration replaced the old elite by an imperial regime committed to economic modernization, Japan adopted innovative policies such as a land tax based on acreage rather than output and the import of modern factories by the government for sale to private buyers once they were proven; with increasing agricultural productivity in the last quarter of the nineteenth century facilitating the transfer of labor and capital out of agriculture, by the early 1900s Japan was outstandingly successful in incorporating the new industrial technology in a modern textile industry and in metal and machinery production and was converging toward the leading industrial powers.

After the 1870s there was a renewed push for formal empire in a scramble for colonies, especially in Africa (Map 1.1). The large profits to be made from the colonial trade contributed to an increasingly popular view of economic power as competitive and of trade as a zero-sum game.[12] Would-be new colonial powers conflicted with established powers: the United States with Spain in Latin America and the Philippines, Japan with China and Russia in the North Pacific, and Germany with

France and Britain across the world. After the 1898 Spanish-American War, the United States gained control of Cuba, the Philippines, Puerto Rico, Hawaii, and Guam. Japan defeated China in 1894–1895, when Taiwan became a Japanese colony, and Russia in 1904–1905, the first victory of an Asian nation over a European nation for centuries; Korea, which had fallen under Japanese influence, became a colony in 1910.[13] Tensions between the European powers mounted until war broke out in 1914.

In sum, the industrial revolution led to an increase in trade as Britain and other industrial nations sought markets for their manufactured goods and bought inputs and food. A global economy was created for the first time. Trade flows responded to price signals, and specialization by comparative advantage contributed to the huge increase in global output and incomes between 1820 and 1913 (Table 1.1). Reductions in transport and other trade costs enhanced the gains from trade.[14] Prosperity was not shared equally, although it is not always easy to identify losers,[15] and the last decades saw rising tensions, with competition for markets and supplies. On the whole, however, there was a virtuous circle in which enterprise, at least for those with some assets, could flourish; policy barriers to trade fell at least until the 1860s, lower transport and transactions costs stimulated trade, and trade was the means for spreading the benefits of the industrial revolution.

The Gold Standard

An important element of reducing transaction costs on a global scale was the development of acceptable means of international payment. Barter is inefficient, requiring dual coincidence of wants. Precious metals are a good medium of exchange owing to their high value/weight ratio, divisibility, nonperishability, and stable value. To avoid the need to weigh the metal at every transaction, it is simpler to use coins than actual gold or silver, but this requires trust in the coins' value. Even more convenient is the use of trusted promises to pay in gold or silver, such as banknotes or transfers between accounts. The creation of an internationally accepted means of payment that increasingly could be transacted without actual movement of the means of exchange was a major achievement of the first global economy.

The international gold standard was established in the 1800s. British leadership played an important role, together with Britain's credible commitment after 1821 to convert pounds into gold (and vice versa) at 113 grains (7.32 grams) of fine gold per pound sterling. Other countries followed; for example, the United States in 1837 set the price of the dollar at 23.22 grains of fine gold (or $20.67 per ounce of gold). The exchange rate between the currencies of any pair of countries on the gold standard was fixed, for example, one British pound exchanged for $4.867 (i.e., 113 divided by 23.22).

Fixed exchange rates reduce uncertainty in trade by making relative prices more easily observable and not subject to change beyond the traders' control. The gold standard also provided an automatic adjustment process to remove imbalances. By the specie-flow mechanism, which had been spelled out by the Scottish economist David Hume, if a country has a balance of payments (BOP) deficit, then gold will flow out, leading to a fall in the money supply and hence in the price level.[16] Lower domestic prices will make exports more competitive and imports less attractive; exports will increase and imports decline until the deficit is eliminated and the gold outflow ceases.

Continually shipping gold from BOP-deficit to BOP-surplus countries was potentially wasteful, but in practice there was little gold movement. If Britain had a BOP deficit, the Bank of England addressed the situation by increasing interest rates to attract greater capital inflows, and when Britain had a BOP surplus the Bank of England lowered interest rates until the outflow of capital removed the surplus. Because the U.K. pound was "as good as gold," other countries held accounts in London and addressed BOP deficits by running down their accounts while they took adjustment measures. Thus, the system worked well to settle BOP imbalances, as long as the imbalances were not large and there was trust in London financial markets.

When did the gold standard become the international monetary system? The answer depends upon how many countries are needed to label it global. With any network based on a standard, the more countries that apply the standard, the more useful it is. The tipping point for the gold standard may have come in 1871 when Germany used the specie that it received as reparations after victory in war against France to adopt the gold standard or in 1879 when the United States restored the dollar's convertibility into gold after the financial disruption of the Civil War.[17] Other countries adopted silver as the basis for their currencies, but the role of gold was decisively strengthened in the 1870s and 1880s when large new silver discoveries in the western United States led to accelerating inflation in countries on a silver standard (Table 1.2). Austria and Russia suspended free coinage of silver, and many Asian countries abandoned their use of a silver standard. Russia and Japan adopted the gold standard in 1897.

The advantage of gold was that supply was limited and to some extent exogenous, but this was also a source of problems. In the late 1800s people worried about whether there was sufficient global liquidity. By the end of the century, Britain's liquid liabilities exceeded its

Table 1.2   Year in which countries adopted the gold standard (pre-1913)

Year	Country	Year	Country	Year	Country
1852	Australia	1878	Belgium	1899	India
1853	Canada	1878	France	1900	Costa Rica
1854	Portugal	1878	Switzerland	1900	Ecuador
1863	Argentina	1879	United States	1903	Philippines
1863	Uruguay	1880	Turkey	1903	Straits Settlements
1871	Colombia	1884	Italy	1903	Siam
1872	Germany	1885	Egypt	1905	Mexico
1873	Sweden	1887	Chile	1906	Brazil
1873	Denmark	1890	Romania	1908	Bolivia
1873	Norway	1892	El Salvador	1910	Greece
1875	Netherlands	1897	Japan	1912	Nicaragua
1877	Finland	1897	Russia		

Source: Meissner (2002).

Notes: Date of free convertibility of currency exclusively into gold. Argentina twice exited, returning in 1883 and 1903; Chile exited, returning in 1895. Economies not adopting gold convertibility before 1913 included Austria-Hungary, Bulgaria, China, Dutch East Indies, Guatemala, Haiti, Honduras, Paraguay, Peru, Santo Domingo, Spain, and Venezuela.

gold stock. In booming economies there was fear that lack of liquidity was hindering growth, a fear highlighted by the slogan in the 1896 U.S. election that the country was being crucified on a cross of gold. In fact, global liquidity was never a major problem. More gold was discovered and, in contrast to the situation in silver standard countries, it was never too much. However, the process did build long cycles into the global economy.

In the nineteenth-century global economy, the most important price was that of gold relative to all other goods (which was, in effect, the inflation rate). During the 1830s and 1840s, increasing demand for gold pushed up the price of gold and hence lowered the price of all other goods. The relative price movements provided an incentive to find gold and a disincentive to produce all other goods. The consequence was heightened prospecting, resulting in the California Forty-niners and the Victoria (Australia) gold rush in the 1850s. The increased supply of gold depressed the price of gold and hence increased the price of all other goods. The disincentive to find gold and incentive to produce other things led to the 1850s and 1860s being boom decades in the global economy. A repeat cycle was now set in motion as the increasing demand for gold to cover the increased economic transactions led to a higher price for gold and greater incentive to find gold. Discoveries in South Africa's Witwatersrand in 1886 and the 1897 Klondike gold rush fueled a global economic boom in the early 1900s.

Symptoms of disadvantages of the gold standard were apparent. The cycles imposed economic hardship, especially during severe depressions such as occurred in 1837 and 1873. Gold rushes wasted resources, as many people prospected, but few prospered; much of the gold was shipped thousands of kilometers to end up in banks' vaults. The benefits were unevenly distributed, to a large extent based on the chance location of gold, so that cities such as San Francisco, Melbourne, or Johannesburg prospered while other regions languished. In the nineteenth-century context, however, unequal distribution of benefits was less important than the advantage of having a widely accepted medium of international exchange and an automatic adjustment mechanism for global imbalances.

There were cracks in the system, even in its heyday between 1896 and 1913 when almost the whole world was on the gold standard. Some countries did not play by the rules, and sought to have some monetary policy independence. When facing a BOP surplus and gold inflow, governments concerned about inflation restricted the increase in the money supply and in the price level by selling bonds to absorb the gold inflow. Governments facing a BOP deficit and worried about the negative short-term impact on economic activity and unemployment bought bonds to offset the reduced monetary supply owing to the specie-flow mechanism. Such efforts to sterilize the monetary consequences of BOP adjustment were relatively minor because under the normal conditions of the 1800s and early 1900s governments saw little need to intervene to curb inflation or unemployment; these were not yet seen as their responsibility. Real challenges to the automaticity of the gold standard only occurred in wartime when governments needed to increase spending, and the simplest, quickest way to finance a budget deficit was by increasing the money supply. Britain suspended convertibility into gold from 1797 to 1821, and the United States did it from 1862 to 1879, but the biggest defection from the gold standard came in 1914.

The gold standard supported the increase in global trade in the century up to 1914 by providing an internationally acceptable means of exchange and a BOP adjustment mechanism. It also facilitated development of international banking and of capital flows from countries with relatively high savings rates to countries with high returns on investment.[18] With rising incomes in Western Europe, savings increased and intermediaries sought to match the savers with borrowers willing to pay a higher rate of interest than was available in the savers' home countries.

Such intermediation accelerated the integration of fertile lands of the Americas and other resource-rich areas into the global economy.[19] European migrants had the knowledge and motivation to turn the North American prairies or the Argentinean pampas into rich farmlands, but they needed capital to build the farm, buy equipment, and purchase initial seed or livestock. The settlers were willing and able to pay higher interest rates on loans than British savers could obtain from British borrowers, so an integrated financial system emerged in which local bank managers in, say, western Canada assessed the loan application and obtained funds from Montréal where large national banks were linked to London intermediaries who aggregated savings deposited in British country banks; each intermediary charged a higher interest rate than it paid, but the spread between end customers was sufficiently large to accommodate a lengthy chain from which every participant benefited (and sufficiently small not to discourage the ultimate borrowers and lenders). Similarly capital raised in London funded North American or Argentinean railways, which were expensive to build but crucial in reducing transport costs from inland locations to the point that a crop like wheat could profitably be grown for export to Europe. The process was enormously beneficial for the global economy, because it lubricated specialization by comparative advantage between the land-abundant Americas and land-scarce but capital-abundant Europe, increasing world output of both food and manufactured goods.

As in the domestic economy, international financial integration introduced new sources of volatility. A recession in England, as in 1836–1837, reduced the supply of savings, pushing up interest rates in London that impacted on the chain of loans leading to mortgages in Ontario (contributing to political unrest in Canada in 1837).[20] These links became stronger as financial integration intensified in the decades up to 1914. Crises occurred when the value of assets was overestimated, whether in commodity booms, the many railway booms and crashes, or real estate (e.g., the five boom-collapse cycles of Chicago real estate in the century after 1830). Easier credit for promoters and gullibility of customers with respect to distant projects in supposedly law-abiding lands added to the potential for bubbles and crises. The occurrence of crises probably added to inequality as the people least able to bear the cost were often among those who were most hurt by the bubble.[21]

The gold standard flourished in the early 1900s. Despite fears of inadequate liquidity, the supply of gold more or less kept pace with demand, although the long-term expansion of supply was cyclical, expensive, and with unequal benefits. The main problem with the gold standard was the constraint on monetary policy independence, which was fairly unimportant before 1914 but overwhelmingly important when war broke out in Europe. This would become an endemic problem for attempts to restore the gold standard after 1918 in an environment where governments were expected to play a more active role in national economic management.

Migration

As well as an unprecedented increase in trade and international financial integration, the development of a global economy between 1815 and 1914 was associated with large migration flows, especially in the later period. Partly people moved to manage the expanding trade, but mainly they moved to settle labor-scarce regions. The process was facilitated by falling transport costs and better information flows, but moving from Europe to the Americas or Australasia involved a lengthy voyage and for most migrants it was a decision not to be reversed.

Before the nineteenth century Europeans had migrated overseas, temporarily or permanently, to establish trading posts, for example, for the fur trade in Canada where the production was mainly done by the native people, or to manage production, for example, on the sugar plantations in the Caribbean. By the 1800s some of these networks were complex and well developed, as in the East India companies that managed the various European countries' long distance trade with Asia. Regional and local trade in Asia and in the tropics was often managed by non-Europeans, for example, Chinese diasporas in Southeast Asia or Indian diasporas in the British Empire.

On a far larger scale was the migration of Europeans to sparsely populated temperate countries, which accelerated over the nineteenth century. Estimates of the number of European migrants are around 300,000 per year between 1846 and 1876, more than 600,000 per year between 1876 and 1896, and more than a million per year between 1896 and 1913. Before 1850 the migrants were mainly from Britain and, especially after 1846, from Ireland.[22] After 1848 they came from Germany and Scandinavia and after the 1880s from southern and eastern Europe. The migrants mainly went to the United States, followed by Argentina, Canada, Brazil, and Australia, although patterns shifted as the frontier of cultivation moved or was closed, and some groups were more attracted to some destinations by similarity of culture or religion (e.g., Italians to Argentina).

The international migration was overwhelmingly economic, pushed by population pressure, unemployment, and poverty in the sending country and pulled by high wages and expected wealth accumulation in the destination country. In market-based economies, large differences in the price of labor plus falling transaction costs offered opportunities for mutually beneficial relocation of labor from low-return to high-return places. In 1870 real wages in Ireland were less than half those in the United States, and real wages in Italy and in Scandinavia were a quarter of U.S. levels (J. Williamson, 1995). Migration was facilitated by falling transport costs and by falling costs of information, as friends who had migrated could report by international mail or by telegraph about conditions in the receiving country, employers could advertise jobs, or governments could encourage immigrants. Despite all the difficulties of travel and initial settlement, the average migrant benefited financially, as did those who remained behind; real wages increased by 112 percent in Italy, 193 percent in Norway, and 250 percent in Sweden between 1870 and 1913, compared with 47 percent in the United States.

The numbers of Asian migrants are even more uncertain than the rough estimates of European migrants. By some counts, 6 million Chinese and 4 million Indian migrants were living outside their homelands by 1914.[23] This does not include Japanese migrants moving to colonies (Korea and Taiwan) or large temporary movements such as for railway construction in western North America or to goldfields.

The consequence of large-scale movement of people was to increase global output as labor moved from less to more productive locations. Distributional consequences could also be expected as the returns to labor would be boosted by reduced supply in the sending country and returns to other inputs such as land or capital would increase in the receiving region. However, in many receiving regions the occupiers of land were expropriated and the benefits went to settlers or the conquering state. Savers in the sending country benefited from higher returns, because capital was complementary to labor in opening up areas of settlement or exploiting tropical resources. This shared benefit across all classes in the European countries was unlike more recent responses to increased migration when the interests of capital and labor have often been opposed.

Many tropical regions were brought into the global economy as suppliers of key primary products. If there was insufficient labor, it would be imported (voluntarily or involuntarily in the form of slaves or indentured workers).[24] Supplying the capital and management for tropical production and expropriating the natural resource rents was profitable, and underlay the scramble for colonies in the late 1800s. Africa, which had European colonies strung around its coast before the 1870s, was by the end of the century almost totally carved up between European empires, with only Abyssinia (Ethiopia) and Liberia remaining independent (Map 1.1).

Conclusions

The development of a global economy between 1815 and 1914 was associated with a great increase in world output, associated with trade and labor migration, and facilitated by falling transport and transaction costs. This expansion largely occurred within a framework of unconstrained economic activity. There were of course many, even in the core countries, who were not at liberty to make economic decisions, for example, the slaves in antebellum United States, and many were driven by poverty to make decisions, for example, the Irish emigrants after 1846 or the indentured Indian workers on the sugar plantations of the British Empire. The Age of Liberty was about freedom to choose, not about freedom from economic hardship, and thus it was more attractive to the wealthy than to the poor.[25]

The emphasis in this and the next three chapters is on Europe, and later the United States, because the process was generated from Western Europe and other regions were brought into the global economy whether they liked it or not. From the 1870s onwards there were growing tensions. The tariff increases of the 1870s and desire to develop infant industries contributed to trade disputes, and a zero-sum view

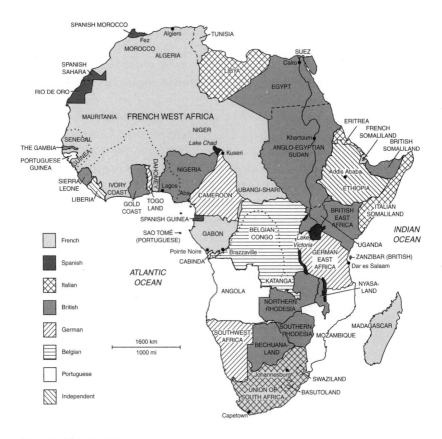

Map 1.1. Africa in 1914

Source: Downloaded from http://www.fsmitha.com/h2/map02af.htm (accessed 18 May 2010).

of colonial trade reinforced an increasingly confrontational approach to international trade. There were many symptoms of increased nationalism, not only in long-established nations such as the United Kingdom or France, but also in newly united Italy and Germany; in countries of relatively recent settlement such as the United States, resistance to migrants by the "native" population flourished as the heirs of European migrants developed a national identity.[26] International tensions were exacerbated by the clash between rising economic powers and established powers, especially over colonies and spheres of influence.

Domestic tensions in the industrialized countries were also brewing as workers demanded a larger share of the benefits of industrialization and the upper classes defended the status quo. Rising inequality sharpened these conflicts. In most industrialized countries, income inequality increased during the 1800s and peaked in the first decade of the twentieth century.[27] Opponents of the system questioned the combination of market forces and individual liberties. Communists wanted to replace the capitalist system by a system based on central planning and public ownership. In practice, despite the evident inequality in the industrialized economies, the response to revolutionary ideologies was limited.

By the second half of the 1800s, real wages were increasing in most of Europe, as well as for most Europeans who emigrated.[28] Despite the obvious health hazards of work in mines or factories, the workers were becoming better off.[29] European workers were more willing to work through trade unions or political parties to reform the system, rather than fight to overthrow it. Moderate social democrats wanted to temper the bad sides of capitalism with a welfare state in which public support would be provided to groups adversely affected by an unconstrained market economy. Some policymakers preempted this agenda, notably Bismarck who introduced the first major social security measures (health and accident insurance and a state pension plan) in Germany in the 1880s and the Liberal government elected in Britain in 1906, which implemented similar reforms (see Chapter 4). However, the actual steps were cautious, and taxation remained low before 1914.

Of all ideologies, nationalism was the most destructive. The trigger that turned international competition into the Great War was the act of a Serbian nationalist against the multinational Austro-Hungarian Empire. The European powers, from liberal democracies to old-style hereditary empires, mobilized their armies and, as the war dragged on, used nationalist propaganda to rally their troops to fight for a dimly understood cause. The cost of a lengthy war between industrial nations was unprecedented and victory went to the alliance of Britain (and its dominions), France, and the United States, which together had greater industrial capacity than their enemies. The defeat and abdication of the German, Austrian and Ottoman emperors, signaled the demise of the *ancien régime* in which power was based on land ownership and hereditary economic and social positions. The struggle for capitalism to replace feudalism, which had been heralded by the industrial revolution in Britain and by the French Revolution, had been settled in favor of capitalism.

CHAPTER 2

War and Depression

✦

The outbreak of the First World War in 1914 marked the end of an era. The catalyst—the assassination of the heir to the Austro-Hungarian throne by a Serbian nationalist—seems almost trivial, but the tensions described at the end of the last chapter had created a tinderbox ready to explode. Most of the major and medium-sized European powers were linked in networks of alliances based on fear of competitors or opportunities for overtaking rivals, and too many major powers saw potential benefits from a short war. Minor powers were enticed to join the fighting by promises of territorial gain.[1] Once set in motion the wheels leading to war were difficult to stop, perhaps because the leaders believed that war between industrialized nations capable of rapid mobilization of troops moved by railways and supported by massive gun power would be brief.

In fact, the Great War, as it came to be called, lasted longer and was far more costly in lives and other resources than anybody foresaw. Industrial technology that had contributed to the expansion of material living standards in the century before 1914 also contributed to the efficiency of killing the enemy. Machine guns had already shown their effectiveness in the U.S. Civil War half a century earlier, but their impact was under-appreciated in Europe. The war saw improvements in military technology in the form of bigger guns, tanks, aircraft, submarines, and poison gas, but the war in Western Europe became bogged down in the trenches of eastern France as generals wasted millions of lives throwing infantry against machine guns to gain, or not gain, a few hundred meters.

A lengthy war became total war. The European powers had been part of a global economy before 1914 and as trade was disrupted, they faced shortages of crucial raw materials and food. Civilian deaths of around 5 million were far fewer than military deaths of around 9 million, but civilian populations faced increasing hardship as food supplies dwindled, especially in continental Europe. The war became global as British imperial troops, the British dominions, and Britain's allies dismembered the German overseas empire.[2] Unable to break the British blockade of its ports, Germany retaliated by attempting to cut off supplies to Britain by submarine attacks on shipping in the North Atlantic. The victims included U.S. ships bound for Britain and, faced with what it considered acts of piracy, the United States declared war on Germany in April 1917.

The First World War marked the end of an era because it was impossible to turn back the clock to the Age of Liberty as it had existed before 1914. After the 1919 peace, the victorious established capitalist powers with their liberal democracies (Britain and its dominions, France, and the United States) faced decades of uncertainty as they tried to restore the pre-1914 world order with little success. Episodes of inflation, labor disputes, and a major depression cast doubt on the efficiency and fairness of the market-based economic system.

Two alternative economic systems, communism and fascism, which advocated much greater state control over the economy and concomitant reduction in individual liberties, gained ground in the 1920s and 1930s. In the Second World War the democracies allied with the Soviet Union to defeat fascist Germany, paving the way for a final showdown between capitalism and communism. That struggle would be won by the liberal democracies, but only after they modified their economies to combine the efficiency of market-based resource allocation with greater equality of outcome and opportunity (Chapter 4). The economic inequality between center and periphery was on hold in the first half of the twentieth century, but became a central feature of the second half of the century as the large European empires disintegrated and the new independent countries, and some older independent countries with new modernizing regimes, challenged the old international order in a variety of ways (Chapter 5). The combination of the battle of economic systems and the challenge of reducing cross-country inequality made the period from 1919 to 1989 the Age of Equality.

The First World War and Its Aftermath

When Austria-Hungary threatened Serbia and Russia began to mobilize, Germany made a preemptive declaration of war against Russia and, knowing that France would support Russia, Germany also declared war on France. Germany aimed for a quick knockout blow against France, which brought Britain into the war when German troops invaded France via Belgium. The basic miscalculation of the German leadership was that, although the German army was capable of rapid advance, the French and British armies were able to hold a defensive line before the German troops could reach Paris; offensive technology was inadequate to defeat well-entrenched defensive positions.

The longer the war lasted, the more important became economic strength and access to global markets. Britain's strength relative to Germany was enhanced by its access to overseas supplies, especially from Canada. German efforts to cut off the supply of food and ammunitions crossing the Atlantic through submarine attacks were inadequate, and ultimately self-defeating as they contributed to bringing the United States into the war. After a final offensive failed in 1918, Germany was exhausted and the war was lost—indeed it was the economic blockade that underlay Germany's defeat as much as anything. When the German high command ordered the fleet to sail out and break the blockade in 1918, the sailors mutinied against what they saw as a suicide mission, triggering the abdication of the German emperor and the surrender of the German army. The semi-industrialized economy of Russia was even less well-prepared to fight a long war; its underrequipped soldiers faced much better equipped German forces, and in the winter of 1916–1917 the front collapsed.[3] In southern Europe the battle lines were more complex, but the end result was determined less by force of arms than by having chosen the right side on which to fight; Italy, Bulgaria, Romania, and Greece all entered the war for old-fashioned nationalist reasons of seeking territorial gains and those that chose the winning side were rewarded.[4]

The 1914–1918 war ostensibly restored the status quo, but it marked the end of an era for many reasons. The established powers, Britain and France, had defeated the rising power, Germany, but the tone of the peace conference was set by the United States, which had been dragged unwillingly into war and saw the peace as an opportunity to establish a new order in Europe based on popular self-determination rather than dynastic empires. The smaller powers had fought for nationalist gains, but the newly imposed national borders were a source of discontent; even some of the victors, for example, Italy, were dissatisfied with the extent of their gains. The territorial adjustments in response to nationalist pressures would work against a lasting peace.

A fundamental difference to the pre-1914 era was the loss of optimism about progress. Even before the grim days of hyperinflation in Central Europe in the early 1920s or global depression after 1929, there was no longer the sense of technical, economic, and political progress as a good and inevitable thing that had pervaded the pre-1914 world— at least the world of the well-to-do. This exacerbated tensions already stoked by increasing inequality, and fueled violent reactions against the pre-1914 economic system. The most important result was the victory of communism in Russia's October 1917 revolution and the establishment of the Soviet Union described in the next chapter, but communist revolutions occurred and were quashed violently in several European countries (e.g., in Germany and in Hungary in 1919). In market economies, conservatives feared revolution; class conflict led to general strikes and other disruption during the 1920s.

The victors of 1918 envisaged the establishment of liberal democracies across Europe, but in the 1920s many of these regimes failed to withstand the challenge of more authoritarian leaders or parties. The challenge was especially potent in countries nursing grudges about their treatment in the post-1918 peace settlement. The attraction of a cooperative approach among workers and capitalists guided by a charismatic national leader underpinned the emergence of fascism in Italy in the 1920s and in Germany and Spain in the 1930s.

The impact in other parts of the world was less dramatic. Germany's overseas colonies had new rulers, but little changed. Japan's influence in Asia increased, but this was part of a longer-term trend, and

Japan was disappointed by the meager gains from its alliance with Britain in the 1914–1918 war. For the United States, the 675,000 influenza deaths in 1918 and 1919 were more than ten times the number of U.S. military deaths in 1917 and 1918.[5] Canada and Australia suffered greater military losses and the 1914–1918 war was an important milepost in their progress toward nationhood, symbolized for Australia by the Gallipoli landings where Australian deaths were blamed on incompetent and uncaring British officers.

The 1914–1918 war had more serious economic consequences for Europe. The physical destruction in the war was most severe in eastern France, which was devastated. The human loss was more evenly spread across Europe, but overwhelmingly concentrated in males aged 15–49.[6] The massacre of young men created a demographic imbalance in the belligerent nations; many girls born at the start of the century would not find a suitable husband, which would affect birth rates and gender roles in Western Europe. The war led to a quantum leap in governments' size, and to the introduction of income taxes to finance the higher spending.[7] Conscription represented a new level of governmental control over men's lives, but at the same time individuals increasingly questioned commands from above.[8] After the war, parties appealing to workers called for legislation reducing the arbitrary power of employers, making labor markets less flexible. In the short-term, and crucially for European history over the next half century, the war was associated with monetary imbalance.

Postwar Monetary Imbalances and Diverging Economic Performance

All of the belligerent nations failed to finance the 1914–1918 war out of tax revenue. Everywhere war was financed in part by money creation, which required suspension of convertibility into gold as inflation rates differed. The problem was not just the inflation rates that were unprecedented in living memory, but the degree to which they differed, especially among the European powers (Table 2.1). The differences reflected policy choices, but also fundamental wartime conditions: the United States and Italy had been in the war for less time than the

Table 2.1   Consumer price indexes in 1919, level in 1914 = 100

Germany	401	Austria	2,492
France	259	Canada	161
United Kingdom	214	United States	172
Italy	273	Australia	149

Sources: Mitchell (1992, 849; 1983, 841, 846).

other countries, Britain had external assets to run down, and France had access to U.S. loans. Germany had neither substantial foreign assets nor access to external loans.

Prewar exchange rates were maintained in principle, but given the differences in price increases they could be maintained only with stringent foreign exchange controls. After the end of the war, the United States was the only major trading nation whose currency was convertible into gold. Effectively currencies had floating exchange rates, but there was a widespread belief that the pre-1914 rates were "normal." Attempts to return to the gold standard, in some cases at the prewar value of gold in terms of the national currency, determined the relative economic performance of European countries in the 1920s and 1930s. Belief in the desirability of fixed exchange rates cast an even longer shadow, which was not extinguished until 1971.

A striking feature of the 1920s was the very mixed fortunes of countries whose economic conditions had been approximately linked by global cycles before 1914. These experiences will be analyzed first for the defeated powers Germany and Austria-Hungary, and then for the victorious powers Britain, France, and the United States. European countries that remained neutral in the war enjoyed higher economic growth in the decade and a half after 1913 than did the European belligerents (Table 2.2); especially striking was the catch-up growth in the hitherto relatively poor Scandinavian countries, as they avoided the disruption of war. Russia exited from the global economy and the capitalist system, and its experience will be dealt with in the next chapter.

Germany had a poor war finance record, partly as a legacy of the rye-steel alliance of the 1870s, which made it difficult to tax these major sectors heavily. Over the five tax years from April 1914 to March

Table 2.2   Average annual growth in real GDP, selected European countries, 1913–1929

Neutrals					
Netherlands	Norway	Switzerland	Denmark	Finland	Sweden
3.6%	2.9%	2.8%	2.7%	2.4%	1.9%
Belligerents					
France	Hungary	Belgium	Germany	United Kingdom	Austria
1.9%	1.7%	1.4%	1.2%	0.7%	0.3%

Source: Broadberry and Harrison (2005, 33).

1919, government spending amounted to 164 billion marks while tax revenue was 30 billion marks. During the war itself, price controls ensured little open inflation, but in 1919 prices increased rapidly. There was some attempt to strengthen finances, but taxes covered only 34 percent of government spending in 1920/1. On top of this precarious situation, Germany was required to pay reparations to the victors; in 1921 the amount was set at 132 billion gold marks (Germany's GDP in 1913 had been 50 billion marks), of which 1 billion was to be paid immediately.[9]

How to pay? The only real option was to reduce domestic absorption in order to reduce import demand and release goods for export, so that the trade surplus would generate gold for reparations. This might be self-defeating if the attempt to increase net exports pushed down the world price of German exports; the "transfer problem" became the subject of a heated debate, but other considerations were more urgent.[10] Living standards were low and cutting domestic consumption still further was an unpalatable step for the German government, which had already moved from Berlin to the small town of Weimar out of fear of revolution. In January 1923 to punish the German government for falling behind in reparation payments, French and Belgian troops occupied the Ruhr, Germany's industrial heartland, with the threat of taking reparations in kind if they were not paid in gold. The German government urged passive resistance by the workers and supported them with unemployment payments that were financed by printing money.

The consequence of these monetary steps was accelerating inflation. The wholesale price index (1913 = 100) had risen to 3,500 by the end of 1921 and to 147,480 by the end of 1922. In 1923 the situation exploded, and by November 1923 the price index reached 72 million. On 15 November the exchange rate was one U.S. dollar for 4,200,000,000,000 marks.

Hyperinflation led to economic collapse. Market mechanisms work poorly when relative price changes are hidden by hyperinflation. Long-term investment is discouraged. Money does not serve as a useful store of value or means of deferred payment. People resorted to extreme measures to protect themselves, spending their wages as soon as they were earned, almost irrespective of what they could buy, because deferred spending would buy less. By the end of the episode people were wallpapering their houses with money because it was cheaper than buying wallpaper, and in a famous photo a woman is feeding her stove with bundles of paper money, which was worth less than the firewood that she needed to heat her apartment.

Not everybody suffered equally. The hyperinflation hurt creditors whose savings were in financial assets and people on fixed incomes, so the middle class and pensioners were especially hard-hit. Workers were by and large sheltered because wages increased as prices increased, and the frequency of payment increased such that many workers were paid daily. Wage flexibility helped to keep unemployment low; in Germany unemployment in 1922 averaged 1.4 percent, compared with 14 percent in Britain. Landowners were also sheltered, as their revenues were linked to current market prices. The rich (or the lucky) benefited from speculation.

Hyperinflation was halted in November 1923 by a mixture of foreign support and currency reform. Under the Dawes Plan concluded in April 1924, French and Belgian troops left the Ruhr, reparations were rescheduled, and the United States negotiated a loan. U.S. banks lent money to Germany to pay reparations so that France could repay loans to the United States.[11] Germany adopted a tight monetary policy based on a currency reform.

The November 1923 currency reform introduced a new currency, the Rentenmark, which was equal to 1,000,000,000,000 marks. The parity rate was set equal to that of the prewar gold mark, which meant that Germany returned to the gold standard at the old rate—a psychological boost that was practically meaningless insofar as the new currency could have been given any value. The Rentenmark was backed by land, which was another psychological ploy; people could not demand land for banknotes. The true key to German monetary stability after 1923 was neither the choice of exchange rate nor the hypothetical backing in land, but conservative monetary policy, including no financing of government budget deficits.

After stabilization, government spending was cut and interest rates increased, leading to a rapid increase in unemployment. Economic collapse, increased insecurity, and a drastic redistribution of wealth continued to undermine political stability even after inflation had been tamed. The consequence was that despite relative political stability over the next five years, Germany was not well prepared to face another round of economic instability after 1929, when the world economy went into recession. Hitler's National Socialist Party (Nazis) came to power in 1933. The longer-term consequence was a fear of inflation, which remains strong in Germany to this day, and memories that the only solution is an independent central bank with a credible commitment to price stability.

Germany's wartime allies, Austria-Hungary and the Ottoman Empire, ceased to exist. In the 1919 peace treaty the multiethnic empires were dismembered in the name of national self-determination. The newly created (or restored) countries, Yugoslavia and Poland, included part of the Austro-Hungarian Empire, as did Italy and Romania. The core of the Austro-Hungarian Empire was divided into three main successor states. Austria and Hungary had hyperinflation and did not stabilize the currency until after economic collapse. Czechoslovakia controlled its money supply and did not experience hyperinflation. The Czechoslovak economy performed much better than the economies of Austria and Hungary during the 1920s and 1930s, and by 1938 it had the sixth-largest industrial sector in Europe. Unfortunately that was insufficient to prevent the country's occupation by Germany after 1938, a fate that Austria and Hungary avoided by becoming German allies once again.

The lesson from the hyperinflation episodes is that hyperinflation is a monetary phenomenon. The immediate consequences of hyperinflation are so severe that it seldom lasts long. The only solution is monetary stabilization. The long-term consequences are always large. Yet hyperinflation recurred in some countries after the Second World War, in Yugoslavia and the USSR in the early 1990s, and in Zimbabwe in the first decade of the twenty-first century. There are specific reasons why hyperinflation arose in these cases, as in Germany, Austria, and Hungary in the early 1920s, but the deeper question is why do some governments have the will or the power to avoid hyperinflation and others do not.

In the 1920s none of the victorious powers suffered from hyperinflation or anything like the economic collapse of Germany, but Britain, France, and the United States did have vastly differing experiences from one another. The major contrast is between the Roaring Twenties in the United States and more negative experiences in Western Europe. The economic outcomes were against a common background that included loss of optimism about progress, dissatisfaction with the war's outcome, U.S. isolationism, and mounting internal conflicts in Europe. The major driver of economic performance, however, was the monetary imbalances; at the prewar gold value of the dollar the United States was running large BOP surpluses, and the crucial question posed to British and French policymakers facing unsustainable BOP deficits at the old exchange rates was how their currencies could return to the gold standard.

For Britain the government's goal was to return to the gold standard at the old parity, that is, an exchange rate of $4.86 to the pound. Given that British prices had risen by 50 percent more than U.S. prices during the war and that the market exchange rate in 1919 was well below $4 to the pound, achieving the goal required a serious reduction in domestic absorption to bring prices back in line with U.S. prices at the desired exchange rate. The British government ran a contractionary fiscal policy (budget surpluses) and succeeded in reducing wages by 40 percent in the first half of the 1920s, allowing a return to the gold standard in April 1925. To maintain the exchange rate the government maintained high interest rates to attract capital inflows. Contractionary policies over the decade 1921–1931 led to economic stagnation in the United Kingdom, even during the global boom of the second half of the 1920s (Table 2.2).

Two smaller countries, Sweden in 1924 and the Netherlands in 1925, returned to the gold standard at prewar rates. The immediate economic consequences were similar to those in Britain, but far less dramatic because Sweden and the Netherlands had not suffered major fiscal dislocation during the war.

France ran significant budget deficits during the first half of the 1920s, based on expected reparations. The deficit was financed by short-term debt, which became harder to roll over, and by printing money. The inflation rate accelerated and reached an annual rate of 350 percent in first half of 1926, at which point the government embarked on monetary stabilization by raising taxes, cutting spending, and increasing interest rates. In 1928 France returned to the gold standard at the current exchange rate (i.e., the franc was set at 20 percent of its prewar gold value). A similar story played out in Belgium, whose franc was stabilized and returned to the gold standard in 1926 at one-seventh of its prewar value.

Stabilization always involved short-term economic hardship, but the countries that did not attempt to return to the old U.S. dollar exchange rate and devalued their currency performed much better over the 1920s than those that deflated in order to achieve the old exchange rate. Indeed, the degree of undervaluation of the French franc at the end of the decade provided some cushion against the global depression of the 1930s, which Britain did not have until it quit the gold standard in 1931. Meanwhile, the return to the gold standard only increased Britain's economic troubles. The continued deflationary policies contributed to the declaration of a general strike in 1926, which was defeated by upper-class volunteers and the army, leaving bitterness on all sides. Even in the economically more successful countries there was a malaise, which in France centered on a sense of not having gained much from winning the war and on the visible destruction of the country's industrial centers and lost generation of men.

The United States had experienced rapid economic growth in the 1870s and 1880s and was probably the world's largest national economy by 1914. The U.S. economy was integrated into the global economy, but domestic economic developments differed from those in Europe. Rapid growth created a visible group of extremely rich individuals and families (John D. Rockefeller, Andrew Carnegie, Andrew Mellon, J. P. Morgan, the Vanderbilts, the Astors, etc.), who made money in oil, steel, coal, railroads, and other industries and were often referred to as robber barons by critics who believed they acquired their wealth by abuse of monopoly power and other unethical means. Following the 1893–1897 depression the Progressive movement targeted the rich through measures such as an income tax and antitrust legislation. Although the 1887 Interstate Commerce Act and 1890 Sherman Antitrust Act preexisted the movement, enforcement only became rigorous after Theodore Roosevelt became president in 1901, culminating in the breakup of Rockefeller's Standard Oil monopoly in 1911. The introduction of an income tax, initially levied on the rich, followed the Sixteenth Amendment of the Constitution in 1913.[12] The outbreak of war divided the Progressives, and after 1919 the movement lost momentum.

The war's legacy and events in Europe fostered isolationism, especially as the 1920s boom in the U.S. economy was in large part driven by new goods produced first and foremost for domestic consumers. The spread of new technologies and processes, such as electrification of factories and introduction of the assembly line, and expansion of industries such as automobiles, aircraft and movies drew on wartime technical change and rising disposable incomes. Canada enjoyed a similarly prosperous decade, with rapid growth in primary product exports such as newsprint, wheat, and newly important minerals like nickel.

Economic development in the United States during the 1920s was a continuation of the industrial revolution. The new car factories and other industrial establishments resembled Adam Smith's pin factory in their ever-greater division of labor, substitution of capital for labor, and technical change. Although the automobile's initial technological development had been in Europe and Britain, France, Germany, and Italy all had more cars than the United States before 1914 (Table 2.3), Henry Ford in Detroit revolutionized the industry; by 1927 more than 15 million Model T Fords had been produced on an assembly line,

Table 2.3   Private cars in use, 1910–1970 (thousands)

	France	Germany	Italy	United Kingdom	Canada	United States
1910	108	55	22	132	6	10
1929	930	422	170	981	1,031	23,121
1950	1,700	516 + 75*	342	2,258	1,913	40,339
1970	12,900	13,941 + 1,160*	10,181	11,515	6,602	89,243

Sources: Mitchell (1992, 714–723; 1983, 713–717).
Note: Germany in 1950 and 1970 consists of West Germany + * East Germany.

with interchangeable parts and a standard paint job (as Ford wrote in his autobiography, "Any customer can have a car painted any colour that he wants so long as it is black" [Ford and Crowther, 1922]), and marketed aggressively through a national network of dealerships and competitive pricing. Similar approaches revolutionized other consumer durable goods industries producing refrigerators, washing machines, and vacuum cleaners.

Prosperity brought social changes in North America as car ownership sparked a move to the suburbs, industrial growth encouraged improved educational standards, and gender roles began to be transformed by labor-saving household appliances and convenience foods such as frozen vegetables, which reduced the drudgery of housework.[13] The level of mass consumption distinguished the North American economies from those of Europe, where cars remained a luxury and electrical household appliances were far less common.[14] The imagery of the new lifestyle was spread by the success of the U.S. film in an age when the cinema became the main center of public entertainment.

The gap between GDP in the United States and in other countries widened in the 1920s. A rich natural resource base contributed to this success, but more important for the theme of this book, the United States actively embodied the principles of a market economy and representative democracy based on individual liberty. There were, of course, flaws in this idealized picture (e.g., the treatment of black Americans or of the native peoples). The Progressive era had seen some steps to counter extremes of inequality and market failures such as abuse of monopoly power or employment of child labor, but economic success blunted the attraction of communism and demands to meliorate the market economy were less extreme in the United States than in Europe. Labor unions grew in importance after 1870 and some workplace disputes were bitter and violent, but by the 1920s the antisocialist American Federation of Labor rather than the class-based and more ideological Industrial Workers of the World (the "Wobblies") was the dominant union.

A puzzle for economists was why the gold standard appeared to have been so successful before 1914 and so unsuccessful after 1919. By the time most countries were back on the gold standard in 1928, some countries were already starting to leave the gold standard. The crucial concept for understanding this outcome is the Impossible Trinity; a country cannot simultaneously have a fixed exchange rate, capital mobility, and an independent monetary policy, because only one interest rate is consistent with the fixed exchange rate given the trade balance and capital flows. The Impossible Trinity posed no major problem pre-1914 because governments accepted automatic adjustment, even if they fudged a little by sterilizing to bend the rules. In 1914 capital mobility was suspended as countries adopted independent monetary policies to finance the war. With the return to peace and capital mobility, governments were less willing to give up monetary policy independence than they had been in the 1800s.

Monetary policy in the 1920s was characterized by sterilization. In principle a country with a BOP surplus accumulates reserves, adding to its monetary base and pushing up prices until reduced international competitiveness eliminates the surplus. This is unless the surplus country sterilizes the increase in money supply by offsetting contractionary monetary policies, for example, selling bonds to suck cash out of the economy. Concerned by the threat of inflation, the United States sterilized its BOP surpluses throughout the 1920s, leading to an inflow of gold without the accompanying increase in the rate of inflation. Deficit countries wishing to limit increases in unemployment also sterilized; instead of allowing the outflow of gold to reduce the money supply, they took steps to increase the money supply and reduce the rate of unemployment.

By 1928 the gold standard had been restored, with some fifty nations on the gold standard (Eichengreen, 1992, 188–189), but global imbalances were increasing rather than being corrected. Less flexible
domestic markets for goods and, especially, for labor, as trade unions'
power increased and workers' rights were better protected by law, reduced the effectiveness of what had been automatic economic adjustment mechanisms before 1914. The system was unstable due to global
imbalances and thus vulnerable to real shocks, such as the steep fall in
commodity prices in 1928–1929, which drove Australia and other primary product exporters off the gold standard in 1929. The U.S. recession and 1929 stock market crash (to be analyzed later in this chapter)
ended the boom in the world's largest economy. Lack of automatic adjustment or exchange rate flexibility contributed to making the 1930s
depression global.

In sum, the decade after 1919 illustrated the potential importance
of monetary policy. Allowing budget deficits to increase and financing
the deficit by printing money led to hyperinflation in Germany, Austria, and Hungary with dreadful consequences for the political future.
Trying to maintain an overvalued fixed exchange rate led to economic
stagnation in Britain. France had a shallower recession because it
returned to the gold standard in 1928 at an exchange rate that made
French producers price-competitive, although reluctance to change
that rate until 1936 despite devaluations all around meant that the recession lasted longer in France (Mouré, 1991). Lack of international
cooperation to reduce global imbalances (sterilization in the United
States in the 1920s, an undervalued French franc after 1928, and widespread sterilization by 1929) contributed to economic instability. In
general, and especially in Europe, the 1920s were characterized by a
lack of confidence in capitalism and a sense of living on borrowed
time—and it would get worse in the 1930s.

Authoritarian Regimes and the Rise of Fascism

The 1914–1918 war saw the end of the absolute monarchies that had
accompanied feudal and precapitalist economies in Europe. The modern industrial economy was incompatible with the type of privileged

political system represented by the Russian, German, Austro-Hungarian, or Ottoman emperors. The end of the autocratic empires appeared, briefly, to signal the triumph of liberal democracy as embodied in the French Revolution, the American Constitution, or the evolution of parliamentary democracy in Britain. The 1919 Peace of Versailles clearly envisioned the prevalence of this type of regime, and initially at least the successor states to the empires embodied the idea.

Almost immediately, however, parliamentarianism came under attack from both the left and the right. The Russian experiment with liberal democracy lasted less than a year as the February 1917 revolution overthrowing the tsar was followed by the October revolution. The Communists justified the dictatorship of the Party, representing the workers, as necessary to ensure the equality of economic outcomes that a market economy could not produce and that the elite could prevent in a parliamentary system.

Authoritarianism on the right followed soon after. The second communist regime in Europe, that led by Béla Kun in Hungary in 1919, was overthrown by force and replaced by an authoritarian government under Admiral Miklós Horthy. Horthy remained as head of state from 1920 to 1944.[15] In its opposition to pre-1914 feudalism and privilege, the new regime was of the twentieth century, but it was antidemocratic as well as anti-Communist, foreshadowing the formal emergence of fascism in Italy in 1922.

In Italy Mussolini came to power in 1922, initially compromising with parliamentarianism as leader of a coalition government. In 1925–1926 the fascist government became more assertive in crushing opposition and limiting press freedom and individuals' civil liberties, although even then the monarchy was not abolished. According to Mussolini, fascism rejects "democracy, the conventional lie of political equality, the spirit of collective irresponsibility and the myth of happiness and indefinite progress . . . The present century is the century of authority, a century of the Right, a Fascist century."[16]

The economic appeal of authoritarian regimes was enhanced by the bleak economic conditions in the 1920s and 1930s. Against the decisiveness of a charismatic leader, liberal democracies appeared sluggish and indecisive. Against the call for action from a dynamic leader, parliamentarians in frock coats and top hats seemed incapable of action. On a psychological level, young men across Europe were attracted by the spirit of self-sacrifice and communal duty to which fascism and communism appealed, whether in defense of national values or of proletarian equality; for many, romantic ideals were more attractive than reasoned debate as a guide to political action.

Across Europe liberal democracies were replaced by a variety of authoritarian regimes. Dollfuss in Austria, Antonescu in Romania, Franco in Spain, and Salazar in Portugal all embraced traditional bases of authority, especially the established Church. Mussolini coexisted in Italy with king and pope. The most revolutionary was the National Socialist Party in Germany, whose leader, Adolf Hitler, acknowledged only the popular will embodied in himself. The hyperinflation of the 1920s and the feebleness of parliamentary governments in Germany paved the way for Hitler's rise to power, but a catalyst was the depression of the 1930s.

In East Asia, Japan followed a similar course of adopting a more authoritarian and militaristic system. Although Japanese expansion was hidden behind an anti-Western slogan of creating a Greater Asian Co-prosperity Sphere, there was little doubt that expansion into northern China in the 1930s was nationalistic. The Japanese regime shared Italy's dissatisfaction with its portion of the victors' spoils from World War I and Germany's desire for control over natural resources. Expanding from its Korean colony, Japan faced weak opposition from China and the French, British, and Dutch imperial troops in Southeast Asia.[17] Thailand after 1937 also had a xenophobic regime based on a charismatic leader, Phibun, who admired Mussolini and Hitler and allied his country with Japan in December 1941.[18] As the fortunes of war reversed, anti-Japanese opposition mounted and Phibun was ousted in July 1944.

The Depression of the 1930s

By 1928 the gold standard had been reestablished, and yet almost immediately the world economy went into recession. Three explanations for this dramatic contrast between the pre-1914 and the interwar gold standard were: (1) the gold standard was less stable than before 1914 due to exogenous changes in technology and economic behavior, (2) the shocks of the late 1920s were exceptional, and (3) policymakers were inept. Each explanation has some plausibility and probably all contributed to the severity of the depression. The depression of the 1930s had a big impact on policymakers designing a post-1945 system and on policymaking in the following decades; how they explained the depression would color their view of the appropriate policies to avoid a repetition.

The initial signs of depression were country-specific. Many primary product exporters such as Australia (wool), Chile (copper), and Cuba (sugar) were hurt by declining commodity prices in the second half of the 1920s, and they were forced to exit the gold standard in order to avoid sudden loss of gold stocks, which would generalize the direct unemployment in the export sector to the economy as a whole. After the depression became global in 1928, the impact on individual countries reflected country-specific structures of production or demand or the strength of the financial sector or valuation of their currency. Nevertheless, the extent of the depression and the inevitability of contagion effects for all economies linked in the world economy made this a global phenomenon.

The central national actor was the United States because the U.S. economy was now the largest in the world, the decline in output was larger in the United States than in any other major economy, and the impact was transmitted by U.S. policy decisions about, for example, import tariffs.[19] The U.S. economy in 1929 had been through a decade of economic expansion, the Roaring Twenties, which had seen substantial structural changes. Instead of a simple division between consumables and investment goods, consumer durables such as cars, refrigerators, washing machines, and vacuum cleaners had brought some investment-like features to consumption, for example, replacement decisions could be delayed on a car but not on bread. Changes in the structure of production and distribution had reduced wage and price flexibility. Most workers were now on a formal contract, often backed by union negotiators, and the development of more complex value chains and large retailers led to fixed price lists on which the agent at the point of sale had no authority to haggle. Both of these developments added to the potential instability of GDP and employment, as reduced labor demand fed through a decline in the quantity employed rather than in the price for labor and as goods prices became less flexible.

The depression in the United States saw a dramatic decrease in output and increase in unemployment. By the spring of 1933, 15 million people were unemployed, almost a quarter of the workforce, and the gross national product had decreased from $103.8 billion to $55.7 billion. The poor were hit the hardest, both in the inner-city suburbs and in rural areas; by 1932 Harlem had an unemployment rate of 50 percent, and 40 percent of the farms in Mississippi were on the auction block. Farmers in Oklahoma and other western states were doubly hit by economic downturns and by the Dust Bowl.[20] Public financial support for the unemployed was minimal.[21]

Although the depression was worldwide, no other industrial country except Germany reached so high an unemployment rate as in North America. In Canada, 20 percent of the workforce was unemployed in 1933 (Figure 2.1), and between 1929 and 1933, the gross national product dropped 43 percent. Primary product exporters such as Australia and Chile suffered even sharper downturns, but were helped by recovery in export prices (e.g., rising wool prices in 1932 helped Australia). Unemployment in Britain peaked around 20 percent; following a decade of sluggish growth, the (cumulative) social impact was perhaps more severe, but the percentage decline was less than in the United States. In France, helped by an undervalued currency, the depression did not begin until 1931, and devaluation also contributed to the mildness of the depression in Japan. Devaluation like protectionism was, however, not possible for all countries, and this contributed to postwar policymakers' concern with discouraging "beggar-thy-neighbor" (i.e., zero- or negative-sum) policies.

What triggered the depression? The early Keynesian view emphasized drops in investment and exports, leading directly to lower demand and output and reinforced by multiplier effects. In the national income accounting that became popular after the depression:

$$Y = C + I + G + (X - M) = C + S + T$$

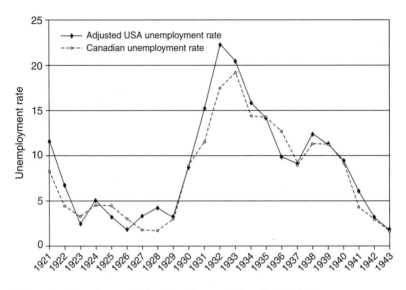

Figure 2.1. Unemployment in the United States and Canada, 1921–1941
Source: Zagorsky (1998), figure 2. Reprinted with permission.
Note: Official statistics, adjusted to provide a common treatment of relief workers.

where Y is national income (which is equal to aggregate demand and aggregate supply, or GDP), C is private-sector consumption, I is private-sector investment (expenditure on goods not consumed this year), X − M is net exports, G is government expenditure, T is tax revenue, and S is savings (income left over after consumption and taxation).[22] If S, T, and M depend on Y, and I, X, and G are autonomous, then a decline in investment (or exports) leads to a decline in aggregate demand (Y), which causes a decline in consumption (C), which further reduces Y, which leads to a further decline in C, and so on. The extent of this indirect effect depends upon the leakages from the circular flow of income, and the size of the leakages depends on the marginal propensity to save, the marginal propensity to import, and the tax rate. In the United States, with low marginal propensity to import and tax rate, when private-sector investment and government spending fell sharply in 1929 and the following years, the multiplier was likely to have been large.

The Keynesian view was challenged by Milton Friedman and Anna Schwartz (1963), who pointed to the drastic decline of the U.S. money supply, which fell by a third after 1929 and was exacerbated by bank failures as more than 20 percent of U.S. banks folded. Both the Keynesian and the monetarist explanation imply policy failures. For Keynesians, fiscal policy (increasing G or reducing T) could have increased aggregate demand to offset the negative impact of lower investment or exports. For monetarists, expansionary monetary policy could have offset the reductions in the money supply that drove down the level of economic activity. Others, such as Christina Romer, have pointed to the 1929 stock market crash as a trigger, because it reduced wealth and hence led people to cut back on aggregate demand, although the implication in terms of the need for offsetting public policy remains the same as for Keynes or Friedman. The trigger may even lie in the years before 1929 when the economic boom generated overenthusiasm and insufficient attention was paid to the riskiness of investments; the bubble burst when some projects turned sour, loans were defaulted upon, and the troubles of banks and other creditors led to an overreaction.[23]

The U.S. government reacted to the post-1929 depression with neither expansionary fiscal policy nor expansionary monetary policy. The principal response was to increase net exports by taxing imports. Congress announced a tariff revision and the president agreed. There was open season for any member of Congress whose voters wanted protection from imports, no tariff was refused, and the U.S. average tariff rose to more than 50 percent.[24] The Smoot-Hawley Tariff of 1930 could have increased net exports and hence domestic output and employment, but it was not given the opportunity. Each cut in U.S. imports was a cut in the exports of its trading partners, all of whom reacted by raising their own trade barriers, often specifically targeting U.S. exports such as cars, tires, or Hollywood movies. Retaliation reduced U.S. exports and nullified the impact of the U.S. tariff on output and on unemployment. Globally, the outcome was that any country's short-term advantage from higher trade barriers was quickly wiped out by an upward spiral of protection. By 1933 world trade had been reduced to a third of its level in 1929 (Figure 2.2). Beyond the very short term, no

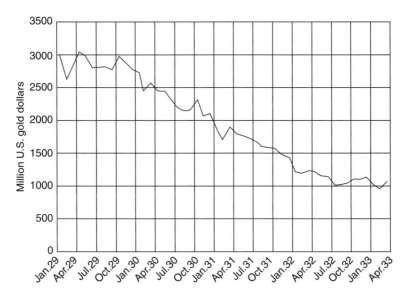

Figure 2.2. World trade, January 1929–April 1933, monthly values in million U.S. gold dollars of 1929

Source: League of Nations *Monthly Bulletin of Statistics,* February 1934, page 51.

Notes: Values are for total imports of seventy-five countries, including all of the major trading nations. The peak was $3,039 million in April 1929 and the trough $944 million in February 1933.

country benefited from protectionism, but all countries suffered from the loss of gains from trade. Some countries tried to moderate the lost gains from trade by forming trading clubs, and imperial preferences such as among the British dominions and colonies were strengthened.[25] Countries without colonies sought spheres of influence, such as Germany's formation of a trade bloc with some Eastern European countries, although this exacerbated intra-European tensions by promoting a competitive rather than a cooperative attitude toward trade.

The gold standard could not withstand these challenges. Kindleberger (1986) saw the problem as one of lack of leadership, as the United States refused to acknowledge the role and responsibilities of the largest economic power, especially the role of lender of last resort. Eichengreen (1992) prefers to see the problem as one of lack of cooperation; for example, in the late 1920s U.S. tight monetary policy and inflows of gold into France with its undervalued currency inevitably increased deflationary pressures on other countries. The two explanations both emphasize the instability of the system in the early 1930s and its vulnerability to shocks.

Financial markets became characterized by capital flight as investors, not without reason, feared default or devaluation. Debt defaults occurred in Latin America in 1931 and Central Europe in 1932 as primary product exporters simply gave up on using much-reduced export earnings to service foreign debt; a consequence was the exclusion of developing countries from world capital markets for the next forty years (and the creation in 1944 of an International Bank for Reconstruction and Development, later renamed the World Bank, to fill the gap). When the largest bank in Austria, Creditanstalt, went bankrupt in May 1931, investors shifted to Germany out of fear that the Austrian currency would be devalued; the capital flight was self-fulfilling as the pressure on the BOP forced Austria to leave the gold standard and allow currency depreciation. Similar pressures quickly built in Germany, which introduced currency controls in July, encouraging nervous investors to take their capital to London. By September investors' nervousness about Britain's commitment to the fixed exchange rate forced Britain off the gold standard. In Kindleberger's (1986) view a timely loan to Austria in 1931 could have stopped the contagion before it started, but Britain no longer had the financial strength to lend to a country in financial trouble and, when sterling came under pressure, the old response of raising interest rates to attract capital flows into London was inadequate, and the United States, which had become the world's leading economic power, was not prepared to act as lender of last resort, and no private lender would lend to Austria.

Even allowing for the size of the initial shocks through commodity and stock markets and reaction to the overexpansionary bubbles of the late 1920s boom and the systemic weaknesses of the restored gold standard, economic policy in all of the major powers was poor. Passive responses or contractionary fiscal policies (to cut spending as revenues fell) or monetary policy characterized not only the United States. In France, Germany, and Britain, governments toyed with public works projects, but did little in the way of countercyclical macroeconomic policy. France was to some extent cushioned by the undervalued currency, and for Britain the situation improved after leaving the gold standard in 1931. In Germany the adoption of a deflationary policy by the government in 1930–1932 and the feeble attempts of two short-lived governments in 1932–1933 to boost the economy contributed to it having the highest unemployment rate in Europe and paved the way for a government promising more radical solutions.[26]

Recovery

In the United States the trough came in 1932. President Franklin Delano Roosevelt came to power in January 1933 promising his New Deal. A more expansionary monetary policy put pressure on the U.S. dollar in 1933, and the United States exited from the gold standard. The New Deal saw some increase in government spending on public works, but both the monetary and the fiscal policy stimuli were quantitatively minor.[27] The United States also looked to reduce tariffs, but did not want to do this unilaterally out of fear about the negative impact on net exports. Thus, under the Reciprocal Trade Agreements Act the United States began to negotiate reciprocal tariff reductions, first with Canada and the United Kingdom. Output regained its 1929 level in 1937, but the economy then entered a new recession as unemployment increased in 1938.[28] Recovery was only really completed when government spending began to increase rapidly after the end of the decade, associated with preparation for the war that came to the United States in 1941.

A similar story of initially conservative policy responses followed by a cautious shift to aggregate demand stimulation, but on far too small a scale to make much impact characterized Britain and other European economies. In 1930–1932 Germany pursued similarly deflationary monetary policies (as the gold standard required of a BOP-deficit country) and introduced a minimal expansion in fiscal policy in 1932. However, the outcome in 1933–1938 in Germany, unlike elsewhere, was a rapid fall in unemployment reaching virtually zero in 1938, when the unemployment rate was still in double digits in the United States and in the United Kingdom.

How important was policy in ending unemployment and, more specifically, how important were the economic policies of the National Socialist (Nazi) government that came to power in January 1933? Four sets of arguments have been advanced.

First, the Nazis' policies were a continuation of the 1932 fiscal policies. Owing to time lags before macro policies feed through to the real economy, the Nazis received the political benefit without deserving it. The recovery was, however, too pronounced and the 1932–1933 policies too limited for this to be a major explanation.

Second, public construction increased rapidly from 1933, reinforced by public policy. Housing projects were supported after June 1933 by marriage loans which increased housing demand from newlyweds.[29] Increased public spending on transport projects (waterways, railways, public buildings, and the Autobahn network) was validated by abolition of the motor vehicle tax in April 1933 and promotion of the people's car *(Volkswagen)*. At least 80 percent of the workers hired on public construction projects had to be from the unemployed.

Third, labor market policies were strengthened. Voluntary labor service, introduced in 1931, was extended and in 1933 became obligatory *(Reichsarbeitsdienst,* RAD); young men performed physical work for six months without pay, which reduced unemployment and prepared the men for military service. Intensive propaganda discouraged women from being in the labor force, apart from domestic service before marriage. Labor markets became more regulated; independent trade unions were liquidated in May 1933 and replaced by the German Labor Front, an obligatory association for 20 million workers that emphasized the common role of blue-collar and white-collar workers. Labor mobility was monitored; in 1934 migration to urban areas required a permit, and after 1936/7 labor books recorded workers' employment records and had to be shown to get a new job. These restrictions were widely accepted by workers because of the Nazis' success in cutting unemployment, but at a cost of reduced individual liberty.

Fourth, rearmament began secretly in 1933 and was pursued openly after 1935, when conscription was introduced. From 1935 to 1939 the economy was moving to a war footing, raising the question of whether Germany's recovery began earlier than in the United Kingdom or the

United States because Germany moved to a war economy sooner. Rearmament may be part of the story, especially in 1935–1938, but hardly enough to explain the rapid reduction in unemployment from 5.6 million in 1932 to 2.2 million in 1935 when rearmament was clandestine and limited.[30]

Both the public construction policies and rearmament appear to be critical elements of the Nazis' success in reducing unemployment and increasing real output after they came to power in January 1933. In this respect they provided the strongest evidence of the potential success of Keynesian policies and of forgone opportunities in other market economies.[31] Labor market planning also played an important role as the RAD and conscription drew men out of the workforce and propaganda reduced the number of women looking for paid work. This more overtly fascist element was of less applicability to the democratic countries.

National socialism (like other variants of fascism) emphasized national unity and prestige. For Hitler economic success was an instrument to achieve national goals, and the latter took priority (e.g., Jewish policy and revenge for the military defeat in 1918). The essential economic policy characteristic was corporatism, emphasizing cooperation between business, workers and government. Fascism was strongly anti-communist, and faced the challenge of how to convince the workers to accept fascism. Fascism was also strongly pro-planning, and faced the challenge of how to get the capitalists to accept fascism. The Nazis succeeded in bringing unemployed resources into production and hence increasing GDP. Workers were bought off by maintaining high consumption levels (as a share of GDP) and by public provision of sports, vacations, and so forth.[32] Industrialists were allowed to operate as cartels and benefited from public construction and rearmament projects. However, these compromises meant that Germany was not well prepared for war—it had far less equipment and men than the combined forces of Poland, France, and Britain and was far from self-sufficient in many crucial primary products.

Germany was driven to war by the Nazis' political goal of gaining *Lebensraum* (living space) in the East. However, given its lack of preparation for a long war of attrition, Germany could only win if its superior technology allowed a lightning war *(Blitzkrieg)*. Poland was invaded on 1 September 1939 and defeated in thirty-six days. Full-scale war with France began on 10 May 1940 and was won by 22 June. Russia was invaded in June 1941, but despite initial successes the German advances were halted and reversed at Stalingrad between July 1942 and February 1943. Germany's problems were exacerbated by declaration of war on the United States in December 1941. From 1943 to 1945 inevitable defeat was drawn out by unwillingness to accept unconditional surrender, at the cost of huge war damage to Germany itself. In sum, over his whole twelve-year rule, Hitler was disastrous for Germany's economy. One outcome of the eventual peace was the partition of Germany, which lasted from 1945 to 1989.

Both Soviet communism and German fascism offered a challenge to market-based economies with individual liberties and to the democratic political systems of Britain, France, and the United States. A common origin lay in the experience of World War I when mobilization of the belligerents' economies encouraged a belief in the efficacy of central planning. This belief failed to recognize the critique that planning worked well in wartime because of the voluntary support of the population, and when that support was withdrawn, as in Russia in the winter of 1916–1917, the war economy collapsed. The authoritarian regimes did relatively well in responding to the global depression of the 1930s, although at the cost of creating inflexible economic systems with poor long-term growth potential.

Although both communism and fascism assigned a central role to the state, they had different motives. Communists emphasized inequality; they were more concerned about "freedom from" (hunger, oppression, etc.) than "freedom to" (make profits, choose your job, etc.). Fascists emphasized society (the nation) as being above (and threatened by) individualism. The two ideologies also differed in communism's emphasis on public ownership and fascism's corporate philosophy of workers, capitalists and the state working for the common good. Communism aspired to be internationalist and universalist in its appeal, while fascism was avowedly nationalist and supremacist. In practice, both Stalin and Hitler were autocratic and their regimes were totalitarian and personalized.

In both the Soviet Union and Germany in peacetime a high degree of compulsion and propaganda was necessary to obtain the compliance of large parts of the population. Both systems were well suited to total war as long as they maintained popular support—in Russia for defense of the Fatherland and for Germany to avenge the inequitable peace of 1919 and to delay unconditional surrender and another round of retribution. After 1945 communism gained ground in the wake of the Soviet military victory: Eastern Europe, China, North Korea, Cuba, and Vietnam became communist and many other countries were influenced by the Soviet economic model (Chapter 5). Fascism was discredited, but survived in Spain and Portugal until the mid-1970s, and regimes in Argentina, Thailand, and elsewhere pursued policies reminiscent of fascism. In peacetime both systems faced long-term problems of legitimacy and of efficiency.

The Economic Failure of Fascism

Fascism, because it set the nation above all else, was fundamentally opposed to other "isms" such as communism, feminism, or liberalism, which placed class, gender, or the individual at center stage. In order to pursue the national interest, fascist regimes embodied the nation in a leader. The undemocratic regime without alternation of power or succession arrangements had difficulty guaranteeing property rights, because no guarantee is credible when the government's power is unlimited and doubly so when a guarantee relies on the decisions of a mortal being. The lack of coercion-limiting institutions had a negative impact on investment and was an obstacle to sustained long-term peacetime growth in fascist economies. A second source of economic weakness, which fascists shared with communists, was belief in the benefits of scale economies and of the wastefulness of competition, while failing to appreciate the benefits of the market as a decentralized processor of information or the benefits of competition as a force for increasing productivity and screening new ideas. In consequence, the fascist economy was unresponsive to changes in demand and lacked innovativeness. The longer the regime was in power, the more serious these shortcomings became.

The rise and fall of fascism as an alternative to liberalism or communism was concentrated in a few decades. The most virulently nationalist and racist of the fascist regimes, in Germany and in Japan, were inherently confrontational, as their leaders used force to expand the operation of their nations by incorporating neighboring territory and to subdue "inferior" races.[33] They both suffered from hubris as their expansionary military plans outran their capacity, and the supremacist regimes were defeated militarily by the melting-pot societies of the United States and the USSR.

Less extreme versions of fascism lasted longer but eventually collapsed under the weight of economic underperformance. Mussolini's Italy grew out of similar feelings of national betrayal by the old leadership as nurtured Nazism in Germany, but the Italian regime was less overtly revolutionary. Power was obtained and maintained by force and the regime was authoritarian, but the monarchy remained in place (and ultimately was the source of legitimately terminating fascism in 1943). The drive for territorial aggrandizement in Ethiopia, Albania, and Greece was less megalomaniacal than Germany's unlimited quest for *Lebensraum* in the east, and anti-Semitism was less pronounced and far less murderous in Italy than in Germany. The economic consequences of a longer spell in power were, however, clearer as the Italian economy slipped behind other Western European economies during the 1930s.[34] Italian military failures in Greece or North Africa, which soon required aid from Germany, were rooted in economic shortcomings, and the Italian home front quickly collapsed in 1943, at least until German forces established a holding line.

The economic weaknesses of fascism are best exemplified by Franco's Spain. The fascist regime established by force in the late 1930s proved long-lasting, but this reflected specific historical circumstances. Despite German and Italian assistance during the 1936–1939 Spanish Civil War, Franco remained neutral in World War II. In 1945 fascist Spain was treated as a pariah; a United Nations resolution banned Spain from membership and recommended that UN members withdraw their ambassadors from Spain. As late as 1950 President Truman stated that "there isn't any difference between the totalitarian Russian government and the Hitler government and the Franco government in

Spain" (quoted in Calvo-Gonzalez, 2007, 743). The Spanish economy stagnated in the 1940s, with real per capita income in 1949 only 4 percent higher than in 1940—in contrast to many other neutrals whose economies benefited from the war. However, in 1951–1953 U.S. policy reversed as Spain was identified as a valuable location for military bases, safe from threat of a Soviet land attack but within striking distance of the USSR. The boost to confidence owing to the implicit regime guarantee was reflected in breaks in financial time series, leading to increased investment and an acceleration of economic growth (Calvo-Gonzalez, 2007). During the 1960s the regime became more technocratic, shedding some elements of fascist centralization and economic control. Nevertheless, by the 1970s the Spanish economy was lagging, and upon Franco's death in 1975 the regime was replaced by a "normal" Western European market system and representative democracy—a change associated with robust sustained economic growth over the remainder of the century. One of the most dynamic sectors of the newly liberalized economy in the final decade of the twentieth century was the financial sector that had been repressed under fascism.[35]

A similar picture could be drawn of fascist regimes in Thailand, Argentina, Portugal, and elsewhere. There may be arguments over definition—were these despotic conservative regimes or truly fascist regimes?—but in no case did the economic system provide a serious challenge to the attractions of the liberal market economy or the centrally planned economy of communism. After 1945 this would be the main contest.

Conclusions

What lessons did the policymakers who would design the post-1945 economic system take from this opinion-forming period? The most dramatic institutional contrast between the post-1919 and post-1945 eras was between the U.S. failure after 1919 to participate in the League of Nations, which hence had little relevance, and its active promotion of the United Nations, whose charter was signed in San Francisco in 1945 and whose headquarters was established in New York. For all its weaknesses and inefficiencies, the United Nations provided a forum in which the great powers could talk on a regular basis, contributing to a peace that underlay the unprecedented prosperity of the post-1945 decades. In the economic sphere, there was a need for international cooperation to prevent trade wars (i.e., to create an international trade organization) and to prevent competitive devaluations (i.e., to create an international monetary fund). Without international monitoring and cooperation, individual countries would face prisoners' dilemmas and pursue mutually harmful strategies.

The economic uncertainties in the two decades after 1919 enhanced the sense of class conflict and, among the ruling classes in Western Europe and North America, a fear of communists. Although the record was uneven, these fears inhibited constructive action to address concerns about economic inequality, which in turn nurtured grievances among the less well-off that family and friends lost in the Great War had died for nothing. The pusillanimity of liberal democracies fed the rise of right-wing authoritarianism and, in its most extreme manifestation, Nazism. The populations of France, Britain, and Germany would respond to the call to arms in 1939, as they had in 1914, but the postwar response to the demands for equity would be much more constructive than in 1919, and surprisingly consensual. Most dramatic was the 1945 British election that wartime leader Winston Churchill lost by a landslide to his socialist opponents; the new government nationalized industries that it saw as key (e.g., railways, coal mining, steel), but essentially allowed the market economy to recover from war.

After 1945 liberal democracies dominated the political scene in the high-income countries, and there was little fundamental disagreement in Western Europe, North America, Japan, and Australasia over the desirability of a market-based economy modified by public policies to address market distortions and to provide a degree of equality of opportunity and of outcome by provision of a welfare state. The need for macroeconomic policies to moderate the business cycle and prevent unemployment levels such as those seen in the 1930s was acknowledged, and their design would be influenced by new (Keynesian) theories and by national experiences of recovery. At the same time, revulsion against the hardships of the 1930s led the majority to accept a role of the government in providing support for those disadvantaged by the market economy (the old, the disabled, the involuntarily unemployed, and so forth). Although the establishment of a welfare state in liberal market economies clearly contained an element of buying off the working class, over the long run it became an integral part of a system that offered a combination of the efficiency of the market economy, the political attractiveness of democracy and individual rights, and moderation of the inequality of the pure market economy.

Before analyzing these developments in Chapter 4, it is necessary to examine the main contestant that the market economies faced. After the defeat of fascism, Soviet communism provided the principal alternative model of an economic system, offering a system that claimed to match or exceed the market economies' output performance while promising greater equality of outcomes (Chapter 3). After its military success in 1941–1945 and with its achievements in the 1950s, the Soviet model provided an attractive alternative for many aspiring low- and middle-income countries. On the other side, even after the depression of the 1930s the United States remained far more prosperous than any other country and would be the leader of the market-based economies after 1945.[36] The battle of systems, and its geopolitical counterpart in the Cold War, would dominate international relations for more than four decades.

CHAPTER 3

The Soviet Economic Model

✦

As capitalism evolved between 1815 and 1914, workers were brought together in factories and in towns. They began to organize and call for political and social change to give them a larger share of the benefits of economic growth and a say in how they were governed. Karl Marx provided the intellectual basis for socialism and communism by pointing to the contradictions of capitalism, which would lead to its eventual replacement by a system in which the means of production would be publicly owned; in the first stage of this socialist system inequality might remain, but in the final stage (communism) each would be provided for according to his or her needs. Among socialists, the major split was between those calling for changes within a market economy (what I will refer to as social democracy), who were willing to wait for capitalism to evolve and self-destruct, and communists wanting to overturn capitalism.

Sections of the ruling class and of the growing middle class sympathized with some of these demands and, whether from humanitarian motives or to preempt more radical change, in the decades before 1914 working conditions in the industrialized countries were improved by legislation on workplace safety, the length of the working week, child labor, and so forth, and the electorate was gradually extended to include a larger share of the population. For revolutionaries, such reforms were too little and too slow. Revolutionaries were unwilling to await the evolution of capitalism into socialism and fought to hasten progress toward a communist society. The most influential of the revolutionaries was Lenin, because he led the first successful communist revolution, in Russia in October 1917.

Although the Russian revolutionaries were opposed to the inequalities of capitalism, they had no blueprint for establishing a communist economy. The outcome of the debate over economic strategy was the adoption after 1926 of an industrialization strategy based on maximizing capital formation at the cost of current consumption. Opposition of farmers was overcome by the forced collectivization of agriculture. The strategy was successful in creating the economic conditions for military victory in the Second World War, and this success was followed by the spread of communism to countries in the Soviet sphere of influence and to countries with modernizing governments seeking a path to rapid economic development. This chapter analyzes the Soviet growth model, its outcomes, and its spread in the 1940s and 1950s; the problems with central planning, which became clearer in the 1970s and 1980s, will be taken up in Chapter 7.

Revolutions in Russia

Russia had been a major power in 1815 because of its size and as a consequence of some economic and military modernization in the 1700s, but it fell behind Western Europe in the 1800s. Attempts at reform, such as the emancipation of serfs in 1861 or the industrial reforms in the early 1900s, were too little too late. Some industrial development occurred, but the Russian Empire remained predominantly rural and its agriculture backward. In 1913 agriculture accounted for more than half of the gross domestic product (GDP) and employed three-quarters of the labor force (R. Davies, 1998, 10).

A revolution in 1905 was put down by force, but the outbreak of war in 1914 provided a more fertile ground for revolution as poorly equipped and poorly led Russian soldiers were outfought by the German army even though the eastern front was of secondary importance to Germany. In the winter of 1916–1917 many soldiers gave up, and a revolution in February 1917 replaced the absolute monarchy with a republic. The republic led by Kerensky was, however, too slow to repair the chaotic situation. It in turn was overthrown in October 1917 by the Bolsheviks, the radical communists led by Lenin, who advocated power to the workers' councils *(soviets)* and replaced the Russian Empire with the Union of

Soviet Socialist Republics. The Bolsheviks rallied popular support with the slogan "Peace and Land." To end Russia's war the Bolsheviks signed a humiliating peace treaty with Germany, and they declared that the land belonged to the peasants. In the ensuing civil war between 1918 and 1921 the communists' Red Army triumphed over assorted opponents, who after 1918 were supported by Western powers.

Under War Communism between 1918 and 1921, the communists nationalized productive enterprises, centralized decision-making and allocated resources by command. Banks and large industrial firms were nationalized. Compulsory labor service and central allocation of workers were introduced, and the government rationed goods and services. The peasants were in principle given output quotas, but in practice food requisitioning was arbitrary and the peasants often received little or nothing in return. Such draconian actions provided food and equipment to the Red Army, but at a cost of undermining producers' incentives to grow or make more. Despite the focus on public ownership and allocation by the state, the War Communism system had important elements of a mixed economy. In the countryside private ownership remained intact after the redistribution of land to peasant households. Everywhere, black markets flourished. Thus, War Communism is usually interpreted as born of emergency during the civil war and driven by necessity rather than by ideology (Dobb, 1960 [1948]; Nove, 1972; R. Davies, 1998, 17–21). War Communism was more improvisation than planning, and without any coordination mechanism the system was unsustainable. Government activities were financed by printing money, and by the start of 1921 prices were 16,800 times their 1914 level.

In 1921 with the civil war more or less won, the economy was on the verge of collapse. In particular, as the peasants were unable to obtain manufactured inputs or consumer goods in return for their crops, farm output shrank and in the winter of 1921–1922 famine swept across southern Russia causing perhaps 5 million deaths (Wheatcroft and Davies, 1994). Lenin retreated from War Communism, relaxing controls and tolerating small-scale private business. After 1921 agriculture, retail trade, and small-scale industry were all decentralized, operating in a market setting, while the state retained control of the large enterprises accounting for three-quarters of industrial output.

The State Planning Committee drew up mandatory output plans for a few key industries and organized the state order system, while control of the financial system enabled the state to allocate capital and credit. Otherwise, most resource allocation, including labor, was market-determined. The authorities introduced a parallel currency, *chervonets,* which was fully convertible into gold, and coins containing 8.6 grams of .900 alloy gold were minted in 1923; after the old ruble was withdrawn in the March 1924 currency reform, the Soviet Union had a stable currency, which was internationally traded. Foreign trade increased, although a state trading monopoly continued to exist and, in part because of restrictions on access to the major market economies, trade never reached even half of the 1913 level. By 1928, however, both agricultural and industrial output had surpassed 1913 levels (R. Davies, Harrison, and Wheatcroft, 1994, 42).

The post-1921 New Economic Policy encouraged economic recovery and allowed the regime a breathing space, but it was clearly a stop-gap measure. Among many who had supported the Bolshevik Revolution as a path to equality, the conspicuously wealthy capitalists *(Nepmen)* and rich peasants *(kulaks)* symbolized what was wrong with the New Economic Policy. A fundamental problem facing Russia's leaders was that the country's comparative advantage lay in agriculture, but industry seemed more dynamic (a similar dilemma would face Third World leaders after 1945). Exclusion from world markets accentuated the low returns to agriculture and increased the incentive to diversify the economy, but there was uncertainty about how to industrialize.

With Lenin's death in January 1924, the debate over economic strategy became linked to the leadership succession struggle. The immediate policy question of whether the New Economic Policy was a temporary measure or a longer-term economic strategy evolved in 1924–1926 into a debate on how to industrialize in an agrarian economy without inciting a peasant revolt. In the long run farmers may be encouraged to produce more food by being rewarded with manufactured goods, but in the short run workers released from a more productive agriculture need to be fed while they build and equip the first factories. The historical debate among communists revolved around the question of whether primitive accumulation occurred slowly and organically in Britain or was funded by exploiting India. The former could be reproduced elsewhere, while the latter implied the need for a new development model for countries without rich colonies.

The Soviet industrialization debate pitched the two sides into an urgent argument over how to promote industrial development in an agrarian economy.[1] Bukharin and others wanted to retain the New Economic Policy and even went as far as encouraging farmers to "Get Rich!" The priority was to increase the supply of food, which could best be done by increasing the price of food and allowing the more productive and responsive *kulaks* to become rich. Eventually socialism could be built at a speed acceptable to the population. This gradualism was too slow for Preobrazhensky and Trotsky, who argued that the priority should be to squeeze capital from the *kulaks* to fund industrial development.

By 1926 Stalin was the dominant political figure. He had initially sided with Bukharin in the industrialization debate, but once he had secured power he adopted a rapid industrialization strategy. In 1926–1927 Stalin increased investment by a third by squeezing the rich, and he directed capital to industrial projects. The increased tax burden on *kulaks* was followed by a grain crisis in 1927–1928, as farmers produced less or tried to hide what they had produced, and by greater use of compulsion to obtain grain for the state. In 1928 the First Five Year Plan emphasized investment in heavy industry. In 1929 the forcible collectivization of agriculture began.

The Soviet Growth Model

Stalin's development strategy was to maximize the increase in output, addressing distributional issues by state allocation of consumer goods. Soviet policymakers mobilized resources and directed them to the greatest extent possible to producing investment goods, such as factories or machinery, which would increase future output, rather than to producing goods or services for current consumption. The scarce resource was capital, which was generated by extracting forced savings from those living above subsistence, and the planners managed the abundant labor force by directing workers to where they were needed.[2]

The basic Soviet growth model can be seen in a later formulation by Evsey Domar and Roy Harrod. Assume that the incremental capital-output ratio ($k = \Delta K / \Delta Y$) is technologically fixed, that is, the stream of output resulting from a one-unit increase in the capital stock is at any moment in time determined by technology, and that the savings rate, $s = S/Y$, is a policy variable.[3] The rate of growth in output can now be written as $\Delta Y / Y = s/k$ because: (1) $\Delta Y = \Delta K / k$ by assumption, and (2) the savings equals investment identity ($S = I$) means that $s \cdot Y = \Delta K$ and $Y = \Delta K / s$. The conclusion is that increasing the share of income that is saved rather than consumed is the key to increasing the growth rate.

The Soviet planners took this a step further, allocating investment funds to capital goods industries rather than to consumer goods industries. If the goal is long-term growth rather than short-term living standards, the logic of starting as far upstream in the production process as possible is impeccable. As a first step, it is better to make sewing machines than to produce clothes, better to produce machine-making equipment than machines, and better still to make steel for the equipment industry or hydropower for the steel mills.[4] The workers would be fed by food obtained under state orders from collectivized farms. In brief, Stalin's model was heavy industry plus collectivization.

The immediate problem with this growth strategy was that people cannot eat or wear steel; a high savings rate implies a cut in current consumption that must be borne by the first generation for the benefit of future generations. Workers were exhorted to work for the common good, but many had to be forced to work; a huge system of labor camps was built up across the Soviet Union, and forced labor constructed many of the large infrastructure and new industrial projects. Food was forcibly taken from farmers who resisted collectivization, destroying their crops and slaughtering their animals rather than hand them over to fulfill state orders. Millions of farmers were deported from their villages, and during the famine of 1932–1933 millions died. Stalin's model could be imposed only by force, as an economic strategy associated with a totalitarian regime.

The Outcome

Little attention was paid to events in the Soviet Union during the 1930s. The USSR was outside the global economy. In contrast to the 1920s when many foreign experts had worked in the USSR, foreigners were kept out of the areas worst affected by the 1932–1933 famines and were increasingly restricted in their movements. With the rise of fascism in Germany and Spain, many socialists in Western Europe were unwilling to criticize the USSR and saw in it what they wanted to see, emphasizing the economic successes without counting the costs. The USSR was little affected by the depression in the market-based economies; unemployment was negligible in the USSR because all adults were allocated work by the state. An industrial sector was constructed, including the world's largest steel plant in the new town of Magnetogorsk. Machine tool and tractor factories were built, as well as factories to produce guns and tanks. Militarily, and also little noticed in Europe, the USSR came out on top in a skirmish with Japan on the Korean border in 1938 and in a major tank battle on the Mongolian border in 1939, in both cases because of the superiority of Russian heavy guns and armor.

Stalin was well aware of the country's economic backwardness compared with Germany. Nevertheless, strengthening the power of the leader took priority; the show trials of the 1930s that removed all opposition, including many of the senior generals, further undermined readiness for war in the west. Stalin tried to buy time by signing in August 1939 a nonaggression pact (the Molotov-Ribbentrop Treaty) with Nazi Germany, despite the ideological gulf between the two regimes. In the following months the USSR occupied territory of Poland, Latvia, Estonia, Finland, and Romania while condoning Germany's annexation of the remainder of Poland and of Lithuania. Whether the geographical buffer provided by the annexed lands and the breathing space of almost two years while Germany was at war and Russia at peace enabled the USSR to better withstand German invasion remains debated. In June 1941 Germany invaded the USSR and, despite initial success, was ultimately defeated, unlike in 1914. The result, as with the Soviet victories over Japan in 1938 and 1939, was largely because the Soviet industrial complex could produce tanks, guns, and planes to a common blueprint in large quantities (Table 3.1).

What does a centrally planned economy do well? In the 1930s massive industrial complexes, hydroelectric dams, and infrastructure

Table 3.1   Military production during World War II (thousands, 1939–1945)

	USSR	Germany	Japan	United States	United Kingdom	Italy
Tanks	103	46	5	100	29	3
Guns	482	320	160	549	390	10
Mortars	352	79	8	102	101	17
Machine guns	1,516	1,176	450	2,614	939	125
Military aircraft	112	90	55	192	95	13

Source: Harrison (1998, 15–16).
Note: Tanks include self-propelled guns.

projects such as the White Sea–Baltic Sea Canal were built by Soviet workforces in the thousands, ignoring the costs in human lives. A centrally planned economy can produce large quantities of a standardized product, such as the tanks that won World War II. It can direct labor to a clear task, such as winning a war.

In peacetime, the USSR was successful at mobilizing resources to achieve well-defined goals such as sending the first person into space— Yuri Gagarin in 1961. It also produced star performers in the arts or chess and many Olympic medal-winners, although it was less successful in sports that required a mix of technique and improvisation (Edelman, 1993). The USSR never won a major trophy in the country's most popular sport, soccer.[5]

The economy was also successful in satisfying basic needs such as housing, heating, primary and secondary education, or basic healthcare. Between 1950 and 1965, the urban housing stock of the Soviet Union doubled. Infant mortality rates fell from 182 per thousand live births in 1940 to 81 in 1950 and 27 in 1965, and other health indicators also improved markedly. Primary education became universal, and the number of pupils aged 14–17 increased from 1.8 million in the 1950–1951 school year to 12.7 million in 1965–1966; higher education enrollments increased from 1.25 to 3.8 million over the same period.

By the 1960s the Soviet Union had ensured almost universal satisfaction of basic needs.[6] In this sense equality had been achieved, although attempts to measure the distribution of income suggest that it was not so different from that in some Western European countries (Atkinson and Micklewright, 1992). Poverty did not officially exist in the Soviet Union, but many households enjoyed little more than satisfaction of basic needs, even with all adults working.[7] The Soviet elite, the *nomenklatura* of high party officials, clearly enjoyed higher living standards, although it was difficult to identify the extent of their wealth because their privileges often came in access to services or housing rather than modern consumer goods.

What does a centrally planned economy do badly? Motivation may not be a problem after a revolution or in a defensive war. In such emergency situations, with the support of the people, the system is good at mobilizing resources, but in the long term incentives are lacking. A standing Soviet joke was that the state pretended to pay people and people pretended to work. The planned economy is also poor at allocating scarce resources. Managers are tempted into wasteful practices in order to satisfy the planners (e.g., cutting quality or ignoring other specifications when their targets are set only in quantity terms), and are more concerned with avoiding failure than with innovating. Moreover, managers had no incentive to consider anything outside the plan, so that little consideration was paid to occupational safety and no attention was given to environmental degradation.[8] Consumers have no power, and their time outside the workplace is not valued; excess demand for consumer goods is addressed by queues (or corruption). Moreover, although the planned economy could produce standardized cars or refrigerators, it was poorly designed to respond to consumers' wants beyond the satisfaction of basic needs.

The fundamental weakness of central planning in processing information, especially as circumstances change, had already been pointed out by "Austrian" critics in intellectual debates in the 1930s and 1940s. In the view of Friedrich von Hayek (1937), no central planner or absolute dictator could process all information about goods and services that producers and consumers need to guide their choices, and the outcome would inevitably be inferior to that from a decentralized market system in which relative prices convey all the necessary information. The role of competition is to transmit evolving possibilities and preferences into relative price changes in a way that no individual can predict because knowing the winner of each competition is beyond the capacity of any centralized information processing system.[9]

In the long-term, a fundamental weakness of centrally planned economies was their poor capacity to innovate. Despite investment in education and pursuit of science by identifying talented science students and providing scientists with good facilities, day-to-day innovations in the factory rarely happened. Some major inventions occurred in centrally planned economies (e.g., the transistor radio in the USSR, the floppy disk in Hungary, or contact lenses in Czechoslovakia), but these goods were developed and mass produced in the United States and Japan without significant recognition of the original inventor. In contrast, a stream of more or less important innovations comes out of the high-income market economies. The hierarchical centrally planned economy had little appetite for risk; once an innovation had passed up the decision-making hierarchy and been rejected, the inventor had nowhere else to turn in order to produce the new good. In market economies, competition among venture capitalists ensures that capital is often available for inventors and entrepreneurs, many of whom fail, but those who survive can reap huge rewards. In the USSR the only real competition was in the Cold War, which stimulated innovations with military use or to outshine the United States (e.g., *Sputnik* and the first man in space). With poor management and lack of innovation, the incremental capital/output ratio, k in the Harrod-Domar model, is not constant; diminishing marginal productivity of capital is not offset by technical change.

A final flaw in the Soviet system was its imperviousness to reform. Although the weaknesses were apparent by the 1960s and many blueprints for reform were drawn up, none of the blueprints was seriously implemented. The problem was that the centrally planned economy was an economic system; attempts to tinker with individual bits tended to worsen the functioning of the system as a whole. What was needed was fundamental systemic reform, but too many people, especially those in the elite, feared the cost of reform. The deep freeze of the Brezhnev era delayed, but could not avoid, the dénouement that will be analyzed in Chapter 7.

The Spread of Communism

The hopes of Lenin and other Bolsheviks that the contradictions of capitalism would lead to communist revolutions in Western Europe were misplaced. Apart from the short-lived regime of Béla Kun in Hungary, no communist revolution succeeded. In 1921 the Soviet army reclaimed Mongolia, which had briefly returned to Chinese influence in 1917, and the Mongolian People's Republic was established in 1924, but little attempt was made to apply the Soviet economic model until after 1945.

The spread of communism began after the Soviet military victory in 1945. As part of the spoils of war, the USSR claimed Eastern Europe as its sphere of influence. It annexed the Baltic states and Moldova as republics of the USSR, as well as incorporating a slice of Polish territory, and supported the establishment of communist regimes elsewhere in Eastern Europe, including the eastern zone of Germany. By the end of the 1940s Bulgaria, Czechoslovakia, Hungary, Poland, Romania, and East Germany all had economic systems designed on the basic Soviet model and were tied into a network of planned international trade through the Committee for Mutual Economic Assistance (Comecon). They were also tied together in a military alliance, the 1955 Warsaw Pact, which was based on mutual assistance against foreign aggression, but which was only invoked to suppress opposition to communism in Hungary in 1956 and Czechoslovakia in 1968.

The only Eastern European countries in which an indigenous communist movement came to power by their own efforts in resisting German occupation were Yugoslavia under Tito and Albania. Both had difficulty coming to terms with Soviet hegemony. In 1948 Yugoslavia left the Soviet camp, and Tito pursued a different economic strategy, replacing Soviet-style central planning with a more decentralized system of workers' self-managed enterprises. Albania split with the Soviet Union in 1960 in protest against de-Stalinization, and allied itself with Maoist China, adopting an ultra-centralized and closed economic system.

In Asia, Korea was divided between a Soviet-administered north and a U.S.-administered south. The regime in the north refused to participate in national elections, and declared a Democratic People's Republic of Korea in 1948. In June 1950 northern troops invaded the south in an unsuccessful attempt to unify the country as a communist state.[10] After an armistice in 1953 the status quo was reestablished, and since then the Korean peninsula has remained divided (and, in the absence of a peace treaty, technically still at war). The North Korean government pursued an autarchic policy with complete state control over the economy, and a highly personalized political system centered on Kim Il-sung, president until 1994, and since then on his son, Kim Jong-il.

The success of the Soviet Union in industrializing rapidly and restoring Russia's international prestige made communism attractive to low-income countries in what would become known as the Third World. In China and in Vietnam communists led the battle for independence from Japanese invaders or French imperialists, and communist governments were established in China in 1949 and in Vietnam in 1945, although from 1954 to 1975 the communist government controlled only the northern half of Vietnam. Soviet propaganda in the 1950s highlighted the genuine economic success in Central Asia, which was contrasted with the poverty in Third World countries that had less enlightened rulers. The 1959 Cuban revolution was an armed revolt against an unpopular dictator, but after the new government nationalized land and expropriated foreign companies, the United States imposed economic sanctions and in April 1961 sponsored the unsuccessful Bay of Pigs invasion, after which Cuba sought Soviet support and the revolutionary government merged with the old Communist Party. Cuba subsequently became a frequent Soviet proxy in Third World countries.

In most of these countries the advent of central planning was followed by improved economic performance. The new modernizing governments were successful in mobilizing resources and in meeting immediate goals of reconstruction or basic needs satisfaction. The gap between North and South Korea or between East and West Germany was less pronounced in the 1950s than it would become in the 1960s and after. China prospered in the early and mid-1950s, and economic conditions were much improved over the chaos of the 1930s and 1940s.

Cuba was successful in diversifying the economy between 1960 and 1964, and improving health and education services.

Conclusions

The Soviet economic model was the great economic experiment of the twentieth century. The Soviet planners aimed to improve on the functioning of the capitalist economy by mobilizing resources and controlling their allocation. The specific path selected by Stalin in the late 1920s involved rapid industrialization, based on collectivization of agriculture and squeezing rural living standards in order to achieve a rapid buildup of heavy industry (e.g., steel, hydroelectricity, machine building). For three decades the strategy was economically successful, reflected in military victory and satisfaction of basic needs of the population. In the 1950s communism was a plausible challenger to capitalism and with the launch of *Sputnik* and the first man in space seemed poised to even overtake American technological leadership.

There had been a high price in terms of individual freedom, recognized in the Baltic countries, Ukraine, and other regions that had suffered most during the collectivization and industrialization drive after 1928. In Soviet propaganda, these costs were justified by victory in the Great Patriotic War, which suggested that the suffering had been worthwhile. The economic successes of the 1950s offered hope that past suffering would be rewarded with future prosperity and equality, but during the 1960s and 1970s it became ever clearer that reality was stagnation without equality, supported by political repression.[11]

In Eastern Europe the assumption of power by communist governments had a mixed reception in the late 1940s, but outside Yugoslavia the regimes gradually lost popularity. Elections were rigged, but opposition spilled onto the streets in Hungary in 1956 and was forcibly suppressed. East Germans voted with their feet, necessitating construction of a wall in 1961 to keep people in. After the 1968 invasion of Czechoslovakia and refusal of the Soviet Union to countenance leaders who promoted serious reform, the situation was frozen for twenty years.

Communism remained attractive to idealistic leaders in poor countries because of its promise of rapid development. By the end of the

1960s the Cold War struggle between the USSR and the United States appeared more geopolitical than ideological, and radical critics of the USSR complained about it turning into a degenerated communism run by and for the elite. China or Cuba appeared to offer a more attractive model of communism in which a new man would respond to moral rather than material incentives. Their story and that of other communist regimes during the Cold War will be taken up in Chapter 5, but before that we will look at the response of the leading capitalist economies in the post-1945 era to the challenges from the "Second World" of communist countries.

CHAPTER 4

Multilateralism and Welfare State
in the First World

⋆

The response of the major capitalist countries to peace in 1945 was more cooperative and purposeful than in 1919. In stark contrast to the post-1919 isolationism of the United States, designing the post-1945 global system was led by the United States, whose relatively undamaged economy dominated global output to an extent never seen before or since. A range of new multilateral institutions provided the institutional support for an international economic order based on individual rights that in crucial respects represented a return to the globalization of the pre-1914 Age of Liberty. Unlike pre-1914 capitalism, however, there was widespread acceptance of the need for government action to address the inequalities and uncertainties of capitalism, both internationally and domestically, as to varying degrees countries adopted welfare state policies.

Such an approach to the inequality associated with capitalism had been embarked upon by Germany in the 1880s and Britain after 1906, when governments introduced elements of social security to help those most disadvantaged by the economic system. Although partial social security measures predated these reforms, the German laws of the 1880s and their consolidation over the following decades greatly reduced the transaction costs of accessing social insurance (Lindert, 2004, 174). Despite these steps in two major European economies, little further progress was made in creating a welfare state in the confrontational atmosphere of the 1920s and early 1930s when conservative political parties became obsessed with the threat of communism and fears of creeping socialism. Such fears fed class conflicts and political polarization. In the democracies the effect was to block meaningful reform, as in France and Britain where left-wing parties gained ground in elections but did not come close to systemic change, or to provoke a military solution, as in Spain. The only successful moves toward creation of a welfare state were in the fascist countries and in smaller democracies, notably the Scandinavian countries.

Despite the lack of progress toward establishing a welfare state in the large market-based liberal democracies, the preconditions were being put in place as all political parties lost confidence in the unregulated market economy during the 1930s and as democrats sought an alternative postwar vision to set against the appeal of fascism. After the Second World War the demands for governments to address the uncertainties and inequality of capitalism became overwhelming.

The long economic boom of 1948–1973 provided the setting for a dramatic extension of the welfare state in all high-income countries. The boom itself was unexpected and provided a fillip to belief in the value of market mechanisms, which were under a serious cloud in the late 1940s and 1950s. In many countries, the 1960s were a decade of affluence, optimism, and individualism, especially among the generation that had no memories of the 1930s depression. The end of the boom and slower growth, increased unemployment, and inflation after 1973 stimulated a reassessment of the balance between market mechanisms and government intervention, but little serious challenge to the fundamental combination of market economy plus welfare state as the desired system.

Social Security Measures before 1945

The first modern social security system dates from Germany during the 1880s, when Bismarck enacted three major laws to protect German workers against sickness, injury, and old age. An 1883 law created health insurance for all workers earning less than 2,000 marks per year. An 1884 law provided employer-funded insurance against industrial accidents (extended to farmworkers in 1886), with victims receiving a pension equal to two-thirds of their earnings, or in the case of death widows and orphans were paid compensation. An 1889 law created a pension system funded by workers, employers, and the state. The coverage of these measures gradually expanded, and in 1911 the compulsory insurance measures were combined in a National Insurance Code.[1]

Bismarck's legislation explicitly aimed to encourage the less well-off members of German society to see the state as working in their interests and not just serving the interests of the rich. In part this was to counter the rising influence of socialists and communists. It may also have served the self-interest of the employers, who contributed much of the funding, but in return probably had a healthier and more productive workforce.[2] The creation of a welfare state substantially reduced the large emigration from Germany to the United States; the number of emigrants per thousand population fell from 2.47 in 1865–1884 to 1.01 in 1885–1913, the largest decline in any European country (Khoudour-Castéras, 2008, 215).[3] In general, the creation of a welfare state certainly did not prevent Germany from enjoying healthy economic growth in the three decades after 1883.

Nevertheless, this early experiment in ameliorating the distributional consequences of an efficient market economy led along a false trail that ended in the Nazi variant of fascism. Combined with the high tariff protection granted to Germany's grain farmers and heavy industry in the 1880s, the welfare state was part of a process of creating a more corporatist economic system in Germany than in the earlier industrializing European countries such as Britain or France. The system created in Germany between 1871 and 1914 emphasized working together for the common national goal, but failure in the 1914–1918 war discredited the monarchy and the old landed aristocracy and military leadership. At the same time, military defeat and a sense of an unjust peace created fertile ground for the more radical nationalism that triumphed in Germany in 1933. Nazism offered a solution to the problems of capitalism that built on the pre-1914 emphasis on working together for the good of the nation.

Britain was the other leading European economy to adopt social security measures on a substantial scale before 1914. The government elected in 1906 introduced major reforms, which improved the conditions of the working class, introduced elements of social security, increased taxation of the rich, and ended the veto power of the aristocrats in the House of Lords. Creation of a welfare state providing some measure of equality of opportunity and insurance against inequality of outcome was, however, not consolidated.

In nineteenth-century Britain, political conflicts between the rising industrial class and the old aristocracy were won by the former as parliament was reformed to broaden the electorate and to make the membership of parliament more representative of the distribution of population. Party politics built on competing manifestos became embodied in the Conservatives of Disraeli, who looked to a strong state maintaining the existing order, and the Liberals of Gladstone, who were the heirs of Adam Smith. In the Age of Liberty some radicals advocated a public role in promoting equality of opportunity through provision of education and health-related improvements in access to water, sewage, and so forth, but neither party saw correcting the outcomes of the market economy as an important duty of the government. Support of the poor and disadvantaged was the domain of private charities.

Pressure for improved working conditions in the factories and mines and on the railways led to permanent organizations of workers, and the political arm of the labor unions, the Trades Union Congress (TUC), acted as a pressure group in the interests of labor. In 1899 the TUC voted to set up a political party, which since 1906 has been called the Labour Party. In 1906 Labour helped the Liberals win a landslide election victory. The reformist government abandoned the small-government liberalism of Gladstone. It introduced labor market reforms (minimum wages, labor exchanges, eight-hour working days for miners, and protection of trade union funds) as well as old-age pensions and health and unemployment insurance, financed by increased taxation of the wealthy. In sum, they established the foundations of the welfare state in Britain, although the project would only be seriously furthered after 1945.

Delays in establishing the welfare state were due to the economic instability between 1914 and 1945 and national political developments. After World War I the Labour Party ceased to support the Liberals and in 1918 committed itself to socialism, that is, nationalization of key industries. Fear of communism fed class conflicts in Britain and contributed to the bitterness of the 1926 General Strike. By 1931 the Conservative Party had also lost confidence in the market economy. The government abandoned free trade and the gold standard, and introduced public ownership of broadcasting, transport in London, and electricity generation. Thus, the principle of extensive government involvement in the economy was accepted by both of the major parties even before World War II took such involvement to new heights. However, when William Beveridge produced the report *Social Insurance and Allied Services* in 1942, the Conservative chancellor of the exchequer feared the cost of implementing the proposed schemes—an attitude that would contribute to Churchill as the Conservative Party leader losing the election in 1945.[4]

The most successful moves toward establishing a welfare state before 1945 were in Sweden, where the Social Democrat Party in the 1930s laid the basis for what would become the model of social protection in the 1950s and 1960s. In the United States the 1935 Social Security Act marked the birth of the welfare state, providing federal benefits to retirees and grants to states to help the unemployed, dependent children, vocational rehabilitation, and public health.[5] In all high-income countries, however, expansion of the scope of the welfare state came mainly after 1945, and the growth of resources devoted to social transfers peaked between 1960 and 1980. According to Lindert (2004, table I.2), social transfers as a share of GDP in 1930 amounted to 2.24 percent in the United Kingdom, 2.56 percent in Sweden, and 0.56 percent in the United States; by 1960, according to the OECD Social Expenditure database, the share in these three countries was almost 10 percent, and by 1980 almost 20 percent.

The Long Boom, 1948–1973

Despite widespread fears in Western Europe and North America that the post-1945 era would be characterized by high unemployment as the major powers demobilized after war, the quarter-century after 1948 proved to be a golden age of sustained growth with a high degree of equality. In the United States the high rate of productivity growth in the 1930s was harnessed with a reemployment of labor and capital first for the war effort in 1942–1945 and then for peacetime purposes. In Europe, the Marshall Plan helped to kick-start the economies.[6] However, the main source of the postwar miracles was that, despite the physical destruction, levels of human capital were high and with good facilitating policies reconstruction proceeded smoothly and rapidly, especially in the defeated powers, Germany, Italy, and Japan.[7]

Recovery in Western Europe, Japan, and elsewhere was a classic example of conditional convergence or catch-up growth, favored by three circumstances.[8] First, the technological gap between the United States and potential followers was exceptionally large in 1945. The extent of U.S. economic dominance has probably never been matched; in mid-1945 the United States, whose GNP had doubled during the war and whose economy had suffered no physical destruction, accounted for half of the world's manufacturing output and most of its food surpluses (Judt, 2005, 105). Second, the leading group of followers was well placed in terms of human capital and social capacity to take advantage of catch-up opportunities. Third, the external environment was favorable.

The positive external environment was provided by an international system which fostered a rebuilding of the global economy that had malfunctioned between 1914 and 1945. The cooperative attitude among the victors, with the United States taking a leading role, was in stark contrast to 1919.[9] The United Nations was established in 1945 with an inspirational charter and, for all its shortcomings over the succeeding decades, the UN was instrumental in maintaining a world free of major wars, especially at the height of the Cold War:[10]

Preamble to the Charter of the United Nations
(signed by 50 countries, June 1945)

WE THE PEOPLES OF THE UNITED NATIONS DETERMINED

- to save succeeding generations from the scourge of war, which twice in our lifetime has brought untold sorrow to mankind, and
- to reaffirm faith in fundamental human rights, in the dignity and worth of the human person, in the equal rights of men and women and of nations large and small, and

- to establish conditions under which justice and respect for the obligations arising from treaties and other sources of international law can be maintained, and
- to promote social progress and better standards of life in larger freedom,

AND FOR THESE ENDS

- to practice tolerance and live together in peace with one another as good neighbours, and
- to unite our strength to maintain international peace and security, and
- to ensure, by the acceptance of principles and the institution of methods, that armed force shall not be used, save in the common interest, and
- to employ international machinery for the promotion of the economic and social advancement of all peoples,

HAVE RESOLVED TO COMBINE OUR EFFORTS
TO ACCOMPLISH THESE AIMS

Accordingly, our respective Governments, through representatives assembled in the city of San Francisco, who have exhibited their full powers found to be in good and due form, have agreed to the present Charter of the United Nations and do hereby establish an international organization to be known as the United Nations.

At Bretton Woods in 1944, rules were designed for convertible currencies with fixed exchange rates monitored by the International Monetary Fund (IMF), which could provide short-term loans to countries with BOP deficits and would monitor exchange rate changes.[11] Members of the IMF are eligible to join the International Bank for Reconstruction and Development (later rebadged as the World Bank), which would fill perceived gaps in global capital markets by providing loans for postwar reconstruction (which happened much faster than expected) and for development (which turned out to be the bank's major business). Establishment of an International Trade Organization foundered on countries' unwillingness to yield sovereignty over trade policy, but a provisional

General Agreement on Tariffs and Trade (GATT) set out rules for trade policies, and in 1995 a more formal institution was established, the World Trade Organization (WTO).[12] Although the IMF's mandate changed dramatically in the early 1970s, the system designed in the 1940s signaled a new commitment to free and nondiscriminatory markets for currency and goods that has underlain the global economy ever since.

In Western Europe, in contrast to the economic nationalism of 1919–1939, regional economic integration occurred on a grand scale. France, Germany, Italy, and the Benelux countries established the European Coal and Steel Community in 1951, with the idea that if these key industries were under supranational control renewed war in Europe would be impossible. The same six countries signed the Treaty of Rome in 1957 to establish other European communities and had completed a customs union by 1968. Seven other Western European countries, led by the United Kingdom, created the rival European Free Trade Association (EFTA) as a path to regional trade liberalization without supranational bodies. By 1973 the United Kingdom and Denmark had left EFTA to join the European Community (EC), a free trade area in manufactures had been established between the EC and EFTA, and the remaining non-communist European countries had association agreements with the European Community. Foreign exchange controls were gradually reduced during the late 1940s and 1950s, and by 1958 most restrictions on current account transactions had been removed. The European countries retained national currencies and on occasion there were major realignments (the French franc in 1958, the British pound in 1967, and the French franc and German mark in 1969), but by 1970 there were virtually no tariffs on intra–Western European trade, and monetary impediments were minor.[13]

Even more striking than the unexpectedly rapid reconstruction of economies devastated by war was the pace and sustainability of economic growth after 1948 (Table 4.1). Global output and living standards increased faster than in any other quarter-century in human history. The spread of car ownership (Table 2.2) and other consumer durables underlined the sense of generalized prosperity during the long boom,

Table 4.1   Growth in per capita GDP, annual average rates, 1950–1973 and 1973–1998

	1950–1973	1973–1998
Western Europe	4.08	1.78
Western offshoots	2.44	1.94
Japan	8.05	2.34
Resurgent Asia (excl. Japan)	2.61	4.18
Other Asia	4.09	0.59
Latin America	2.52	0.99
Eastern Europe and Soviet Union	3.49	−1.10
Africa	2.07	0.01

Source: Maddison (2006, 129).
Notes: "Western offshoots" are the United States, Canada, Australia, and New Zealand. "Resurgent Asia" includes 15 high-performing Asian economies.

especially in Europe and in Japan, where such goods had been luxuries before 1939 but were mass consumption items by the early 1970s. Moreover, the quality and variety of cars, washing machines, refrigerators and other kitchen appliances increased dramatically. The social impact was greatest in the evolution of radios and gramophones, from large pieces of furniture to cheap portable transistor radios and record players, and of televisions, from small black and white sets receiving few channels to color TVs able to broadcast real-time news or sports by satellite.[14] Services associated with tourism, eating out, and entertainment accounted for a growing share of consumption spending.

A feature of the growth in the high-income countries during the long boom was the central role of investment in physical and human capital. In countries devastated by war high rates of investment were an inevitable part of reconstruction, but everywhere the capital-labor ratio to which countries were converging was much higher than before the war. This capital-deepening increased labor productivity and was accompanied by significant gains in real wages. At the same time the need for more skilled labor encouraged other high-income countries to follow the United States in making completed secondary education the norm and then in the 1960s greatly expanding tertiary education enrollments. Low fees and financial assistance to students attending state colleges and universities were important elements of promoting equality of opportunity.

The boom was accompanied by massive sectoral change, especially the shift of labor out of agriculture (Table 4.2). In Western Europe there were 30 million farmworkers in 1950, but only 8 million a quarter-century later, and similar shifts occurred in Japan and in Eastern Europe. The sectoral shift from a low- to a higher-productivity sector, as in the Lewis (1954) model, represented a one-time boost to growth in countries where the transition occurred (Temin, 2002). This helps to explain why Britain, where the agricultural sector had already shrunk substantially before 1945, had lower growth than the other large European countries. A counterpart to the decline of farm employment was the increase in manufactured exports from the countries concerned; Britain had supplied a quarter of the world's manufactured exports in the late 1940s, but in the 1970s this share fell below a tenth, as Britain was overtaken by Germany, Japan, and France.

The movement from villages to towns was one source of social upheaval. Increased demand for workers also pushed up the wages of young workers and of female workers, and led to large immigration flows, even in Europe.

The increased wages of young people created for the first time a large group of young people with discretionary spending power. To the shock of many older people, the teens and twenties spent their cash on things that separated them from respectable society, wearing unconventional clothes, paying for unconventional hairstyling, and buying recordings of unconventional music. The social threat from rock and roll or alienated youths turned out to be far less than many older people feared, but the questioning of established conventions would contribute to the Age of Equality by undermining the acceptance of status based on birth. In the 1960s the music of the youth culture became a worldwide phenomenon (at least in the countries where a majority could afford to buy records) with a philosophy of tolerance, anti-materialism, and anti-war.

The cultural phenomenon of the 1960s was short-lived, no longer than the seven years from the Beatles' first hit record in late 1962 to the group's disintegration, but its impact went deep. Many of the fash-

Table 4.2 Sectoral employment of the workforce, 1950–1970 (percent)

| | 1950* | | | 1970 | | | Share of world manufactured exports (%) | |
	Agriculture	Industry	Service	Agriculture	Industry	Service	1950	1970
United Kingdom	4.9	49.4	45.7	3.2	44.8	52.0	25.5	10.8
United States	11.9	35.9	52.2	4.5	34.4	61.1	27.3	18.5
France	27.4	37.0	35.6	13.9	39.7	46.4	9.9	8.7
Germany	23.2	44.4	32.4	8.6	48.5	42.9	7.3	19.8
Japan	41.0	24.2	34.8	17.4	35.7	46.9	3.4	11.7

Source: Crafts and Woodward (1991, tables 1.10 and 1.11).
Note: * France 1954, Japan 1955.

ions soon looked dated, but the repudiation of Western conventions of the 1950s, when men wore suits on weekends and few women wore trousers, had a permanent impact. The student protests of 1968, which often appeared like privileged youths complaining about their lot, had a wider echo in industrial relations. Widespread strikes in France in May 1968 and in Italy's "hot autumn" of 1969, for example, were about hierarchical conditions in the workplace rather than about traditional trade union issues of pay and hours, reflecting students' concerns about alienation more than the materialist concerns of political and labor leaders of an older generation: "Traditional styles of authority, discipline and address (or, indeed, dress) had failed to keep pace with the rapid social and cultural transformation of the past decade" (Judt, 2005, 408).[15] Protests in the United States had a different focus, the Vietnam War, but a common thread was assertion of individuals' right to oppose a policy being prosecuted by the national leadership. In sum, the 1960s youth movements were harbingers of new attitudes toward individuals' status in society and of questioning traditional authority and ways of doing things.

The changing status of women was also dramatic. In 1945 women had fewer social and political rights than men and were paid less for the same work. Even where equal legal rights existed, practice was rarely equal, and in many countries the status of women had retrogressed since the 1920s; driven by fears of national decline and by the high unemployment of the 1930s, women were encouraged to leave the workforce and concentrate on child-rearing. Equal pay was only gradually legislated in the United Kingdom, France, the Netherlands, and the Scandinavian countries in the 1950s and even later in West Germany, Austria, and Southern Europe. The contraceptive pill, which became available in the early 1960s, changed sexual practices and gave women greater control over their reproductive lives, but abortion laws varied considerably, as did divorce procedures and family law.[16] Thus, attitudes changed and women gained greater economic, social, and political equality, but in many areas even as formal restrictions on female participation were lifted, a glass ceiling remained; male dominance in politics, business, law, and other professions would only begin to be eroded in the 1970s.

A final response to labor market disequilibria was migration. Immigrants had long been a feature of economies such as Australia, Canada, New Zealand, and the United States, and in the 1950s and 1960s inflows continued to be large, including many Europeans. A novel feature of the 1950s and especially the 1960s was the growing immigrant population in European countries. In France, the United Kingdom, and the Netherlands the inflows came from their disintegrating empires, especially as falling transport costs enabled the immigrants to move from a lower- to a higher-wage location. The receiving countries responded by tightening their definitions of citizenship.[17] In Germany and Switzerland the immigrants were seen less as fellow citizens than as guest workers who would return home when their jobs were over. Yet this was an unrealistic vision, as the immigrants had children who grew up in the only country they had ever known. Despite official pronouncements that the German Federal Republic was not an immigrant country, 2.6 million foreign workers lived there by 1973 and they were responsible for almost a fifth of births.

Explaining Growth in Market-Based Economies

The long boom was driven by high savings rates and investment in human and physical capital, but—in contrast to the USSR—growth in the established market economies was sustained. In terms of the Harrod-Domar model set out in Chapter 3, the economic problem that the USSR started to face in the 1960s was diminishing returns to capital, or equivalently that the incremental capital-output ratio (k) began to increase (see Table 7.2). In the market economies, the efficiency of capital did not fall, and the incremental capital-output ratio remained constant, around three; diminishing returns were offset by increased productivity.

The process was set out in the neoclassical growth model popularized by Robert Solow (1956). The model is neoclassical in its assumptions about the production function; output depends on inputs of labor and capital, such that additions of one input increase output but at a diminishing rate, and increasing both inputs by the same percentage will increase output by the same percentage (aggregate constant returns to scale).[18] An increase in the savings rate, given the level of investment demand and labor supply, pushes down the market interest rate relative to the wage rate, encouraging substitution of capital for labor; the higher capital/labor allows each worker to produce more output. Thus, in the short run the higher savings rate increases the growth rate of output as the economy transits from the old capital/labor ratio to the new capital/labor ratio, which is associated with a higher output. However, a one-off increase in the savings rate will not affect long-run growth; once the new equilibrium between savings and investment has been reached, the growth rate of output will return to its previous rate, which will be the rate of population growth plus any increase in productivity (shifts in the production function, or "technical change").[19]

Empirical evidence on the neoclassical growth model was provided by growth accounting, that is, decomposing increases in income into parts owing to increased inputs and the residual could be ascribed to increases in productivity. Solow (1957) examined U.S. economic growth between 1900 and 1950, when output increased by 3 percent per annum, the capital stock by 3 percent, and the labor force by 1 percent. Weighting the two inputs by their share in total income (one-third for capital and two-thirds for labor), the growth accounting is that capital accounted for 1.00 percentage points of growth and labor for 0.67, so the residual must have accounted for $3 - 1 - 0.67 = 1.33$. Thus, in explaining U.S. growth in output per head between 1900 and 1950, shifts in the production function (described variously as technical change or increased total factor productivity) were more important than capital formation. This is generally true for the United States and for other high-income countries in the second half of the twentieth century, although less so after 1973.[20]

The neoclassical model highlights the importance for growth in per capita output of technical change, as any shift in the relationship between inputs and outputs is termed, but does not explain such shifts. In the early stages of the long boom the exogenous technical change could be explained by specific beneficial conditions, such as civilian use of wartime technologies, but the market economies also seemed to provide an environment more conducive to innovation than that of the planned economies. The theoretical challenge was increasingly seen to be how to endogenize growth, that is, how to explain growth within the model rather than by some unexplained shift in production relations or an empirical residual.

The sustained relationship can be explained by the existence of increasing returns to scale. Adam Smith (1776) argued that, as the size of the market increases, there are more opportunities for profitable capital formation, which will increase output and set in motion a virtuous circle of higher output leading to increased capital formation leading to higher output and so on and on.[21] Links between capital formation and growth may also be due to the embodiment of new technology in new equipment and to the impact on labor productivity through posing new challenges that keep workers on their toes; much productivity improvement arises from learning by doing (Arrow, 1962; Lucas, 1988), and this effect can be enhanced by continuous upgrading of the capital stock with which people work. The endogenous growth theory of Romer (1986) emphasizes the role of knowledge as a source of increasing returns; the rewards from innovating are related to the size of the market, whereas the costs of innovating are largely independent of the size of the market. An empirical problem with theories relating growth to size is that there is no simple correlation between economic size and economic prosperity—small countries like Switzerland are among the world's richest, while large countries such as India are not—although this can be countered by the observation that all rich small countries have had open economies so that the relevant market size is the global economy.

The Schumpeterian branch of new growth theories emphasizes the role of new goods and new ways of producing things; capitalist growth involves a process of "creative destruction" as entrepreneurs identify new opportunities and existing production facilities lose their value.[22] Growth during the long boom reflected the process, as promoting new goods, in the way that William Hoover or Henry Ford had done in the United States in the interwar years, became a science taught in proliferating business schools and reflected in the new professional area of marketing.[23] The United States kept the lead in these areas but Western Europe was catching up fast. By contrast, planners in the Soviet Union and in the Third World (see Chapter 5) saw such activities as wasteful and concentrated on producing more of the same good rather than seeking new varieties of output and new methods of production.

A symptom of the difference was the age of the capital stock; in dynamic economies new machinery replaced obsolete equipment, whereas in less dynamic economies machinery would be used until it was physically worn out.

A feature of the theories described in the previous paragraph is the role of entrepreneurs, that is, risk-taking firms or individuals who identify new market opportunities and who introduce innovations. The financial sector plays a crucial role in allocating capital, and this involves mediating not only between savers and investors, but also between competing requests for loans from would-be entrepreneurs with risky projects. Some of the many capital-constrained entrepreneurs will have overestimated the economic feasibility of their ideas, but some projects will be good and a well-functioning financial sector will be one that encourages entrepreneurs with ideas but limited capital and can balance risk and returns. A well-functioning market economy is unstable, because loans may turn bad for unforeseen reasons or the investment climate may change. In 1929 or 1973, for example, as investment demand plummeted, the new equilibrium in the neoclassical growth model involved lower capital/labor ratios and slower or negative growth, although these situations still provided opportunities for risk-takers to find good ways of employing the underutilized labor and capital.

During the long boom, world trade grew faster than output. The United States took the lead in dismantling the high tariffs of the 1930s (Figure 4.1), and for Western Europe and Japan (and especially the new industrializing economies described in the next chapter) openness was a key feature of their growth. Simple stories of specialization by comparative advantage seemed unable to explain the link between trade and growth, especially in Europe where countries had similar endowments and the growth in trade was intra-industry (e.g., France sold Peugeot cars to Germany and imported Mercedes cars from Germany) rather than inter-industry trade. Theoretical work shifted from simple export-led growth stories to emphasizing the role of imports in providing access to best-practice technology or intermediate inputs and the role of international competition in punishing producers who do not update their obsolete equipment, all of which should be reflected in improved quality of investment.

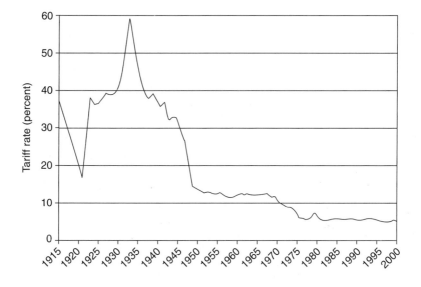

Figure 4.1. Average U.S. tariff, 1915–2000

Source: Compiled from data in *Historical Statistics of the United States: Millennial Edition,* ed. Susan Carter, Scott Sigmund Gartner, Michael R. Haines, Alan L. Olmstead, Richard Sutch, and Gavin Wright (online version). New York: Cambridge University Press, 2006.

The gains from trade were easiest to explain with respect to intercontinental trade, highlighted by the rapid growth of Japan based on exporting manufactured goods (Table 4.2). This was a simple story of specialization by comparative advantage, initially in low-wage manufactured goods, followed by movement up the quality ladder as skill levels and wages increased. Long distance trade was facilitated by reductions in ocean transport costs driven by technical and organizational change. Containerization was introduced first in the United States and then on U.S.-Japan and U.S.-Europe routes in the late 1960s, with massive cost savings from not having to pack and unpack items as they moved over long distances by a variety of transport modes (Levinson, 2006). The growth of open registry shipping to circumvent regulatory and labor laws in high-income countries further reduced shipping costs.[24]

The reestablishment of a global economy was also visible in the growth of multinational enterprises, international finance, and communications technology, although in the 1950s and 1960s many of these changes were embryonic. Before the second half of the century, multinational enterprises were mainly trading companies or resource companies operating where the oil or minerals or crops were to be found. Multinational manufacturing companies, which were primarily based in the United States and to a lesser extent Western Europe and Canada, mostly established subsidiaries in the high-income countries where the markets were largest, but other patterns began to emerge. Companies producing goods with high transport costs, such as Coca Cola, established subsidiaries or licensed local producers in a larger range of countries. Some companies inhibited from exporting to overseas markets by high protective tariffs jumped over the tariffs by establishing local production, especially in Latin America. Electronics and clothing firms began to experiment with relocating labor-intensive activities to low-wage countries such as Singapore or South Korea.[25] The process could be conducted within a firm through direct foreign investment in production facilities overseas or it could be done by subcontracting to local producers; the choice depends upon the trade-offs between retaining control over things like proprietary technology and quality control and the extent to which a local firm or joint-venture partner may be better able to deal with local labor regulations or relations with governments. Banks responded by improving the services offered to customers with cross-border activities, and devising ways to avoid onerous domestic regulations, for example, creating euro-dollar markets in which dollar-denominated transactions took place outside the United States. International communications improved as satellites and other technical change facilitated international telecommunications technology[26] and as air transport became faster and cheaper.[27] All of these developments would become much more important in the final quarter of the twentieth century.

Establishment of the Welfare State

The prosperity of the 1950s and 1960s, perhaps combined with feelings of national solidarity from the wartime experience, facilitated the creation of and extension of policies to share the prosperity and include the economically less fortunate. All across Western Europe governments established cradle-to-grave economic safety nets.[28] In the early postwar era public housing provision was a high priority, especially in Northern Europe, with the number of new houses vying with the unemployment rate in many countries as the most important economic indicator. Public health services and schools were improved and made universally available. The long boom provided the material resources for such programs, while prosperity reduced the claims for unemployment insurance and other welfare payments.

The 1945 British election resulted in a landslide victory for the Labour Party, given a mandate for sweeping reform by soldiers looking for a better world. The distinctive features of the 1945–1951 government's policies were nationalization (of railways, coal mining, steel) and extension of the welfare state (symbolized by the creation of the National Health Service and extension of public housing). Nationalization remained a political football for forty years as the steel industry was denationalized and renationalized, but its economic impact was minor, as the group of state-owned industries remained small (and generally inefficient) and the economy as a whole was market-driven. When Labour returned to power between 1964 and 1970, the main economic project was no longer nationalization but a national economic plan, which was also ineffective in changing the essence of the market economy.[29]

The welfare state became a fixture accepted by both major parties in the United Kingdom. The Conservative governments of 1951–1964 and 1970–1974 showed no inclination to dismantle the welfare state. The Labour government of 1964–1970 extended some of the benefits (e.g., for workers made redundant), but made no fundamental change. The general principles of a social safety net, decent pensions and housing, the National Health Service, and public provision of education were bipartisan. The massive expansion of the free-access university system during the 1960s was begun by a Conservative government and continued by a Labour government.

Elsewhere in post-1945 Europe the mixed economy and the welfare state became the norm. In Eastern Europe the shift toward economic planning and social security initially followed a similar pattern, although under Soviet control it quickly led to the destruction of the market and democracy. In some Western European countries, notably Germany and Italy, many social policies were continuations of systems established under fascism. In Sweden they were an extension of experiments begun in the 1930s. Yet whatever the background there was a general pattern, agreed by all major political parties and reflecting a postwar world in which the extension of state power was widely accepted as desirable. The most memorable opposition was fictional—George Orwell's *1984* and Aldous Huxley's *Brave New World* painted bleak pictures of a future in which individualism is repressed by a depersonalized state— but as long as the managed economy produced high growth and economic security, after three decades of war and economic uncertainty, concerns about government overreach were muted.

The consensus was strongest in the German Federal Republic. Ludwig Erhard, the Federal Republic's first economics minister and chancellor from 1963 to 1966, championed the "social market economy" as the creation of the right-wing CDU. Karl Schiller, the first economics minister from the left-wing SPD after 1966, continued almost seamlessly, declaring that "the welfare state and a dynamic market economy are mutually indispensable" (quoted in Mazower, 1998, 298). Similar patterns emerged in the rich countries beyond Europe, such as Australia, Canada, and New Zealand. Opposition to increased state economic power was strongest in the United States, which had enjoyed greater interwar prosperity than Europe, despite the post-1929 depression, and had suffered the least homeland disruption during the 1941–1945 war, but after 1964 President Lyndon Johnson pushed through a major program of welfare entitlements aimed at creating a Great Society.

In the rich countries, the post-1945 years were an era not only of increased government involvement in the economy whatever the name of the governing party, but also of deep conservatism in the desire for a quiet life. In the 1950s economic innovation in the name of equity coexisted with a reassertion of traditional social values, especially concerning the role of women and the importance of the family. This conservatism was driven in part by political leaders concerned about fears of communism and of declining birth rates, but it was accepted by many people seeking a retreat into domesticity and material comfort after decades of economic disruption and war. The social conservatism of the 1950s would, however, prove transitory as the long boom continued, and the political voices of previously disempowered groups such as women or youths would become louder. The seeds of greater sexual equality were being laid as women received equal voting rights in most Western European democracies.[30] Respect for traditional hierarchies would be challenged in the 1960s by a new generation without memory of depression or war, and in many countries the minimum voting age was reduced from 21 to 18 in the early 1970s.[31] The increasing demands of working women or of articulate students put further pressures on the welfare state, for example, to provide services such as childcare for less well-off working women or to support poor students.

The conservatism of the 1950s was, however, not backward-looking to laissez faire capitalism or precapitalist society. The combination of the managed economy and the welfare state reflected a changed notion of citizenship in a democracy, with economic rights added to political rights. The social security elements of the welfare state contributed to equality by protecting people from drastic income loss owing to unemployment, disability, ill health, or old age, and such protection was seen as a right. By adding some "freedoms from" to the "freedoms to" that had been established before 1914, the Age of Equality built upon the Age of Liberty.[32] However, in many European countries the extension of the welfare state in the prosperous years was bringing it close to its fiscal limits by the early 1970s when the world was struck by major recessions.

The Productivity Slowdown of the 1970s

The 1970s were a critical decade for the high-income countries as the growth that had seemed self-sustaining at historically high rates since the late 1940s slowed down (Table 4.1). More immediately, these countries faced the twin macroeconomic threats of increasing unemployment and inflation. The malaise could be traced to three interrelated developments: the collapse of the fixed exchange rate regime in 1971–1973, a rapid increase in commodity prices in 1972–1974, of which the oil price increases in 1973–1974 (and again in 1980–1981) had the biggest impact, and the productivity slowdown in the leading economies.

The Bretton Woods agreement reestablished a fixed exchange rate system in the world economy, but without the automatic adjustment mechanism of the classical gold standard. Gold had a nominal role, but already by 1960 U.S. gold reserves were insufficient to cover the total potential demands for conversion of U.S. dollars into gold.[33] This did not matter as long as everybody trusted the U.S. paper currency, and the system became centred on the U.S. dollar; the Bretton Woods fixed exchange rate system is often referred to as a dollar-exchange standard to distinguish it from the earlier gold standard. Exchange rates were maintained vis-à-vis the U.S. dollar, which meant that any other bilateral exchange rate could be calculated, but there was no mechanism to change the U.S. exchange rate against all other currencies.

Until the late 1950s there was little need for a BOP adjustment mechanism because all major currencies except the U.S. and Canadian dollars were not freely convertible.[34] After convertibility was reestablished in Western Europe, central banks held foreign currency reserves (primarily in liquid U.S. dollar–denominated assets such as U.S. Treasury bills) which they ran down or accumulated to balance the demand for and supply of foreign currency. A country facing severe BOP deficits could borrow from the IMF for short-term financing of the deficit and, if the disequilibrium persisted, could seek agreement within the IMF for a devaluation of the exchange rate, as Britain did in 1967 and as France did in 1969. A country with recurring BOP surpluses could revalue its currency, as West Germany did in 1969. There was less immediate pressure on a surplus country, which was accumulating reserves, than on a deficit country, which would eventually run out of reserves and credit from the IMF, but a surplus country would not accept claims on a foreign government (essentially U.S. Treasury debt) in return for exports of real goods and services indefinitely. Moreover, as international financial markets grew during the 1960s, participants were able to make one-way bets against currencies of deficit countries or on currencies of BOP surplus countries in anticipation of devaluation or revaluation; the amounts involved in supporting strong currencies increased, and by the early 1970s the size of the capital flows contributed to making speculators' predictions self-fulfilling.

The critical threat to the system arose when the United States began to run recurring BOP deficits in the late 1960s, driven by the cost of financing the Vietnam War and the Great Society program. Increased money creation reduced U.S. competitiveness, and other countries (notably Germany, whose central bank stopped supporting the mark after adding a billion dollars to its reserves on 4 May 1971) tired of accumulating U.S. dollars in payment for their exports. On 15 August 1971, President Richard Nixon imposed a ninety-day wage and price freeze, a 10 percent import surcharge, and formally "closed the gold window," ending convertibility between U.S. dollars and gold. The decision, made without consulting other countries, was referred to by the rest of the world as "the Nixon shock." In return for removal of the import surcharge, which threatened the GATT-based international trading system, the major nations negotiated devaluation of the U.S. dollar. Convertibility between currencies was reestablished in December 1971, although even the symbolic connection to gold was now dead.

The December 1971 Smithsonian Agreement, which set new exchange rates against the U.S. dollar for all major currencies, was a response to the need for devaluation of the U.S. dollar. However, the new set of fixed exchange rates was unstable because countries pursued divergent monetary policies (i.e., the threat to the system in 1971 was not just a U.S.-originating problem). Among the seven largest market economies, Italy and the United Kingdom pursued macroeconomic policies with less concern about inflation and Germany had a greater aversion to inflation both before and after 1971 (Table 4.3). The consequences of these preferences were exacerbated in 1972 by asymmetric pressures of rising commodity prices. In this Impossible Trinity situation, fixed exchange rates could be maintained only by restricting international capital mobility, but no major economic power wanted to reimpose foreign exchange controls.

The outcome was the adoption of generalized floating in early 1973. This may have been the source of some short-term disruption to trade, but more importantly in the medium term the new arrangements permitted the major economies to pursue independent monetary policies

Table 4.3   Consumer price indexes for G7 economies, 1950–1985 (1980 = 100)

	1950	1971	1980	1985
Italy	13.9	28.7	100	190.3
United Kingdom	13.4	30.1	100	141.5
France	15.6	42.1	100	157.9
Japan	16.3	44.9	100	114.4
Canada	28.4	47.5	100	143.0
United States	29.2	49.1	100	130.5
Germany	39.2	64.1	100	121.0

Source: International Monetary Fund, as presented in Mundell (2000, 336).

Note: Seven largest market economies in 1985, ordered by their 1971–1980 inflation rates (from highest to lowest).

unconstrained by any pressure to maintain the international value of their currency. The impact during the remainder of the 1970s was an increase in the global money supply, which accommodated double-digit inflation in the main market-based economies.

As a general phenomenon the commodity price boom was concentrated in the period between mid-1972 and mid-1974 when a variety of commodities experienced large price increases. The *Economist* USD price index for twenty-eight commodities rose 63 percent between 1972 and 1973 and by 159 percent over the period 1971–1974—the biggest annual or three-year increase since the index was begun in 1864, using data back to 1845. After mid-1974 most commodity prices, apart from oil and some foods, fell. The shock to policymakers was that before 1973 macroeconomic policy had been based on shifting aggregate demand, with an assumed trade-off between unemployment and inflation; stimulating demand by expansionary fiscal or monetary policies would reduce unemployment and increase inflation, while contractionary demand management policies would increase unemployment and reduce inflation.[35] The aggregate supply curve was assumed to be stable, or gradually shifting in response to increased labor, capital, and technical change, but in most high-income countries in 1972–1974 the aggregate supply curve shifted sharply in the opposite direction as input prices increased much faster than output prices. The average price level increased and the

level of economic activity declined; the combination of higher inflation and higher unemployment was christened "stagflation." Floating
exchange rates freed governments from the Impossible Trinity constraint on monetary policy, and many increased the money supply
rather than trying to restrain monetary growth, which would lead to
higher unemployment. Apart from inflationary macro policies permitted by floating exchange rates, governments tried a variety of het-
erodox policies, such as wage and price controls or job-sharing, all of
which had at best a short-term impact. Everywhere, as the decade
progressed there was increasing dissatisfaction with incumbent politicians and in some countries increasing social conflict.

The most dramatic commodity price increase was that of oil, driven
by the producers' cartel the Organization of Petroleum Exporting
Countries (OPEC). OPEC had been formed in 1960, but was quiescent
until 1973. In October 1973 Arab members plus Egypt and Syria imposed an oil embargo on countries supporting Israel in the 1973 Yom
Kippur War. Irrespective of the catalyst, supply controls to increase
the price of oil were supported by non-Arab producers too; the shah of
Iran, in a December 1973 interview published in the *New York Times,*
in response to being questioned whether OPEC would maintain high
oil prices stated:

> "Certainly! And how . . . ; You [Western nations] increased the price
> of wheat you sell us by 300%, and the same for sugar and cement . . . ;
> You buy our crude oil and sell it back to us, refined as petrochemicals,
> at a hundred times the price you've paid to us . . . ; It's only fair that,
> from now on, you should pay more for oil. Let's say ten times more."

The Arab oil embargo ended in March 1974, but the price of oil, which
had been $2 a barrel for more than a decade, continued to rise to more
than $10 a barrel.

The consequences were to exacerbate the supply shock that had led
to stagflation in the high-income countries and to provide a massive
income transfer to oil-producing nations, which created a recycling
problem. The sparsely populated oil producers had inadequate absorp-
tive capacity, so they deposited their windfall gains with large international banks. The demand for loans in high-income countries was

negatively affected by recession, such that the excess supply of funds drove down interest rates and forced the banks to seek new borrowers. Most dramatically, the banks reversed their scepticism toward lending to low- and middle-income countries—it was now more than forty years since the defaults of the 1930s and memories of that episode had dimmed. The borrowers included oil-importers trying to smooth consumption (e.g., Brazil or Argentina), commodity producers expecting future prosperity (e.g., Mexico or Morocco), some centrally planned economies (e.g., Poland), and some of the new industrializing economies of East Asia (e.g., South Korea, Taiwan). With low real interest rates, borrowing was rational as long as loans were used for investments that would generate future foreign exchange earnings to service the debt. However, some borrowers were too optimistic and lenders foolishly believed sovereign debt was safe (and required less screening by loan officers); the outcome of such loans was the 1982 debt crisis (Chapter 5).

In 1979–1980 OPEC used its market power to push up the price of oil again, and it surpassed $40 a barrel. The consequences were dramatic. Unlike the confused macroeconomic policy response to the commodity price increases of 1972–1974, in high-income countries (especially in the United States and the United Kingdom) the priority in 1979–1981 was to reduce inflation by controlling the money supply, even though the resulting increase in interest rates would induce a recession. The increase in interest rates, and especially the U.S. interest rate increases, which contributed to appreciation of the U.S. dollar, hurt the debtor nations, most of whose external debt was denominated in dollars and was at a floating interest rate. In 1982 defaults by major borrowers led to a debt crisis. A longer-term consequence of the oil price increases was to stimulate exploration and the discovery of new oil reserves, notably in the North Sea, Alaska, and Mexico, and as these non-OPEC supplies came on line, the price of oil dropped below $10 a barrel by 1986.[36]

For the high-income countries the oil crisis was a catalyst for stagflation after 1973, and the collapse of Bretton Woods enabled independent monetary policies, which in the 1970s were inflationary. The period from 1973 to 1979 was characterized by low interest rates, but also by low investment in the industrialized countries. The fundamental force behind the slower growth rates in Table 4.1 was a slowdown in productivity growth. In the United States, according to Nordhaus (2004), the productivity slowdown in the late 1970s and early 1980s was the biggest slowdown in the second half of the 1900s, a rebound from two decades of rapid productivity growth associated with new technologies (synthetics, aircraft, suburbs).[37]

Conclusions

Concerns that the market-based economy would be under threat in the 1940s and 1950s were gradually dissipated as the long boom continued into the early 1970s. The proven ability of market systems to generate high levels of mass consumption and a wide variety of goods was critical for the contest between capitalism and central planning. Yet the system that appeared so resilient in the high-income countries of North America, Western Europe, Australasia, and Japan was a significantly modified version of the pre-1914 capitalist economy. In all cases, albeit to differing degrees, the price system was the primary resource allocation mechanism, but substantial government intervention moderated the operation of market forces by providing a social safety net for the most needy and by substantially determining outcomes in social sectors such as education, health, and public transport. The combination of high material living standards for the majority of the population and individual liberty and freedom of expression would prove irresistible in the final quarter of the century.

However, some harsh lessons were learned in the economically unstable decade of the 1970s. In particular, the limits of fiscal policy to deliver low unemployment and low inflation were seen. A related issue was the financing of the welfare state as costs of health, education, and pension programs increased, and budget deficits pushed up inflation.

As most high-income countries experienced double-digit inflation at some stage in the 1970s, the costs of inflation were highlighted: the short-run shock to relative incomes, the asymmetrical impact on borrowers and lenders and, most importantly, the long-term negative impact on the working of the market mechanism. If relative price changes are to play a useful signaling function, then the average price level should be fairly stable. The lesson that low inflation must be one of the highest economic policy goals in a market economy had been decisively learned by the 1980s.

The productivity slowdown also highlighted the importance of incentives. The market system only functions well if people respond to price signals. During the long boom most high-income countries maintained punitively high marginal tax rates on the rich, in part to finance increased government expenditures but more fundamentally driven by a desire for equality. In the United States the average federal tax rate for the top 0.1 percent of the income distribution was around 60 percent from 1960 to 1976, before falling to 42 percent in 1983 (Piketty and Saez, 2007). In Europe taxes on the rich were even higher, with the marginal rate reaching 95 percent in the United Kingdom. These peaks began to fall everywhere in the 1970s. Initial moves to deregulation also began in this decade, but the movement would become more pronounced in the 1980s and associated with governments of Margaret Thatcher in the United Kingdom and Ronald Reagan in the United States (Chapter 6).[38]

The limits of the welfare state would be debated in the 1980s. Did unemployment insurance, high tax rates, and other social security and redistribution measures dull incentives? Should benefits be universal, provided as a right, or should they be targeted to reach those most in need, even if the necessary means-testing imposes a stigma on recipients? To what extent should health, education, and pensions be privately funded, and how should the public-private balance be designed to ensure equity and efficiency? The answers to these questions challenged the welfare state as envisaged in the Swedish model or by reformers like Beveridge, but the desirability of the welfare state in some form would remain inviolate.

Finally, for all the negative economic news of the 1970s, the economic system in the high-income countries did not face an existential threat. Economic growth slowed, but income levels remained high, especially in countries such as Germany or Japan whose currencies appreciated after the end of the fixed exchange rate system. The post-1945 productivity improvements and product development were not lost. The institutions underpinning the liberal global economic system remained in place; although there was some protectionist backsliding in the 1970s and early 1980s, the trade liberalization achieved in GATT rounds of multilateral trade negotiations remained intact. These institutions, together with the innovations behind lower transport and transaction costs, would underpin rapid growth of the global market and integration of many more countries into the global market system in the remainder of the century.

CHAPTER 5

Decolonization and Cold War

✦

The cooperation between the united and allied nations fighting against Germany and Japan collapsed quickly after 1945. Within a few years an Iron Curtain divided Europe. The ideological divide would remain for more than forty years, but despite the competition between the two sides—the First World of high-income market economies and the Second World of centrally planned economies—there was no shift in the composition of these two groups.[1] The ideological battleground turned out to be in the Third World.

In the decades after 1945 all across Asia, Africa, and to a lesser extent Latin America, regimes came to power intent on economic modernization. Whether the goal was to increase the living standards of their people or to increase their country's regional or global power, the new leaders recognized the necessity of economic growth if they were to achieve the goal. The wide gap between the industrialized and nonindustrialized countries—or "developed" and "underdeveloped" countries, as they were referred to at the time (Table 5.1)—led to identification of economic development with industrialization. The challenge was to identify policies that could promote industrialization.

In the late 1940s the advantage in the competition between economic systems appeared to lie with central planning. The Soviet Union had emerged victorious from World War II, and postwar reconstruction, as in Western Europe, was surprisingly fast. In the 1950s the Soviet Union continued to project an image of success, as did other countries that adopted central planning after 1945 (see Chapter 6).

Table 5.1 Gross national product per capita, mid-1950s (selected countries, in current U.S. dollars)

First World		Second World		Underdeveloped (above $200)		Underdeveloped (below $200)	
United States	2,343	USSR	682	Argentina	374	Iraq	195
Canada	1,667	Czechoslovakia	543	Cuba	361	Mexico	187
New Zealand	1,249	Poland	468	Malaya	298	Chile	180
Switzerland	1,229	Hungary	387	Hong Kong	292	Saudi Arabia	166
Australia	1,215	Romania	320	Turkey	276	Morocco	159
Luxembourg	1,194	Yugoslavia	297	Brazil	262	Ghana	135
Sweden	1,165	Bulgaria	285	Spain	254	Egypt	133
Iceland	1,146			Japan	240	Indonesia	127
France	1,046			Greece	239	Taiwan	102
Belgium	1,015			Portugal	201	Thailand	100
United Kingdom	998			Philippines	201	Iran	100
Norway	969					South Korea	80
Finland	941					India	72
Denmark	913					Nigeria	70
West Germany	762					Pakistan	56
Netherlands	708					China	56
Austria	532					Afghanistan	54
Ireland	509					Ethiopia	54
Italy	442					Nepal	40

Source: Bhagwati (1966, 10–11), based on GNP data from national statistical offices.

Note: Bhagwati labels all of the countries in the last two columns plus Bulgaria, Romania, and Yugoslavia "underdeveloped"; in Latin America, Africa, and Asia only Venezuela (762), Uruguay (762), and South Africa (381) are not classified as underdeveloped. In the text he observes that "Asia is the most depressed area, trailing behind Africa, the Near East, and Latin America in that order" (Bhagwati, 1966, 17).

In contrast, the poor reputation attached to markets in the prewar depression was difficult to shake off, despite the military success of the United States, the United Kingdom and British dominions. Primary product exporters had suffered especially badly from the volatility of world markets, and a belief that they were condemned to second-class economic status was reinforced by evidence of long-term decline in primary product prices relative to the price of manufactured goods in world markets.[2] The new governments, which started with a fairly clean economic policy slate, sought to promote industrial development by insulating their economies from world markets, a strategy known as import-substituting industrialization (ISI), which was almost universally adopted by the Third World countries of Asia, Africa, and Latin America.

The outcome of ISI strategies was initially positive, as resources were mobilized, industries established, and growth rates increased. Over time, however, the growth rate slowed, often accompanied by BOP difficulties and by increases in unemployment or underemployment and income inequality. Yet ISI strategies were difficult to change because groups that benefited from the policies and had become politically powerful feared that they would suffer from reform. When reform came it was typically after a crisis, and sometimes several attempts at reform were necessary before the strategy was fundamentally changed.

An alternative development strategy was pursued by a handful of East Asian countries that produced manufactured goods for sale in the world market. These new industrializing economies enjoyed stellar growth rates, even through the decade 1973–1982 when the world economy was in turmoil. This outward-oriented strategy was adopted by an increasing number of countries after the late 1970s, most dramatically by China in 1978–1979. The rush to emulate the high-performing Asian economies in the 1980s and 1990s highlighted that even in the Age of Equality people's aspirations were for higher living standards and that economies responding to world prices satisfied these aspirations better than more regulated and more autarchic economies.

The End of Empires

Although the Ottoman and Austro-Hungarian empires collapsed after the 1914–1918 war, the overseas empires of the victorious powers remained.[3] The British and French empires spanned the globe, and even small European countries like the Netherlands, Belgium, and Portugal ran empires far bigger and more populous than their homelands. The United States, technically opposed to colonialism, ran the Philippines as a colony and exercised colonial rule in Hawaii, Puerto Rico, Guam, and other islands, as well as explicit hegemony in the Western Hemisphere.

In Asia, war fatally destabilized the European and American empires, as well as ending Japanese rule over Korea and Taiwan. With varying degrees of imperial resistance, the Philippines, Indonesia, India, and Vietnam became independent in the second half of the 1940s and early 1950s. The new nationalist governments were committed to promoting economic modernization. This attitude was shared by new governments in countries such as China after 1949 and Egypt after 1952 and by Latin American countries, Turkey, and Iran, which were frustrated by their second-rank economic status. The burning issue facing all of these governments was how to modernize their economies.

Should modernizing governments follow the advice of Western governments, the World Bank, and their economists and retain market-based economies albeit guided by planning ministries or should they follow the Soviet model? The need for some planning was taken for granted. The depression of the late 1920s and 1930s had hit primary product exporters especially hard, and fostered distrust of market mechanisms. The intellectual appeal of Keynesian economics also encouraged a search for market failures and use of government policies to correct them. The success of the USSR, both in war and in peacetime (peaking with Sputnik and Yuri Gagarin),[4] convinced many policymakers of the desirability of planning and of promoting industrial development.

At the same time, few countries were willing to adopt communist systems. The majority retained elements of market-determined resource allocation and private ownership. Generous aid from the West encouraged Third World governments to at least pay lip service to capitalism and to democracy.[5] Superimposed on the ideological conflict between the First and Second Worlds were old-fashioned geopolitical struggles for spheres of influence.[6] When Cuban revolutionaries overthrew the government in 1959, this was a threat to U.S. hegemony in the Western Hemisphere, and when the USSR supplied missiles to the new regime it brought the world to the brink of war in 1962. Even after the crisis was resolved by Soviet missile withdrawal, the USSR continued to pour large amounts of financial aid into Cuba in order to ensure the success of the only communist regime in the Western Hemisphere.

Starting with Ghana in 1957, a wave of decolonization swept sub-Saharan Africa, creating a new Cold War theater. The superpowers became involved in the frequent conflicts between competing domestic groups in arbitrarily constructed nations, leading to the most bitter civil wars when fueled by competition for control over natural resource revenues as in the attempted secessions of Katanga from Congo[7] or Biafra from Nigeria. Both superpowers, as well as ex-colonial powers such as Britain and France, were content to support autocratic rulers whose regimes were far from the ideals of either communism or liberal democracy, as long as they were on the right side when it came to votes at the UN, supply of raw materials, or other matters of importance to the major powers.

Influential Third World leaders tried to dissociate themselves from the Cold War clash of systems and superpowers. India, Indonesia, and Yugoslavia led the nonaligned movement, but this was viewed with suspicion by the United States and the USSR, both of which tended to see countries as either their friends or their enemies. By the mid-1960s the low-income countries formed a majority in the United Nations, and they used their voting power to create the UN Conference on Trade and Development and to push for a New International Economic Order; the main outcomes were the 1971 Generalized System of Preferences for developing countries and some attempts to regulate primary product markets, but the former had minimal results because importers made exceptions for any good that threatened domestic producers, and commodity producers were happy with market outcomes when commodity prices began to rise rapidly in 1972–1973.

Import-Substituting Industrialization

Development economics emerged as a distinct subdiscipline aimed at analyzing low-income countries' particular problems and understanding how their economic growth could be accelerated.[8] Theories and policy recommendations were fostered by the same environment that led to the emergence of modernizing regimes in the already independent countries (such as Ataturk in Turkey, Nasser in Egypt, and several Latin American regimes). The market mechanism was held in low esteem and Keynesian economics in high esteem, and the Soviet system was seen as the sole example of successful industrialization in the twentieth century, while industrialization was synonymous with economic development. All development theories emphasized the role of physical capital formation, as in the Harrod-Domar growth model (Chapter 3), where the incremental capital-output ratio (ICOR) is assumed to be a technologically determined constant and growth is a result of increasing the savings rate. Influential books by Arthur Lewis and Walt Rostow synthesized the secret to economic development in an increase from being a 5–6 percent saver to being a 10–12 percent saver.[9]

The development strategy adopted by all Third World countries in the 1950s was import-substituting industrialization. The goal was to promote industrial development, and, given the distrust of international markets, the solution was to produce for the domestic market. Patterns of domestic demand for industrial goods could be seen from imports, and so the strategy was to use trade restrictions to allow domestic producers to displace imports. Even in the late 1960s, Myrdal (1968, 1203) observed that "the obstacles to export promotion in manufactures are so great that import substitution usually offers a more promising prospect."

The implementation details varied from country to country. The Latin American countries, except Cuba, remained committed to private ownership and used the price mechanism (i.e., high protective tariffs) to encourage production of import substitutes. Other governments, such as in India, became more directly involved in resource allocation by raising tax revenue and allocating it to state-owned enterprises, which operated alongside the private sector. Turkey used state-owned banks to direct credit to the desired industries. McKinnon (1973) and Shaw (1973) coined the term "financial repression" to capture the phenomenon of government policies that restrain financial intermediaries' activities, whether by directing credit and imposing interest rate ceilings to encourage aggregate investment and capital-intensive activities or by legislating high reserve requirements which force banks to hold government bonds or cash. In financially repressed economies, governments applied foreign exchange controls to prevent domestic savers from accessing foreign capital markets in search of higher returns. Thus, measures to direct financial resources to desired users, either by bringing more resources under government control or by constraining financial intermediaries' freedom of action, both reduced the size of the domestic financial sector and contributed to delinking the domestic economy from global financial markets.

Countries adopting import substitution strategies experienced an initial increase in growth. New regimes mobilized resources better than their predecessors, and increased investment led to higher growth. Resource misallocation was initially unimportant because the earliest import substitution projects were typically in areas where comparative disadvantage was minor, for example, where transport costs were high or the need for skilled labor low (beer, kitchen utensils, and so forth). Over time, as the domestic market was filled, the economy had to move into more difficult areas of import substitution where comparative disadvantage was more pronounced. In a large economy like India the positive period lasted longer than a decade, but in a small economy like Cuba the easy projects were exhausted in less than five years. In all ISI economies, resource misallocation costs increased over time.

Resource allocation responds to relative prices. If import-competing industrial goods are favored, then agriculture and export sectors are disfavored. In the ISI countries, farm productivity grew slowly as farmers had little incentive to make investments or to risk trying new seeds or other innovations. Because imports into low-income countries tend to be capital-intensive, ISI strategies rewarded owners of capital more than laborers and tended to make the distribution of income more unequal. Capitalists were often willing to share the benefits of industrialization with their workers in order to encourage loyalty, but this opened up large wage gaps between the few relatively well-paid workers in the modern sector and other workers. In Brazil factory wages in the south were more than five times wages in the northeast, and workers moved from the northeast to Rio de Janeiro or São Paolo in search of a job even if the probability of success was not high. Thus, many countries' labor markets became characterized by underemployment, as people moved to the cities and undertook low-productivity activities (such as selling shoelaces or washing car windscreens) to keep themselves alive while they waited for a job in the modern sector.[10] The negative impact on income distribution and the high-profile urban poverty supported critiques of the market system, but the real problem was the price distortions caused by ISI.

The two most important prices in a market economy are the exchange rate and the interest rate. Most ISI countries had overvalued currencies at the official exchange rate. Demand for foreign currency was artificially low due to foreign exchange controls, and balance between demand and supply was maintained by requiring all foreign exchange earnings to be surrendered to the state, which would allocate the scarce foreign currency to, for example, industries that required imported inputs. Together with high trade barriers the distorted exchange rates disconnected domestic prices from world prices, as well as encouraging black markets for currency and corruption among officials involved in the system. The cumulative effect of distortions due to disconnecting from the world economy were emphasized in an influential set of case studies coordinated by Little, Scitovsky, and Scott (1970) for the OECD. Countries pursuing ISI strategies not only forwent potential gains from specialization and trade, but also suffered chronic resource misallocation through poor project selection. Little and Mirrlees (1969), in another very influential book, highlighted the difficulties of evaluating projects when prices are artificial and that appropriate opportunity cost prices for a small economy are world prices; for an imported good the world price indicates the cost of obtaining an extra unit of the good and for an export the world price indicates the benefit of producing an extra unit of the good. There are many sources of market failure, whereby market prices do not precisely capture social cost and benefit, but these divergences are unlikely to be as large as the policy-induced price distortions in ISI economies. In sum, an overvalued exchange rate that discriminates against trade (because exports are less competitive and imports are restricted by controls) not only forgoes short-term gains from trade but also, more seriously, leads to resource misallocation through poor choice of investment projects, which will damage long-term growth.[11]

The interest rate is important not just as the price of saving and investment, but also in allocating capital among competing uses. Assessing the empirical evidence from many low- and middle-income countries, Fry (1988) concluded that savings were fairly unresponsive to interest rate changes; low interest rates have a negative but small impact on the level of savings. A far more serious problem was adverse selection. In a financially repressed economy, banks that cannot charge a higher interest rate to compensate for risk will lend to the least risky would-be borrowers. Public officials directing capital may also be cautious if they fear criticism for directing capital to risky projects, some of which will fail; it is safer to support low-risk projects even if their returns are low. If the scarce capital is allocated to relatives or cronies of the president whose political skills are better than their management skills, then the adverse selection problem may be even more severe. Fry assembled evidence that capital in ISI countries was allocated not to projects with the highest social return, but to safer, less productive projects. Potential entrepreneurs with high-return projects willing to pay higher interest rates than borrowers with lower return projects could not obtain credit because banks were unable to charge above the artificially low interest rate. In sum, in a financially repressed economy where interest rates are artificially low, not only will there be less private savings, but also there is likely to be misallocation of the scarce capital; in countries adopting ISI strategies in the 1950s and 1960s, the latter was the more severe problem.[12] Misallocation of capital did not have an immediate effect after the adoption of ISI, but it explains poor long-run growth performance.

All countries pursuing ISI strategies ran into economic difficulties, but the symptoms varied. In Latin America the dominant symptom was high inflation as governments printed money, often to support the living standards of poor people hurt by food shortages due to an underperforming farm sector.[13] In India the situation was brought to a head when the monsoons failed in the mid-1960s; the stagnant export sector was unable to provide sufficient foreign exchange to pay for imports and India was forced to accept large-scale food aid from the United States—a humiliating outcome from a development strategy intended to increase self-sufficiency. In Egypt bread riots threatened the government and encouraged an opening up of the economy in the 1970s. Iran, with its oil wealth, faced no serious BOP constraint, but the pace of change and blatant inequalities led to unrest, which was suppressed by a brutal security apparatus, and in 1978 to a revolt that replaced the modernizing regime with a conservative theocracy.

The situation with respect to agriculture began to improve in the 1960s as a result of the Green Revolution.[14] The development of new high-yielding varieties of rice and wheat allowed many low and middle-income countries, including India, whose wheat yields almost doubled between 1965 and 1970, to greatly increase their food output. This was not a universal pattern, because some countries' policies discouraged adoption of the new technology and the new seeds were unsuited to some countries' conditions (especially the arid countries of Africa, which continued to suffer severe droughts in the closing decades of the century). There were also negative side effects of increased need for fertilizer and narrowing of the gene pool for major grains, but by any criteria the Green Revolution was one of the most positive developments in the second half of the twentieth century. The new technology averted fears of world hunger for the rest of the century and, although famines continued to occur, especially on the edge of the great North African desert, they were the result of poor distribution, not global food shortages.

For many countries, especially in Latin America, the end of the road for ISI strategies came with the increase in oil prices in the 1970s.

Oil importers like Brazil could not earn foreign exchange to cover the higher fuel bills and after decades of ISI had little scope to reduce non-oil imports; the short-term solution, facilitated by the recycled revenues of oil-exporting nations, was to borrow from foreign banks. Brazil, Argentina, and other oil importers ran up large debts, which were used primarily to support consumption rather than for productive investments that would generate foreign exchange earnings to repay the debts. Oil exporters like Mexico and Venezuela were tempted to borrow on the strength of expected future oil revenues and invested in ISI projects, which also did not generate foreign exchange earnings. When interest rates and the U.S. dollar rose in the early 1980s, the borrowers who had persisted with ISI policies could not meet their external debt payments.[15] On 12 August 1982 Mexico announced that it was no longer able to meet its debt obligations, and by October 1983 twenty-seven countries, owing $239 billion, had rescheduled their debts to foreign banks.[16]

The resolution of the debt crisis over the next dozen years involved a series of plans to share the burden between borrowers and lenders. For the lending banks, avoiding outright default was important because they would face bankruptcy, and it was better to be repaid part of what they were owed than to be paid nothing. For the banks' governments, especially the United States, the aim in 1983–1989 was to prevent a domestic banking crisis triggered by failure of major banks due to underperforming overseas loans. The plans allowed banks to gradually wind down their exposure to manageable levels, for example, U.S. money center banks' outstanding loans to Latin America fell from $56 billion in 1983 to $44 billion in 1989. Meanwhile, the borrowers were granted partial rollover of loans aimed at keeping their economies functioning while the causes of the debt accumulation were addressed.[17] In the eighteen national negotiations under the Brady Plan between 1989 and 1994, about $61 billion of the $191 billion private lender debts were forgiven, primarily at the cost of the lending banks' shareholders (Cline, 1995). For the borrowing countries, even repaying part of their debts involved harsh squeezes of living standards to free up resources to produce exports and to reduce import demand; the process, known as the "lost decade" in Latin

America, highlighted the shortcomings of an ISI strategy and the need for economic reform.[18]

Reforming an economy based on ISI was not easy, because many groups benefited from the status quo and would lose from reform, while the main beneficiaries of reform, potential exporters and consumers, were either not yet identified or poorly organized politically. In India initial attempts at reform in the 1970s were limited and the process continued through the 1980s as governments continued to respond to pleas to support ailing enterprises rather than undertake thoroughgoing reforms; only in the 1990s were substantial reforms implemented.[19] Brazil also went through a stop-go cycle of reform and backsliding during the 1980s and early 1990s, before undertaking sustained reform. Mexico bit the bullet earlier with major reforms in 1986 that were maintained by the promise of a free trade agreement with the United States and Canada (NAFTA was eventually signed in 1993). Although speed of implementation varied, the global trend toward abandoning ISI strategies was clear by the 1980s.

The Newly Industrializing Economies

The Third World countries pursuing import-substituting industrialization ran into constraints on economic growth that were not encountered by the First World countries engaged in the global economy. Surprisingly for many observers who saw this as evidence of the bias in the international system in favor of rich countries, a handful of poor countries that adopted outward-oriented development strategies also grew rapidly by integrating into the global economy. First among these were the city-states of Hong Kong (the equal-largest developing country exporter in the 1950s with India, despite its tiny area and small population) and, after becoming independent in 1965, Singapore. These could be ignored as special cases, but by the mid-1970s it was becoming clear that Taiwan and South Korea were also growing rapidly on the basis of exporting labor-intensive manufactured goods.[20] In 1979 the OECD coined the term "newly industrializing countries" to capture the phenomenon of these and other countries such as Israel and Yugoslavia enjoying export-led growth.[21]

Hong Kong was the only low-wage economy pursuing free trade policies in the 1950s and 1960s, and it was also one of the fastest growing, but it was ignored as a colony with specific characteristics—even though the location became a negative factor when China shut itself off from the world in the 1960s. The other three high-performing Asian economies all changed from more inward-looking to more outward-looking trade policies in the first half of the 1960s. This was less dramatic for Singapore which had long been a trading city, but had been governed by Malaysian trade policies before it seceded from the federation in 1965. South Korea and Taiwan, on the other hand, had adopted import-substituting industrialization policies in the 1950s and then rejected this development strategy, adopting trade policies that gave roughly equal incentive to produce for the domestic market and for the export market. In both cases, growth dramatically increased after the policy shift in the early 1960s and was clearly led by manufactured export growth.

Even more dramatic were the sustained high growth rates of the four Asian Tigers (as they became known) during the 1970s when the world economy was in disarray. Clearly they were not at the mercy of international markets, and success was due to domestic factors. By the end of the decade South Korea and Taiwan were among the heavily indebted countries, but they experienced no debt crisis because the loans were invested in export-oriented factories that earned the foreign currency to pay off the debts and leave good profits. For them the recycling of oil wealth and availability of loans at low real rates of interest provided an opportunity, not a trap, and they were able to seize it.

There can be little doubt that the high-performing Asian economies represent an economic success story. Their success was even more striking insofar as in the 1950s nobody foresaw the Asian economic miracles. South Korea and Taiwan were basket cases with low per capita incomes, and many feared that they would become permanently dependent on U.S. aid; even in the 1960s Gunnar Myrdal (1968) wrote them off as having little hope of economic prosperity.[22] After the event there was an active debate over the role of government in the development of the newly industrialized economies, but by the end of the century the high-performing Asian economies were clearly market-driven. The motor of success was specialization according to comparative advantage, which for low-income labor-abundant countries meant production of labor-intensive manufactured goods for sale on world markets. Individual governments may or may not have played an active role in promoting some activities, subsidizing credit for exporters and so forth, but the crucial policy was creating a more or less level playing field between producing for the home and for the export market and in liberalizing labor and (usually later) capital markets so that workers could be transferred from existing employment into the factories. Other secrets of success included conservative macroeconomic policies that kept inflation under control so that relative price changes could be readily observed, and in some cases undervalued exchange rates which enhanced export competitiveness.[23]

The speed of growth was historically unprecedented, but it was not a miracle. The high-performing Asian economies increased their capital and labor inputs by saving and working more and by investing in human and physical capital; it was a simple story of increasing inputs in order to produce a larger output—"perspiration not inspiration."[24] Robert Lucas (1993) saw the "miracle" as a readily explainable example of catch-up growth, aided by the extent to which learning-by-doing was possible in the export activities. Others (e.g., Matthew Higgins and Jeffrey Williamson, 1996) emphasized the demographic dividend that followed a drop in birth rates; savings rates and participation rates were higher because a larger share of the population was of working age. Apart from the demographic change, the blueprint for success can be copied if a government has the political will to dismantle the controls that favor certain economic activities, most often import-competing industries.[25]

The performance of the four Asian Tigers made a huge impression on policymakers elsewhere, especially as import-substitution strategies faltered. Both Taiwan and South Korea had been poorer than Ghana when the latter became independent in 1957 (Table 5.1), but by the 1980s they were many times richer; the four Asian Tigers also overtook the richest South American countries.[26] The success was all the more striking for having been completely unpredicted.

During the early 1980s there was a debate about whether the four Asian Tigers' development model could be generalized. Cline (1982), for example, argued that there was a "fallacy of composition"; a few small economies could develop on the basis of exporting labor-intensive manufactures, but if many countries adopted the same strategy, it would be self-defeating because the increased supply would depress the world price of manufactured goods and might invoke a protectionist response from the importing countries. Indeed, there were signs of protectionism during the late 1970s and the 1980s, mostly in nontariff barriers or other trade-restricting agreements, but these were gradually dismantled, before many of the practices were outlawed in the Uruguay Round of multilateral trade negotiations that concluded in 1994.[27] During the 1980s several Southeast Asian countries abandoned ISI in favor of more outward-oriented policies, and this was followed by rapid sectoral change and economic growth in Malaysia, Thailand, and Indonesia. The biggest recruit to the high-performing Asian economies was China, which dramatically reformed its development strategy after 1978. China's success in exporting manufactured goods over the next three decades definitively put to rest concerns about a fallacy of composition. Chinese exports reduced the price of clothing, toys, travel goods, and many other labor-intensive manufactured goods below what it would otherwise have been, but the negative impact on prices was far too small to undermine the overall strategy or to deter other low-wage countries from adopting an outward-oriented strategy, such as Vietnam after 1986. Meanwhile, the original Tigers, moving up the quality ladder as their wages and skill level increased, continued to grow rapidly.

China

The development debates of the 1950s and 1960s largely ignored China, even though it was the world's most populous country and impoverished by centuries of poor governance. In part, this was because China was a communist country and had an anomalous role in the Cold War. During the 1950s China was a close ally of the USSR, but after the Sino-Soviet split in 1960 China became increasingly inward-looking and suspicious of both superpowers. In 1978–1979 China replaced the Maoist development model with an open door policy, setting in motion a decades-long process of rapid growth that propelled China to becoming a major player in the global economy of the twenty-first century.

After the 1949 revolution, the People's Republic of China followed the Soviet development model based on collectivization of agriculture and promotion of heavy industry. China received substantial bilateral support from the USSR in the form of technology and equipment, until the Sino-Soviet split in 1960. Apart from the Soviet connection, development was an autarchic version of ISI; China operated largely outside the global economy, and most foreign businesses within the country had closed down by the mid-1950s. The Chinese economy was successful in the early and mid-1950s, mobilizing resources and achieving growth with equity, reflected in widespread improvements in literacy, health care, housing, and other basic needs. However, by 1957 there were signs of slower growth and decreasing economic dynamism.

In 1958 Mao Zedong launched the Great Leap Forward, aimed at bringing the communist economy to the next stage through more centralized farm decision-making (communes) and a rural industrialization program. In the following years (1959–1961) China experienced a major famine, partly due to bad weather, but exacerbated by the limited government response (and lack of independent media to publicize the misery and push officials into action) and by the absence of a market mechanism to direct food. The disaster led to the temporary eclipse of Mao Zedong by President Liu Shaoqi and Deng Xiaoping, who advocated a more pragmatic approach: "I don't care if it's a white cat or a black cat. It's a good cat so long as it catches mice." In 1966, however, Liu and Deng were purged as Mao sought to revitalize the revolution through a Great Cultural Revolution.

China's economic problems were blamed on officials, intellectuals, and others who had perpetuated old elitist ways of thinking and acquired excessive power, while losing touch with the lifestyle of the ordinary people. In order to create a classless society with all working together for the common good rather than personal material benefit, such class enemies were sent to work on farms or in factories as part of a reeducation process. The economy became even more autarchic, and chaotic as ideologically correct Red Guards took precedence over technically more competent managers, engineers, instructors, and so on. The early 1970s saw some restoration of order, helped by rising revenue from primary product exports such as oil, and a counterpart was improved relations with the West, highlighted by President Richard Nixon's 1972 trip to China and meeting with Mao Zedong. There was, however, no major change in China's economic strategy until after the death of Mao Zedong in 1976.

Mao's death set off a great debate about economic strategy. The "Gang of Four" leaders who supported continuation of Maoist policies were quickly sidelined. Mao's successor, Hua Guofeng (1976–1978) used foreign borrowing to import factories (mainly from Japan). This offered a quick fix to modernize China's outdated industry, but risked debt problems if oil revenues fell in the future. In 1978 Hua was replaced by Deng Xiaoping, who dumped the foreign contracts and initiated a strategy based on agrarian reform (replacing the communes with a household responsibility system under which a family took responsibility for a plot of land and could retain output above the plan requirement) and an open door policy (gradual reduction of restrictions on foreign trade and permitting foreign investment in joint ventures but not foreign debt).

The reform era in China will be analyzed in Chapter 7, but it had an important influence in the Third World. At first there was little outside recognition of the extent of change in China, which had been an insulated enigma for three decades.[28] The agrarian reforms drove the economy in the early 1980s and not until the mid-1980s did the open door policy start to have a significant impact. After that, however, China's sustained growth and increasing participation in world trade became hard to ignore. Although the USSR itself would abandon central planning by the end of the 1980s, China's reforms were already a signal that the centrally planned economy was no match for an economy in which resource allocation was guided by market forces.

The mechanics of China's economic growth are simple. During the 1950s economic growth was fairly rapid and driven by increased productivity, but after 1957 growth slowed. From 1957 to 1978 the contribution of total factor productivity was negative. In contrast to this ISI phase, after 1978 the annual average growth rate more than doubled (9.5 percent in 1978–2005 versus 4.4 percent in 1952–1978), and more than two-fifths of the post-1978 growth was due to increased productivity (Table 5.2). In the decade 1985–1995 productivity gains were the most important source of growth, as labor was transferred from low-productivity agrarian employment into production of manufactured goods for export, where the worker's output valued at world prices was much higher. The pattern reflects the massive gains from specialization according to comparative advantage when the economy first started to export manufactures in the mid-1980s. After 1995 capital formation became a more important source of growth, in line with Krugman's observation about the earlier new industrialized economies relying on perspiration not inspiration. China's huge reserves of literate low-wage labor meant that expansion of labor-intensive manufactured exports would drive Chinese economic growth for decades, with huge implications for the global economy.

Table 5.2   China's GDP and sources of growth, 1952–2005

Period	GDP growth per annum	Share of GDP growth attributable to		
		Physical capital	Education-enhanced labor	Total factor productivity (TFP)
1952–1957	6.5	12.7	14.9	72.4
1957–1965	2.4	93.1	49.5	−42.6
1965–1978	4.9	67.7	36.7	−4.4
1978–1985	9.7	40.6	26.6	32.8
1985–1990	7.7	38.8	21.5	39.7
1990–1995	11.7	33.3	9.5	57.3
1995–2000	8.6	52.7	10.5	36.8
2000–2005	9.5	57.1	10.6	32.3

Source: Perkins and Rawski (2008).

Conclusions

A striking feature of the second half of the twentieth century was the priority given to economic development in countries previously on the periphery of the global economy. In the 1950s, governments in Asia, Africa, and Latin America universally pursued import-substituting industrialization with the aim of accelerating economic growth. Although impressed by the Soviet Union's economic achievements and pressed to take sides in the Cold War, many governments of poorer countries preferred to remain nonaligned and some, notably India, combined a democratic political system and individual liberties with substantial economic planning. In the international economic sphere, these governments pushed for a new international economic order that would correct perceived inequities in the global economy by intervention in commodity markets and preferential tariff treatment, but these measures failed to have an impact, just as insulation from global markets by ISI led to increasingly disappointing economic performance.

In the 1950s and 1960s all regions of the world experienced historically high growth rates. In 1973–1998, unlike the boom in the 1950s and 1960s, there was no global pattern of economic performance (Table 4.1). The most striking group is the high-performing East Asian economies whose respectable growth record before 1973 became even more positive in the final quarter of the century, despite the 1997 Asian crisis. Latin America experienced slow growth in the 1980s (a "lost decade" for the region), but improved economic performance in the 1990s and early 2000s. Eastern Europe and the former USSR had the worst record, in large part because of the huge disruption of system change. Africa also experienced slow growth, continuing a process of divergence between the very poorest countries and the rest of the world.

In terms of the competition between economic systems, there is no question which side South Korea and Taiwan were on in the Cold War. Whatever the economic role of their governments, it fell far short of Soviet-style central planning. Moreover, although there were debates about the role of government, there was little doubt that the key to the new industrializing economies' success was specialization in response to price signals in the global market. The timing was helped by the dismantling of tariff and nontariff barriers by the major market economies and by the dramatic reductions in ocean freight rates and air transport described in the previous chapter. Even so, the strategy was far more soundly based than the ISI strategy, which everywhere ran into problems owing to resource misallocation.

The high-performing East Asian economies were those that abandoned import-substitution policies in favor of outward-oriented development strategies, following the path previously taken by Japan of pursuing their comparative advantage in labor-intensive manufactured goods. Following the success of the original four Asian Tigers, Malaysia, Thailand, Indonesia, and China adopted similar strategies in the late 1970s and early 1980s. The equality in Maoist China was no match for the prosperity in neighboring Taiwan as a rallying call for the people. Yet, apart perhaps from Hong Kong, there was a strong concern for social cohesion in the high-performing Asian economies. The extent to which they have a model that successfully balances prosperity and equality will be examined in Chapter 8.

Although the superiority of an outward-oriented development strategy became widely accepted, the model was not universally adopted. Within East Asia the adoption rate was mixed, with countries like Myanmar and North Korea shunning meaningful reform. Despite the major reform in India in 1991, other South and Southwest Asian countries' economies remained unreformed. In Latin America, more market-friendly and outward-oriented policies were widely adopted during the 1980s, although a split emerged between countries embracing globalization, led by Chile and later including the two largest countries, Brazil and Mexico, and those countries resisting globalization, led by Venezuela. In Africa the picture was depressingly less positive. The vital question is why, when the menu of good economic policies was widely accepted, so many countries failed to reform their interventionist systems based on a discredited ISI strategy.

Before taking up these stories in Chapter 8, it is necessary to examine developments in the First and Second Worlds in the 1980s. A conservative reaction in the high-income countries of North America, Western Europe, and Australasia sought to roll back the government's place in the economy (Chapter 6). Together with the collapse of central planning in the Second World in 1989 (Chapter 7), this reinforced a new consensus that closed, more or less planned economies were no match for open, market-based economies. However, reactions to the reforms of Thatcher and Reagan indicated that few were willing to throw out the welfare state commitment to equality in the name of greater efficiency.

CHAPTER 6

The Conservative Reaction in the West

.⁺.

The long boom of the 1950s and 1960s came to an end in the 1970s. The trigger was the increase in primary product prices, and most of all the increase in the price of oil in 1973–1974. Keynesian macroeconomic management, based on fine-tuning aggregate demand to mediate a trade-off between inflation and unemployment (the Phillips Curve), was ineffective in the face of a supply shock that led to "stagflation," the joint increase in inflation and unemployment. The economic malaise provided an opportunity for criticizing attempts to maintain unemployment at artificially low levels and the welfare state. Friedman (1968) provided an early influential critique of why the Phillips Curve trade-off was not a constant relationship; as governments maintained low unemployment by allowing inflation, people became accustomed to inflation and built inflation expectations into their economic calculations, including wage demands, thus creating an upward spiral for wages and prices. The welfare state was criticized as a source of the excessive deficit spending that fueled inflation, and even more for blunting economic incentives and hence slowing the growth and reducing the efficiency of market economies.

The symbols of the conservative reaction were the governments of Margaret Thatcher and Ronald Reagan in the 1980s.[1] The failure of a middle-of-the-road Conservative government in 1970–1974 and the labor disputes and weak Labour governments of 1974–1979 provided an opening for a free-market prime minister in Britain. In the United States the tight monetary policy of Paul Volcker, appointed in 1979 as chairman of the Federal Reserve Board with a mandate to cut inflation, created the worst recession since the 1930s and provided an opportunity for a radical reformer. The second oil shock in 1980 reinforced the perception of a need for change. In both the United Kingdom and the United States international affairs added to the economic malaise; Britain struggled to adjust to the loss of empire, and the United States had in half a decade suffered defeat in Vietnam and humiliation in Tehran as U.S. diplomats were held hostage and a rescue mission was bungled. Other countries did not have similarly strongly ideological right-wing leaders, and this added to the influence of the Thatcher-Reagan agenda as a beacon to critics of the managed capitalism and extensive welfare state that had become universal in the high-income countries by the 1970s.

Both Thatcher and Reagan offered radical solutions to the loss of national confidence.[2] In the economic sphere they offered monetarist macroeconomic policies, tax cuts (especially for those paying high marginal tax rates on their income), deregulation, and a general focus on market forces rather than government directives to allocate resources. Both were hostile to welfare programs, which they saw as a prime source of the excessive size of the public budget and as contributing to a dependency culture and lack of individual initiative, and to labor unions. Both pursued a forceful and overtly nationalist foreign policy, with Mrs. Thatcher going to war with Argentina over the Falkland Islands and Mr. Reagan adopting the expensive "star wars" antimissile program to drive the Soviet Union toward ruin.

Despite the common ground, there were differences between the United Kingdom during Thatcher's leadership (1979–1990) and the United States during Reagan's presidency (1981–1988). In Britain, although tax reductions were generally popular, the welfare state and especially the National Health Service were also popular, so it was difficult to balance tax cutting with monetary restraint without losing popular support. During the 1980s the dilemma was resolved by selling public assets. Resistance to measures promoting inequality was stronger in the United Kingdom than in the United States, and the threat of introducing a new regressive tax whose burden would fall more heavily on the poor than on the rich contributed to Thatcher's fall. In the United States, privatization was less important because there had never been as much state ownership as in Europe, and tax cuts led to macroeconomic problems that had global ramifications. Also, the strength of right-wing groups stressing a social agenda and religious agenda (e.g., on abortion) forced Reagan to respond in areas that were absent in British politics.

The Thatcher Government in the United Kingdom

In Britain the negative impact of global recession after 1973 was compounded by domestic economic disasters in the 1970s, whose origins lay in the uneasy marriage between the labor unions and the Labour Party. When the 1964–1970 Labour government sought a cooperative approach to wage-setting similar to that in some European countries, such as the Netherlands or Germany, the labor unions were unwilling or unable to cooperate.[3] The consequences of a wage scramble by individual unions became more harmful in the poorer economic conditions of the 1970s, culminating in the 1978–1979 "winter of discontent" when strikes were more widespread than at any time since the 1926 General Strike.

Faced with double-digit inflation, the voters were seeking a government that would act decisively to bring down the rate of price increase.[4] The Thatcher government adopted a monetarist approach, limiting expansion of the money supply, even though the resulting high interest rates led to a severe recession in the early 1980s. Unemployment rose dramatically, which the government's supporters ascribed to excessive wage demands. Attempts by trade unions to gain pay increases were strongly resisted; car workers in 1979, steel workers in 1980, rail workers and civil servants in 1982, the print unions in 1983, and, most dramatically, the lengthy and bitter coal miners' strike in 1984–1985 were all defeated.

Margaret Thatcher became the first Conservative prime minister committed to rolling back the state. Nationalized industries were privatized and other activities were deregulated. Despite talk of rolling back the welfare state, however, little was actually done beyond limited attempts to introduce market forces into the provision of social services. The only major privatization in the social sphere was sale of public housing, which mainly involved selling the better-quality state-owned housing to the tenants best able to buy and could be viewed as a move to better targeted support rather than elimination of public housing for those unable to afford their own homes.[5] The policies were popular insofar as deregulation delivered cheaper transport and phone calls, but there was little support for rolling back social services.

The massive sale of shares in British Telecom in 1984 was followed by the privatization of gas, water and electricity, bus services, steel, cars (Jaguar and Rover), aero-engines (Rolls-Royce), British Airways, and the British Airports Authority. Between 1984 and 1996, the largest public flotations (television, gas, airports, airlines, steel, water, electricity generation and distribution, rail, and nuclear energy) raised around £50 billion at 2000 prices, and there were also many smaller disposals and secondary offerings. By the time Mrs. Thatcher left office in November 1990, one in four of the population owned shares and more than forty former state-owned businesses employing more than 600,000 workers had been privatized.

The consequences of privatization remain controversial. In many cases there were trade-offs between raising revenue and improving efficiency. Efficiency would be most improved by increased competition, whereas the value to new shareholders would be highest if the privatized enterprise held monopoly power. The dilemma was heightened because privatization played an important fiscal role, bringing millions of pounds into the public budget and reducing the public sector borrowing requirement despite increases in military spending and failure to significantly reduce other spending. To many observers revenue seemed to be the main goal, as privatized enterprises were left with substantial monopoly power in industries which were at best only partially deregulated.[6]

In cases such as the railway track, air traffic control, and the London Underground, privatization was an unsatisfactory solution to the general problem of the efficient provision of public services which are natural monopolies, and public involvement was subsequently increased. However, a natural monopoly is not always easy to define and may be eroded by technical change, as in the provision of telecommu-

nications, where deregulation has been associated with increased efficiency.[7] The postal service is an intermediate case; British (and most
other) governments have retained the state provider's monopoly of
letter delivery, but allowed competition in other mail services that are
efficiently provided by many private courier services.

The Thatcher government used tax reform to increase economic incentives at the cost of greater inequality, but this was unpopular. Initially the government combined income tax reductions with the introduction of a more regressive value-added tax (VAT); the VAT increased
prices, such that the monetary squeeze to reduce inflation had to be
tighter and the ensuing recession and unemployment were more severe. Despite spending on the military, including the Falklands War,
and failure to substantially reduce other expenditures, large revenues
from the sale of state assets enabled the government to avoid further
tax increases. In the early 1990s the threat of introducing a new flat tax,
the poll tax, contributed to Thatcher's fall from power.

Despite the fact that Thatcher was twice reelected, she never obtained a majority of the popular vote and her longevity in office was in
large part due to a split in the Labour Party, as members who despaired
of the old alliance with the labor unions and commitment to nationalization left to form the Social Democrat Party. The new party never
managed to displace the old Labour Party, but the Labour Party itself
could only return to power after it had dumped its commitment to
public ownership and reinvented itself. When Tony Blair became
prime minister in 1997 as the head of what he termed "New Labour,"
his program looked more like that of a European social democrat than
that of the 1918–1994 Labour Party.

The Reagan Presidency in the United States

Major differences between the Thatcher and Reagan reform agendas
were Reagan's overriding commitment to tax cuts and the relatively
small scope for cutting the welfare state or privatizing state enterprises in the U.S. system. Soon after entering office in 1981 President
Reagan cut the top marginal tax rate from 70 percent to 50 percent
and bolstered business investment tax allowances. Over the next few

years the business tax relief was rolled back, but the cut in income tax rates was maintained. In 1986 the administration introduced a far-reaching tax reform, which cut the top marginal rate on both wage and capital income from 50 percent to 28 percent. Reagan's successor, George H. Bush, pushed the top rate up to 31 percent, and Bill Clinton increased it to 40 percent, so that the Reagan tax rates of the late 1980s were the lowest since the depression of the 1930s.

Reagan, like Thatcher, pursued a tight monetary policy in order to bring inflation down from the high rates of the 1970s, although this was an inherited policy run by Paul Volcker, the Federal Reserve chairman who had been appointed by Reagan's predecessor, Jimmy Carter. The combination of tight monetary policy and lax fiscal policy led to a rapid rise in U.S. interest rates and in the external value of the U.S. dollar. Among other consequences, this was disastrous for the low- and middle-income countries that had borrowed heavily in the 1970s and whose external debt was denominated in U.S. dollars at interest rates which were often tied to U.S. interest rates or to the closely related London Interbank Offered Rate on dollar-denominated assets, LIBOR. The strength of the dollar also reduced the price-competitiveness of U.S. producers.

The Reagan administration was the most protectionist U.S. government since 1930, renouncing U.S. principled leadership within GATT in favor of more nationalist policies to protect domestic producers. The 1980s saw a proliferation of orderly marketing arrangements, voluntary export restraint agreements (VERs), and other trade restrictions, which contravened the spirit of the GATT. They typically involved an implicit threat of higher trade barriers if the exporter did not agree, and they sometimes bought agreement by permitting exporters to operate as a cartel, gaining added profits in return for limiting the quantity exported. The United States negotiated or imposed restrictions on imports of steel, semiconductors, cars, lumber, machine tools, and many other items, covering almost a quarter of U.S. imports, often in a nontransparent way.[8] These trade measures flew in the face of any commitment to market forces and, although publicized as protecting U.S. workers, they mainly benefited U.S. corporations in certain sectors; the losers were U.S. consumers, adding to the increased inequality resulting from the changes in income tax structure, and in the longer term the rules-based global trading system. The Reagan administration also initiated a major shift in U.S. trade diplomacy by negotiating bilateral deals (with the Caribbean Basin countries, Israel, and Canada), which undermined the multilateral trading system based on the principle of treating all GATT members equally.

The Reagan administration continued some of the deregulation measures that had been begun by the Carter administration, but its main commitment to market-driven outcomes was shown by challenges to organized labor. An early high-profile indication of this hostility was the response to the August 1981 air traffic controllers' strike, which was met by mass redundancies and the destruction of an apparently powerful union.[9] After that, labor was far less assertive.

The main legacies of the Reagan administration were the cuts in marginal tax rates and the defense buildup that may have contributed to the collapse of the rival superpower, the USSR. These came, however, at the cost of macroeconomic imbalances. Tax cuts were expected to encourage greater economic activity and hence greater tax revenue, but the expected boost to tax revenue as a result of lowering tax rates, a principal claim of supply-side economists, failed to materialize. Unlike the Thatcher government in the United Kingdom, when it cut income taxes the Reagan administration could not introduce an offsetting indirect tax because sales taxes were state-run, and it did not have the windfall revenues from privatization or from North Sea oil that the British government enjoyed during the 1980s. Despite rhetoric about decreasing the size of the federal government, expenditure cuts were far smaller than the reduction in tax revenues; although nondefense spending was cut from 17.1 percent of GDP to 15.6 percent of GDP, defense spending was increased from 5.1 percent to 5.6 percent of GDP. The net effect was an increase in the budget deficit from 2.6 percent of GDP when Reagan came into office to 6 percent in 1983.

Although the rhetoric indicated opposition to the welfare state, there was little real rollback (admittedly from a much lower starting point compared with the European high-income countries or Canada or Australia), and when Ronald Reagan was succeeded by his vice president, George H. Bush, there was a rhetorical shift toward a more compassionate conservatism—much as happened with the succession of Margaret Thatcher by John Major in the United Kingdom. Nevertheless, the Reagan reforms did represent a significant challenge to the Age of Equality, as the interests of the rich and entrepreneurial were given priority and the interests of unionized workers and of the average consumer were ignored.

Clinton and Blair

After a brief and undistinguished period under the successors of Reagan and Thatcher, both the United States and the United Kingdom turned to leaders committed to retaining and even extending the welfare state. Neither Bill Clinton nor Tony Blair attempted to reverse the measures taken to deregulate the market economy or the commitment to low inflation maintained by a strong central bank, but their vision of a market-oriented economy in which the state provided a measure of social security and ensured health care and education for all seemed to fit the majority viewpoint in both countries in the final decade of the twentieth century. Both Clinton and Blair proved to be electorally successful, even though they both faltered in their attempts to improve the public health care system.

Taking the last two decades of the twentieth century together, there was no sustained attack on the welfare state in the high-income countries. If anything the principle of a safety net was extended and the egalitarian side of the welfare state was emphasized, alongside an increased recognition of the benefits of market mechanisms. Old-age pensions, for example, were reformed in the direction of universalism and away from targeting through means tests, despite the increased budgetary costs. The main justification was to remove the disincentive to work or save for pension-age individuals with high marginal tax rates.[10] At the same time people were encouraged to save by tax-sheltered pension plans, compulsory payments by employers into pension accounts, and so forth.

Even supporters of state intervention recognized limits to social engineering, highlighted in many countries by public housing projects from the 1950s and 1960s that bred crime and other social catastrophes. However, public provision of health and education, at least for the less wealthy and at elementary school, remained unquestioned. As people lived longer and studied more, spending on health and education grew faster than incomes, and the impact on the public budget was eased by encouraging, or requiring, private expenditures on nonessential medical procedures, individual hospital rooms, higher education, and so forth. In sum, debates about the nature of the welfare-state remained at the center of many countries' domestic politics at the end of the twentieth century, but there was no serious debate about the desirability of a market-based economic system to provide efficiency and individual choice (liberty), with a welfare state to ensure some degree of equality.

A striking gap between rhetoric and action in the Reagan and Thatcher era was that the conservative governments committed to market mechanisms were also nationalist and willing to intervene to protect domestic economic interests. Unlike the United States, Britain as an EU member had little room for maneuver on trade policy, but the 1980s were characterized by frequent trade spats over French turkey exports to Britain and other British complaints about the operation of free trade within Europe. Indeed, it was this nationalism that triggered the fall from power of Margaret Thatcher, after the Foreign Minister resigned over her Europe policy. By contrast the governments of Clinton (1993–2001) and of Blair (1997–2007), which were ostensibly more market-skeptical and reliant on the votes of import-threatened blue-collar workers, were more internationalist. After multilateral trade negotiations had stalled during the 1980s, President Clinton led the completion of the Uruguay Round in 1994, which created the World Trade Organization, and he also restored normal economic relations with Vietnam, extended the U.S.-Canada free trade area to include Mexico in the North American Free Trade Area and oversaw the last stages of China's 2001 WTO accession.

There was no attempt to reverse the financial deregulation of the 1980s despite its association with huge incomes for people who produced no tangible output. Financial deregulation had already been associated with the savings and loan (S&L) crisis in the United States during the second half of the 1980s, a global stock market crash in

1987, and the Japanese asset market bubble in 1988–1989 which would be followed by a dismal decade for Japan. Nevertheless, there was no serious questioning of the benefits of less regulated global financial markets. In keeping with the general tenor of their governments, both the United States and the United Kingdom became more concerned about how to provide support for those least able to protect themselves against harmful consequences of global capital mobility.[11] Foreign aid, which had been cut back under Reagan and Thatcher, was increased by Clinton and Blair.

Financial Development and Financial Crises

The long boom in the 1950s and 1960s was driven by the real sector, and productivity gains were passed on as real wage increases. Even during the productivity slowdown of the 1970s, income inequality did not increase greatly in the high-income countries. One reason for the relatively stable distribution of income and wealth in the high-income countries from the mid-1960s until the early 1980s was the long bear market in the main stock exchanges. The Dow Jones Index, for example, stood at 874 at the end of 1964 and at 875 in 1981, despite the rapid inflation of the 1970s. The next eighteen years saw a bull market that took share values to record highs, measured by cyclically adjusted price-earnings ratios. Other financial markets also boomed, during a period of unprecedented financial market change.

The financial sector was the most regulated sector in the high-income countries, even though it generally remained under private ownership. Financial sectors are regulated for a number of reasons, perhaps the simplest of which is the problem of asymmetric information between depositors in a bank and the owners of the bank. An important intermediation function of retail banks is to collect small liquid deposits and lend them out as less liquid loans; because banks borrow short-term and lend long-term and because small depositors are uninformed about the bank's balance sheet, it is essential that depositors do not panic and demand to withdraw their money in a sudden bank run, which would make concerns about the bank's liquidity self-fulfilling. To discourage bank runs, depositors may be offered some form of protection, for example, insured deposits up to a certain amount. Such guarantees raise moral hazard problems, which governments address by prudential regulation, but it is difficult to strike a balance between ensuring prudence on a bank's part and encouraging a desirable degree of risk-taking by loan officers.

Early bank regulations were aimed at ensuring prudent behavior by screening the owners of banks, limiting the types of assets that financial institutions could hold, and requiring a minimum share of assets be held in currency or government bills. By restricting entry and behavior, such regulations reduced competition. During the depression of the 1930s, many governments further tightened regulations in order to protect depositors. The U.S. Banking Act of 1933 founded the Federal Deposit Insurance Corporation (FDIC) for insuring bank deposits, established controls over the interest rates that banks could charge, and separated commercial and investment banking (an element usually referred to as the Glass-Steagall Act). These regulations were interconnected, as the interest ceilings and separation of roles were intended to limit competition, allowing banks to make added profits to cover their premiums to the FDIC and also reducing the risk of bank failure (and of large FDIC payouts).[12] The predilection for controls continued through the 1950s and 1960s, for example, U.S. mutual savings banks and savings and loan associations were exempt from the original interest rate ceilings but had ceilings applied in 1966.

As economic activity grew during the long boom, institutional innovations allowed market participants to evade some regulations. The euro-dollar market that emerged in London in the 1950s allowed fairly unregulated banking in dollars.[13] The pace of change increased during the 1970s. With the generalized floating of the major currencies, a currency futures market was launched in Chicago in 1972. The recycling of petrodollars led to global competition among the largest banks for these deposits and for new customers.

In the 1980s the two major financial centers, London and New York, were in the forefront of deregulation. In the United States deregulation actually started with reform of the stockbrokers' commission system in 1975. However, the interest rate ceilings became more strictly binding in the late 1970s as equilibrium interest rates increased. Rich depositors evaded interest rate controls through money market accounts that provided higher returns while still providing liquidity, and such instruments gradually became more available to people with more modest assets. Formalizing the deregulation, the Monetary Control Act of 1980 began a six-year phaseout of the interest rate ceiling on deposits that was completed in March 1986. Meanwhile, the Garn–St. Germain Act of 1982 deregulated the savings and loan industry. The banking industry pressed for repeal of the Glass-Steagall Act, although this was delayed until 1999.

In the United Kingdom one of the first acts of the Thatcher government in 1979 was to end exchange controls. Deregulating capital flows gave a boost to cross-border investing, which in turn put pressure on anti-competitive practices such as stockbrokers' fixed commissions. The big bang reforms in the London financial markets in 1986 led to lower transactions costs and heralded further financial developments. In both the United Kingdom and the United States, as stockbrokers lost fee income and commercial banks sought to break out of their limited business activities, financial conglomerates emerged. Restrictive laws were rescinded. In the United Kingdom, building societies were allowed to demutualize, which permitted these formerly specialized mortgage institutions to become for all intents and purposes diversified banks. In the United States, following the repeal of the Glass-Steagall Act in 1999, Citibank became the largest financial institution on the basis of universal banking activities.

The final ingredient behind unprecedented financial innovation was the historically low interest rates after the early 1980s. These resulted from monetary policies in the countries with the leading financial centers, the United States and the United Kingdom, and hence obtained in global financial markets in the 1990s and early years of the twenty-first century. Easy credit provided the backdrop to aggressive development of financial vehicles; options and swaps (bond swaps, interest swaps, credit-default swaps) permitted almost unlimited menus of degree of risk and could be profitable because of the low cost of money. The financial innovations centered on new methods of spreading risk, although with ever more complex derivatives, even large investors made foolish decisions in the 1990s based on ignorance.[14] The removal of Western European countries' exchange controls in the years up to 1992, and liberalization of capital flows elsewhere, contributed to the creation of an increasingly integrated global financial market.

The innovations allowed informed market participants to find the best price for their financial transactions and to select their exposure to risk. One of the great advantages of the market economy is the financial sector's ability to intermediate savings and investment with some precision and efficiency, and increased financial sector sophistication helped firms to perform well during what was a boom period in the 1990s and the early years of the twenty-first century for the United States, the United Kingdom, Australia, and many other economies. Many startup entrepreneurs made fortunes, as venture capitalists were willing to take on the risk of lending to unproven small businesses. Consumers went on a buying binge, driving up house prices as they obtained cheap mortgage loans, and using credit card debt or second mortgages to finance further discretionary expenditures. Among the biggest beneficiaries were the companies in the financial sector and their employees who received ever larger bonuses. The period saw a sharp increase in income inequality in most high-income countries.[15]

Low interest rates and a long credit-driven boom had, however, two drawbacks. The first problem was moral hazard; without oversight by depositors, institutions had an incentive to accumulate high-return (and presumably high-risk) assets or, at a minimum, not to pay due diligence to their accumulation of risk because all the rewards of success accrued to the institutions' employees and owners while the costs of poor decisions would be partially borne by taxpayers. Low interest rates encouraged highly leveraged positions, as financial institutions acquired funds at low interest rates and sought new borrowers without adequate risk assessment. Second, the longer a credit boom lasted, lenders and regulators had less and less knowledge of institutions' asset position and solvency. Small depositors were, explicitly or implicitly, insured by governments, but financial institutions were unsure of the riskiness of their holdings—yet they continued to ignore warning signals, often with the optimistic justification that "it is different this time."[16]

A first sign of danger was the U.S. S&L crisis of 1986–1989. The S&L institutions, which specialized in lending to homebuyers, took on too much risk, lending to customers who were willing to borrow at interest rates that would have been profitable for the S&Ls, but who turned out to be unable to service their loans. When a borrower defaulted, the S&L could foreclose and seize the house as collateral. However, if too many houses in a town were being sold off, house prices would fall and the institution would not be able to realize the presumed value of the collateral. Hundreds of S&Ls went bankrupt, leading to the insolvency of the Federal Savings and Loan Insurance Corporation by the end of 1986 and to the Financial Institutions Reform, Recovery, and Enforcement Act of 1989, which initiated taxpayer involvement. By 1995 more than a thousand S&L institutions had failed, and the cost to the taxpayer of reimbursing depositors was $153 billion (Curry and Shibut, 2000). At the time the crisis was blamed largely on the institutions' weaknesses and the cupidity of some owners. After the bailout, the problem was declared solved. However, the bailout reinforced beliefs that deposits in the financial sector were safe, while scapegoating and punishment of a few high-profile owners did little to remove moral hazard.

A second symptom of shaky financial foundations was the recurrent financial crises of middle-income countries during the 1990s.[17] These had specific national roots, but also reflected the globalization of financial markets and in several cases similar issues to those that would strike the high-income countries in 2007–2009. Capital flows accentuated the boom and bust in Mexico and Thailand after reform ushered in a period of high growth (1986–1993 in Mexico, 1982–1996 in Thailand); foreign capital was attracted to the booming economies, but when doubts about the sustainability of high returns led to capital outflows the governments were unwilling to accept that the growth was unsustainable and reduce domestic demand or take other measures to stem the capital outflow. Treating the capital outflow as temporary and running down foreign exchange reserves led to a severe exchange rate and financial sector crisis in Mexico in 1994 (the tequila crisis) and in Thailand in 1997 (initiating the Asian crisis).

The 1997–1998 Asian crisis illustrated the moral hazard problems and the costs of governments not responding when circumstances turned sour. Thailand had the fastest-growing economy in the world between 1982 and 1996. The growth was firmly founded on export-oriented development, and liberalization of capital flows led to inflows of capital into the booming economy. The lightly regulated domestic financial sector was increasingly tempted to make optimistic loans. Finance companies would offer high interest rates to depositors and lend out at higher rates for projects based on assumptions of continued growth. Office buildings in Bangkok were particularly favored as the boom drove up demand for office space and high rents offered a good return on construction projects. However, when export growth slowed in the first half of 1996 and office demand lagged new supply, rents plummeted and the value of new buildings fell, and nonperforming loans increased. International lenders withdrew their money from Thailand out of fears of default or exchange rate loss, creating a self-fulfilling prophecy of currency depreciation. The Thai authorities reacted slowly, running down reserves rather than raising interest rates or taking other measures to discourage capital outflow, and when the reserves ran out the currency collapsed in July 1997. The crisis affected other Asian countries, which experienced a financial crisis as foreign creditors reassessed the country risk or a trade shock as Thailand's exports became more competitive following the devaluation.

The Asian crisis also showed the resilience of soundly based economies. Although there were contagion effects (stemming from increased competitiveness of exports from countries forced to devalue in the crisis, or from reassessment of risk across the region), the Asian crisis was not regionwide. Economies with sound financial systems, such as Hong Kong, Singapore, and Taiwan, or with capital controls (e.g., China) were relatively little affected. The countries most affected were those whose financial institutions had been the least prudent in their lending decisions and now had the most nonperforming loans (Thailand, Indonesia, Malaysia, and South Korea). Even these economies quickly resumed economic growth once the financial sector's balance sheets had been restructured, although the economic burden of a sharp fall in economic activity often fell disproportionately on poor people who lost their jobs and had little social security protection. The political consequences are difficult to assess; the short-term chaos following the end of the Suharto regime in Indonesia led to an improved political situation, while the election of a populist prime minister in Thailand led to political conflicts which undermined the country's democratic institutions.

The debt-financed equity boom in the United States burst in 2000 with the dot-com crunch, but consumers continued to happily run up debt and governments were happy that people were happy.[18] After the turn of the century the asset bubble shifted to housing markets. The phenomenon of negative aggregate saving in the United States, Australia, and elsewhere caused only minor concerns, despite aging populations and inadequate public pension funds. Governments, as in Mexico before 1994 or Thailand before July 1997, were eager to accept the praise for good times. Governments fueled leveraging by maintaining low interest rates and subsidized the bubbles by tax codes which gave tax breaks for mortgage payments and favored corporate borrowing over financing through sale of shares.

Conclusions

The depression of the 1930s led to new attitudes toward the role of the government in market economies. The pre-1914 gold standard had contributed a mindset in supporters of market forces that, despite the severe depressions of the 1800s and the increasing inequality, the automatic discipline of the market was the way to ensure the best economic outcome and that government intervention in the marketplace would pose a threat to individual liberty. These attitudes were jettisoned by fascist regimes which cared little for individual rights, but also were increasingly questioned in liberal democracies. The New Deal in the United States or the policies of popular front or social democrat governments in Europe, with the possible exception of Sweden, had limited economic impact in the short-term, but represented a sea change in ideas that would become the norm even for conservative governments after 1945.

The 1930s and 1940s were a watershed in acceptance of the use by national governments and international economic institutions of professional economists in managing the economy. President Roosevelt appointed the first economic advisor to the U.S. president, Lauchlin Currie, and in Britain economists like John Maynard Keynes began to be heeded. At the international level, institutions like the IMF and World Bank were primarily staffed by economists, as were some agencies of the United Nations. Central banks became more professional, and the importance of monetary policy was universally recognized by the late 1970s. Improved economic management at both the macro and micro level allowed market economies to become more complex and more efficient in the second half of the twentieth century, without major disruptions, and this, together with establishment of the welfare state, contributed to the attractiveness of the market system. Yet there were limits to the ability of governments to improve the functioning of market economies, which were highlighted by the stagflation of the 1970s.

The conservative reaction in the 1980s called for rolling back the scope of the government in the economy, to some extent a return to the Age of Liberty when regulations were looser and taxes lower than they had become in the 1960s and 1970s. Despite the rhetoric, there was little rollback of the welfare state and certainly no abandoning of the idea that governments had a responsibility to help those disadvantaged by the market. Margaret Thatcher and Ronald Reagan may have felt less inclined to promote an Age of Equality than their predecessors, but their successors maintained a commitment to a market economy plus the welfare state. Although many books were written on the crisis of the welfare state and the growth of social transfers slackened after 1980, in all OECD countries except Ireland and Denmark the share of social transfers in GDP was higher at the end of the century than in 1980 (Lindert, 2006, 236).[19]

Nevertheless, the episode described in this chapter was crucial for the evolution of the world economy in the last two decades of the twentieth century. In the high-income countries some elements of the conservative reaction were widely adopted. Notably the idea of a trade-off between unemployment and inflation was discredited, and prioritizing of low inflation as the goal of monetary policy became almost universal. This was essentially nonpartisan, and the biggest converts were often left-of-center parties as in New Zealand or Australia after 1983. Within Europe a key moment came in 1981 when France elected its first socialist president in the Fifth Republic and despite an initial commitment to Keynesian macroeconomic policies targeted at unemployment reduction, President Mitterrand had within two years reversed the priorities to the extent that French inflation was lower than that of Germany (at the time considered the benchmark for monetary stability) by 1991.

The benefits from deregulation (and privatization) were also widely recognized, although in practice it proceeded on a case-by-case basis. The pace of deregulation and privatization varied from country to country and was often resisted on social grounds or by vested interests. Labor markets became more flexible, raising concerns, especially within the European Union, of whether there was a race to the bottom with respect to protection of workers' rights. In practice, although the power of labor unions was reduced in most countries, labor legislation remained supportive of workers' rights; although a market whose flexibility is important for long-run economic success, the labor market was special because the price of labor, the wage rate, is the critical determinant of most people's income.[20]

Although people in high-income countries could no longer expect to have a job for life and worried about relative price increases in an open economy (e.g., for oil), the economies were generally more stable in the last two decades of the twentieth century. A number of empirical studies established a structural break around 1984, after which the magnitude of fluctuations in the major economic aggregates became significantly smaller.[21] The Great Moderation has been ascribed to better macroeconomic policy, which contributed to reduced volatility of major economic aggregates.[22] Others, however, ascribe it to improved inventory management techniques or sectoral shifts from more volatile manufacturing to less volatile services or simply to luck, that is, the exogenous shocks were smaller between 1984 and 2007 than before or after that period (Ahmed, Levin, and Wilson, 2004). A more dynamic interpretation is that people learned to anticipate and to adapt to the fluctuations that are inherent in market-based economic systems with financial intermediation.[23]

The modern market economy delivered some economic security as well as prosperity. A targeted welfare state moderates inequality by offering protection against individual-specific income loss (due to unemployment, disability, and so forth), a social safety net for the very poor, and support for disadvantaged children (by subsidized education and health care). When crises did occur in high-income countries, they increasingly reflected the difficulty of financial sector regulation. The financial deregulation and innovation that during the 1980s accelerated in the United States and the United Kingdom, and to varying degrees elsewhere, underpinned a positive growth performance, which was highest in the countries with less regulated financial sectors. Financial deregulation also allowed individuals to better manage their own economic security by offering a range of assets to balance risk and return and to plan for retirement or smooth consumption when hit by other economic shocks such as job loss. More innovative financial sectors were also more likely to provide funding to venture capitalists with potentially high-return, but also risky projects.[24] Risk-taking by financial institutions inevitably increases the probability of a financial crisis, which must be weighed against the benefits from financial deregulation and innovation.[25]

Beyond the high-income countries the change in the conventional wisdom was important. The shift in emphasis from the benefits of planning and government intervention to the advantages of market mechanisms in guiding resource allocation was paralleled by growing attention being paid to government failures as opposed to the earlier emphasis on market failure as a justification for public policy. The setting was important because many low- and middle-income countries were abandoning their import-substituting industrialization strategies under pressure of the debt crisis or other symptoms of the failure of ISI and were strongly influenced by the prevailing climate. Even more dramatically, the end of central planning in Eastern Europe in 1989 and the dissolution of the USSR in 1991 created a situation akin to that of the decolonization era of the late 1940s and 1950s when a new generation of policymakers was looking for a development strategy in a situation where they had almost carte blanche. The global shifts toward more market-oriented economic systems are the subject of the next two chapters.

CHAPTER 7

The Collapse of Central Planning

✦

The idealism of the communist revolutionaries and their pride in the establishment of the Union of Soviet Socialist Republics with its vision of a free and equal society is easy to forget when we know how the great Soviet experiment ended. For many Soviet leaders the high point was the Seventeenth Party Congress in 1934, where

> [t]he delegates, apparent "victors" but actually future victims of Stalin, sang enraptured dithyrambs to the leader. Embodying the working class and the peasantry alike, they bore on their shoulders the whole weight of industrialization and collectivization. Deprivation lay behind; the shining future lay ahead. It would be free, egalitarian, plentiful, this society with new productive forces at work, altered productive relationships, and a new socialist man . . . Their belief was genuine and sincere.[1]

The dream would be shattered by the show trials of the next few years when many of the delegates would be executed and the dream of a free communist society destroyed. In other dimensions, however, the USSR continued to be successful with military victory in the 1941–1945 war, in meeting basic needs even in the poorest parts of the Soviet Union, and with high-profile victories in space and in sports. As described in Chapter 3, the Soviet model was exported to Eastern Europe after the defeat of Germany and adopted by China, Vietnam, and other poor countries in the 1950s (Map 7.1).

Nevertheless, the Soviet growth model started malfunctioning as investment became increasingly inefficient. The range of goods produced

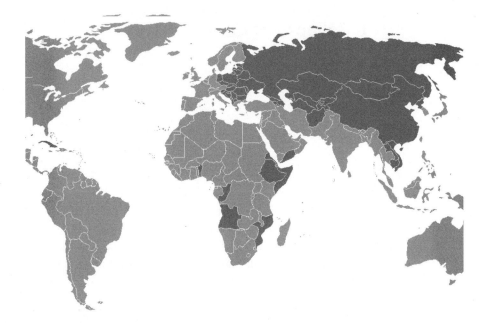

Map 7.1. The spread of communism, late 1970s

was limited as the system failed to respond to consumer wants beyond basic needs. The gap between Eastern and Western Europe widened in the 1960s and became harder to ignore as images of Western consumption appeared on television screens. In an attempt to satisfy demand for consumer goods, factories were commissioned from the West, such as the huge Fiat car factory at Togliattigrad (named after the Italian Communist leader) which began production in 1970 of Fiat 124 models for sale as Ladas and Zhigulis in the USSR, but even these factories quickly fell behind and became caught in a time warp.[2]

Economic decline was briefly reversed in the 1970s as Russia benefited from the increase in the world price of oil. The new prosperity was celebrated by foreign adventures (the invasion of Afghanistan) and by holding the 1980 Olympic Games in Moscow. As oil prices started to slide in the 1980s, so did Russia's economic and military fortunes. Yet the system fossilized as leadership change proved impossible, other than to wait for Brezhnev to die. Even when that happened, he was succeeded by two elderly leaders, who quickly died, before a reformist leader, Mikhail Gorbachev, gained control. Similarly in China, the obvious malfunctioning of Maoist central planning could only be seriously addressed after Mao's death.

The Failure of Piecemeal Reform

Central planning was successful in mobilizing resources, and the Soviet Union benefited from large numbers of rural workers who could be transferred to more productive employment. Robert Allen (2003) argues that the Soviet Union was successful only as long as it could release labor from agriculture, as in Lewis's model of growth with surplus labor. When that supply dried up around 1970, the USSR failed to transform its economy into one where technical change drives growth. Resource allocation was not a problem when the immediate goals were not particularly complex, but in the peacetime economy where basic needs had been largely fulfilled, the negative impact of reduced resource mobilization was exacerbated by resource misallocation.

Central planning was less successful in the longer term because capital was allocated inefficiently, rarely seeking out new opportunities, and because it proved difficult to maintain enthusiasm and individual productivity in the absence of material incentives. The economic growth record is difficult to capture precisely, because Soviet statisticians used different concepts to mainstream national accounts (e.g., focusing on material product and ignoring output of services) and because output was frequently misreported at all levels. Nevertheless, by any measure the rate of growth began to decline in the 1960s and slowed drastically in the 1970s (Table 7.1). The proximate cause of the slowdown was reduced productivity, associated with misallocation of capital, and captured in estimates of the incremental capital-output ratio (Table 7.2).

The Soviet leadership was well aware of the economic problems, and especially in the 1960s frequent reforms were proposed. These had little impact and under Brezhnev's leadership in the 1970s serious reform was abandoned. Rising prices for oil exports helped to mask

Table 7.1   Soviet economic growth data (average annual growth in national income)

	Official data	Khanin's estimates	Western estimates
1928–1941	13.9	2.9	5.8
1950s	10.1	6.9	6.0
1960s	7.1	4.2	5.2
1970s	5.3	2.0	3.7
1980–1985	3.2	0.6	2.0

Source: Fischer (1992, 11).

Notes: The official data were inflated in order to give a better picture of Soviet performance. Khanin's revisions of the official data are the most widely accepted estimates by a Russian economist, although they have been criticized in the West for being nonreproducible. The Western estimates, derived from the work of Bergson and the CIA (synthesized in Ofer, 1987), may be overestimates, in part because the CIA portrayed the Soviet Union as a greater threat than it was.

Table 7.2   Incremental capital-output ratios (ICORs): Russia, 1885–1985

1885–1913	3.1
1928–1940	2.8
1950–1960	3.7
1960–1975	5.0
1975–1985	14.8

Source: Gregory (1994, 129).

Note: Well-functioning economies typically have ICORs in the 3–4 range. —

the economic decline, and the Soviet Union had a brief period of revived confidence as it hosted the 1980 Olympic Games and in 1979 invaded Afghanistan as part of its long-term quest to expand south to an ice-free port on the Indian Ocean. The optimism was short-lived; as oil prices declined in the early 1980s and Soviet troops became bogged down in guerrilla warfare in Afghanistan, the situation became dire.

Reforms were difficult because, as with any reforms people in powerful positions were potential losers from reform and they had blocking power. More importantly in the case of centrally planned economies, the systemic nature ensured that piecemeal reforms had minimal impact.[3] As a system dedicated to achieving the highest possible results during the current planning period, Soviet central planning was inflexible. Operations rarely stopped, whereas in market economies partial closure for technical upgrading is a frequent occurrence. Taut planning meant that intermediate goods were supposed to be supplied in exactly the right quantities; in market economies firms maintain inventories to allow for delayed delivery or wastage, even as they try to minimize these stocks.[4] There was little way to reward good performance, so workers at all levels were closely monitored and the autonomy of subordinates was strongly restricted, which stifled initiative. Enterprises operated under a soft budget constraint, that is, they could never go bankrupt; managers were careful to follow rules and bureaucratic procedures because they had little to fear if their enterprise made a loss, as long as they could not be identified as having made errors. At the same time there were few rewards for managerial success, and hence little incentive to explore new opportunities for improved efficiency or better products. Service was not counted in the national accounts and was not rewarded, and was generally abysmal. In the absence of prices determined by supply and demand, consumer goods were allocated by rationing, which for scarcer, larger items encouraged corruption and a system of mutual favors, and for smaller day-to-day necessities hours were spent in queuing.

The Soviet Union announced an impressive number of reforms, in 1965, 1967, 1972, 1976, 1979, and 1982, but none had a significant impact on the system; nor did they succeed in arresting the declining economic performance, despite significant mathematical advances in planning techniques.[5] In Eastern Europe reforms went further in introducing a role for prices and greater enterprise autonomy, especially in Hungary, but the systemic features remained largely unchanged. Within the Eastern European countries under Soviet influence, whenever reforms were perceived to be going too far, they might be put down by force, as in Czechoslovakia in 1968, or by repression, as in the response to the rise of an independent trade union in Poland in 1980 and 1981. In August 1980 shipyard workers in Gdansk, led by Lech Walesa, formed the unofficial trade union Solidarnošč, which became a national movement and was forced underground after the declaration of martial law in December 1981 and imprisonment of its

leaders. Although Solidarnošč became the focus of opposition in Poland through the 1980s, in the early 1980s it was protesting against
poor economic management, reflected in food price increases, rather
than striving for overthrow of the system.

Even Yugoslavia, which adopted a more decentralized workers' self-
management system in 1950–1951, experienced declines in growth
and efficiency that in the long term were impervious to piecemeal reform. Reforms in the first half of the 1960s reduced the role of the
state, and price reform brought domestic prices closer to world prices.
By the early 1970s Yugoslavia was the most economically successful
among European communist countries, and a candidate to be included
among the fast-growing newly industrialized economies. Yugoslavia's
economic performance deteriorated through the 1970s and 1980s, although with indicative rather than physical planning the symptoms
differed from those in the centrally planned economies, with rising
inflation and currency depreciation prominent in Yugoslavia. Inflation rose from 16 percent in 1978 to 24 percent in 1979 and 37 percent
in 1980; by the mid-1980s inflation was 80–90 percent and had reached
200 percent by 1988.[6] Underlying the poor economic performance
were the familiar culprits of slow productivity growth and resource
misallocation, especially poor allocation of capital. Workers' self-
management provided an incentive to maximize income per worker
rather than enterprise profits, which in combination with the planners' continuing influence over capital allocation led to intense competition for capital but inefficient allocation; as in all financially repressed economies, the Yugoslav planners' allocation of capital was
not necessarily to the most socially desirable use, in large part because
they had no price signals to indicate what that allocation should be.
Poor economic performance fueled political tensions, which were exacerbated after Tito's death in 1980. Economic difficulties encouraged
the federal government to seek assistance in 1988 from the IMF, whose
conditions included a deflationary policy package that added to economic tensions. Political and economic reform accelerated in 1989,
but it was too little too late, as nationalists came to power in the two
largest republics (Milošević in Serbia and Tudjman in Croatia). The
country, and the economic system, dissolved in the 1990s; 300,000

Table 7.3   USSR economic growth record, 1985–1991

	1985	1986	1987	1988	1989	1990	1991
GNP growth	0.8	4.1	1.3	2.1	1.5	−4.0	−13.0

Source: IMF et al. (1991).

people died in the conflicts, and for all but Slovenia much of the decade was lost time in terms of reforming the economic system.[7]

Substantive reform had to come from above, but many among the elite at the top of the Communist Party feared reform. In the USSR the leadership became ossified under Leonid Brezhnev, First Secretary of the Communist Party from 1964 to 1982. Brezhnev's successor, Yuri Andropov, attempted to improve the situation by tackling corruption, but failed to address the causes of economic inefficiency. Andropov died fifteen months after becoming First Secretary, and he was succeeded by another of the old guard, Konstantin Chernenko, who had an even briefer period in office. Finally, in 1985, the Soviet Union had a more dynamic, younger leader, Mikhail Gorbachev, who undertook an opening of the political system (*glasnost*) and reform of the economy (*perestroika*). The 1987 Law on Enterprises, which abolished output targets and made state enterprises self-financing, is often seen as the end of central planning, but state orders still accounted for most of industrial output and enterprises wanted guaranteed inputs. As state orders declined in importance in 1989–1990, output stagnated (Table 7.3). Rising foreign debt led to greater involvement with the IMF and World Bank, but advice on reform fell on deaf ears as Gorbachev hesitated to undertake radical reforms, which might undermine the whole political as well as economic system.

The End of Communism in Eastern Europe

June 4, 1989, was a day of dramatic events. In Iran the Ayatollah Khomeini, spiritual leader of the 1979 revolution, died. In China demonstrations for political and legal reform were forcibly silenced in Tiananmen Square. Many observers expected, or hoped, that these events heralded shifts away from religious fundamentalism in the Islamic world and toward greater democracy and individual freedom in the world's most populous country, but any hopes for rapid change would be dashed over the following decades. Meanwhile, in Poland an election was held on June 4 that set in motion events that would see the end of communism in Eastern Europe by the end of the year.

Elections in the Soviet bloc had long been a farce of unbelievably large turnouts resulting in overwhelming victories for candidates nominated by the Communist Party. In Poland the independent trade union, Solidarnošč, forced underground after the introduction of martial law in late 1981, enjoyed widespread popular support, and in 1989 the government allowed it to field candidates for a number of seats in the parliament. The decision, probably intended as a safety valve to allow some blowing off of steam, resulted in huge votes against the Communist candidates in the contested seats. Although the Communist Party gained a majority in parliament due to the reserved seats, its legitimacy was in tatters. The culture of fear, in which everybody was afraid of voicing independent opinions for fear that their neighbor would report them to the authorities and they would be arrested, was destroyed. Under popular pressure the regime imploded. Non-Communists assumed power, held truly democratic elections, and denounced central planning. In the following months similar displays of popular opinion led to the collapse of every Communist regime in Eastern Europe, with surprisingly little bloodshed outside Yugoslavia.[8]

In abandoning communism, the countries of Eastern Europe asserted the end of the division of Europe that had been characterized by Winston Churchill in the late 1940s as the construction of an Iron Curtain splitting Europe in two. By 1989 a return to Europe was symbolized by joining the European Union, and the priority of EU accession meant that the transition from central planning in Eastern Europe involved relatively little debate over the appropriate institutions. EU accession negotiations involve bargaining over the time horizon for introducing EU law, but no discussion of the nature of that law, because any new member must accept the existing EU rules (the *acquis communautaire*). New members have to be democracies, and have to accept the existing institutional framework for economic activity, which allowed very little national variation by the time that the EU single market had been completed in 1992.

The acceptance of existing institutions was most dramatic in Germany. The German Democratic Republic established under Soviet influence in the eastern part of post-1945 Germany had one of the most rigidly central planned economies. In the immediate postwar reconstruction period the East German economy performed reasonably well.[9] Tensions soon emerged, however, between income equality and retaining trained people, who could command high incomes in the West. As the economic performance gap widened in favor of West Germany, the flow of people from East to West accelerated, until the East German regime responded in 1961 by building a wall (often referred to as the Berlin Wall, but stretching all along the western border) to prevent East Germans from leaving. The East German regime was clearly in power only with the support of the Soviet army, and individual liberty was far more limited than in West Germany. In the summer of 1989, as Communist regimes collapsed in Poland, Czechoslovakia, and Hungary, East Germans found that when they traveled to these countries they could by August drive freely across the border from Hungary into Austria and from there into West Germany, where they could live and work as German citizens. The exodus turned to a flood in September. Combined with mass demonstrations for political change, the possibility that the country might soon be empty accelerated the end of the East German regime. In November 1989 the demolition of the Berlin Wall provided the most dramatic symbol of the end of communism in Eastern Europe and destruction of the Iron Curtain, as well as of the failure of Soviet-style central planning. Less than a year later Germany was reunified as the eastern portion joined the German Federal Republic (former West Germany).[10]

The most difficult economic question in German economic union concerned the currency; the inconvertible East German ostmarks would be replaced by West German deutsche marks (DMs), but at what exchange rate? The decision was essentially a political one of accepting the official 1:1 exchange rate, rather than the black market rate, which had valued ostmarks significantly lower, although limits were placed on the amount of savings that could be transferred into DMs at this rate. This was a windfall gain to East German savers, many of whom responded by dumping their local cars and buying better-quality Western cars. The deeper economic effect was on labor markets, where Germany's strong labor unions insisted on maintaining wage parity between East and West. At the 1:1 exchange rate, East German workers were generally far less productive than West German workers, and with wages that were inflexible downward their workplaces became uncompetitive. More-productive East Germans migrated to the West to work with better facilities, and among those remaining in the East unemployment increased. Rather than see a mass redistribution of the population, the German government responded with increased spending on infrastructure and other assistance to the eastern economy. The net effect of this spending, plus the transfers to East German savers and a rising bill for unemployment and other social benefits, rapidly increased the government budget deficit. With a strong antipathy to inflation, the German government financed the deficit by borrowing rather than by increasing the money supply.

German reunification and restructuring of the formerly centrally planned part of the economy were expensive, but the cost was only partly born by taxpayers; increased debt and higher interest rates passed some of the burden to future German taxpayers. There was also an unanticipated consequence. As capital markets became more integrated in the European Union—a key component of the program to complete the internal market by 1992—an increase in German interest rates attracted inflows of capital from the rest of the EU, pushing up interest rates all across the EU. Given the commitment to fixed exchange rates among the EU countries, this led to a crisis, as some countries were unwilling to accept the loss of monetary policy independence (i.e., they would not accept the high interest rates necessary to maintain the fixed exchange rate), a classic example of the Impossible Trinity. The United Kingdom, Denmark, and Sweden (and Italy temporarily) exited the fixed exchange rate arrangement. This highlighted the options for monetary arrangements within an EU that has freedom of capital movements. A majority of EU members committed to a single currency, which became reality within a decade, while the United Kingdom, Denmark, and Sweden preferred to maintain independent currencies and monetary autonomy. The countries that gave up monetary autonomy had a decade of relatively high interest rates, which left the larger countries (Germany, France, and Italy) with slower economic growth than other large high-income countries.

Successful transition from a centrally planned economy to a market-oriented economy has two central components: market-determined prices drive resource allocation, and enterprises and other decision-makers respond to prices in socially desirable ways. The second point requires government action to ensure that prices reflect social costs and benefits when they might differ from private costs and benefits (e.g., to counter negative externalities such as pollution or to subsidize goods and services with positive externalities, and to restrict abuse of monopoly power), and is generally best served by some form of private ownership of most productive activities. The biggest challenge is that this requires an appropriate institutional framework that protects property rights, ensures law and order, and encourages good governance, while also satisfying social and other goals that vary from country to country.

The transition was relatively simple in East Germany. An appropriate set of relative prices was imported from West Germany as soon as the border came down. Privatization was directed from above by the Treuhandanstalt, a body created in 1990 and disbanded on 1 January 1995 after it had sold 13,800 firms and parts of firms. The privatization process avoided debates over the fairness of privatization of state assets and any incumbent bias; most acquirers were from outside East Germany and were better informed than East German stakeholders would have been about how to find good managers (Dyck, 1997). The broader institutional framework was that which had evolved in the German Federal Republic, a proven successful market economy.

In other ex-Communist countries of Eastern Europe the transition to a market-based economy involved more choices than in East Germany because any external assistance would be minor. A big debate at the time was between shock therapy, introducing market-driven relative prices and controlling inflation at a stroke, and a more gradual transition, which would allow producers to adjust to the new situation. Poland took the first route with a big bang approach on 1 January 1990 when the economy was opened to trade and capital flows and a fixed exchange rate was adopted; the former brought appropriate relative prices (i.e., world prices), while the latter provided an anchor against inflation by preventing monetary policy independence. The shock therapy induced a deep recession, and the government's ability to ease the burden through subsidies was limited because it could not run budget deficits; deficits could not be monetized, due to the lack of monetary policy independence, or financed by borrowing, due to lack of creditworthiness. The benefit of shock therapy was that once the Polish economy emerged from the recession it was better placed to achieve sustained growth, although the government did drop the fixed exchange rate in 1995 in order to allow some macropolicy flexibility. Other Eastern European economies moved with varying speeds toward a similar outcome as prices converged to world prices through liberal trade policies and inflation was brought under control. The process was generally faster and more complete in the Czech Republic, Hungary, and Slovenia, and slower in Southeastern Europe.

There were also debates about the privatization of state-owned enterprises. Small enterprises with little equipment, like bakeries or hairdressers, could be transferred to the employees, but when it came to large enterprises issues of efficiency and fairness clashed. In Poland there was a serious attempt at restitution if precommunism owners could be identified. In some countries, the principle was that all had contributed to constructing the capital of state-owned enterprises, and it should thus be redistributed among the population, for example, by issuing vouchers that could be used to bid in auctions of state-owned enterprises. Such schemes, however, faced problems of asymmetric information, because managers and other insiders had a better knowledge of which were valuable assets. In many cases, workers were given first option on a percentage of the shares of the enterprise in which they worked. Any scheme giving priority to insiders, whether managers or workers, risked ending up with badly managed private enterprises as the Communist-era managers and workers often had little concept of how to find a good entrepreneurial manager. With hindsight, the variations did not make a huge difference; there were gainers and losers in the privatization process, but by the end of the

1990s Poland, the Czech Republic, Slovakia, Hungary, and Slovenia all had economies in which prices were market-determined and private enterprises dominated.[11]

The debate over the speed of transition turned out not to be so important. Some elements of the transition, such as market-driven prices and low inflation, could be introduced quickly, albeit with some pain. Other elements, such as a financial sector with well-trained loan officers and competent regulators, inevitably took more time. The real issue turned out to be about obtaining the right outcome rather than the speed with which the transition was implemented. The most drawn-out processes were creating the legal and administrative institutions necessary for a well-functioning market economy, and in these areas the process was simplified by the common goal of EU accession, and hence acceptance of EU law. The Czech Republic, Hungary, Poland, Slovakia, and Slovenia joined the EU in 2004, Bulgaria and Romania in 2007.

The transition from central planning in Eastern Europe was facilitated by the existence of an accepted model of institutional change. For East Germany the transition was, uniquely, financed in substantial part by the citizens of an affluent market economy, and the creditworthiness of the German Federal Republic meant that the monetary costs could be funded by borrowing rather than inflationary finance. Even under these favorable conditions, the transition costs for the generation of adult East Germans were substantial.[12] Many Eastern Europeans hoped that adoption of Western institutions would bring their living standards to Western European levels. Even though incomes started to converge after the transitional recession, there remained huge differences in wealth as Western Europeans had accumulated physical assets (houses, cars, etc.), financial assets, and human capital (skills appropriate to a market economy) that would take decades for Eastern Europeans to accumulate more or less from scratch.

The Dissolution of the Soviet Union

A striking feature of the collapse of communism in Eastern Europe in the second half of 1989 was the impotence of the Soviet Union. In 1968 Soviet troops had quashed reformers in Czechoslovakia and in 1981 the threat of military intervention lay behind the Polish government's decision to impose martial law, but in 1989 the troops remained in their barracks. Indeed, the Soviet Union was facing increased internal dissent as Gorbachev's *glasnost* policies allowed more open discussion of nationalism in the Baltic republics, Ukraine, and the Caucasus.[13] The creation of elected presidents of the individual republics was in many cases cosmetic as the first secretary of the Communist Party became president, but in Russia, the largest Soviet republic, elections in June 1991 brought to power Boris Yeltsin, who was a more committed democrat and economic reformer than Gorbachev.[14]

The crucial episode came in August 1991 when a conservative group among the Soviet leadership organized a coup d'état to replace Gorbachev by Vice President Yanayev. The conspirators were opposed by Yeltsin, who led popular opposition in Moscow, encouraging the troops not to support the coup and forcing the conspirators to back down. Although Gorbachev remained in power, the initiative lay with Yeltsin, who nationalized Soviet Union property in the Russian republic and replaced the Soviet flag with the Russian flag on public buildings. Other republics followed Russia's lead and made declarations of independence over the ensuing months. On 25 December 1991 Gorbachev formally announced the dissolution of the Soviet Union and lowered the Soviet flag for the last time. The fifteen republics were replaced by fifteen independent nations.

The end of the Soviet Union was accompanied by the definitive end of central planning as formal Soviet planning institutions ceased to exist.[15] In Russia Yeltsin adopted a big bang approach to reform, freeing virtually all prices on 2 January 1992. Since the other former republics continued to use the ruble and borders were still open, they all had to follow Russia's lead and free up prices. Some governments tried to soften the change by keeping some regulated prices and by allocating some goods by state orders, but all of the Soviet successor states were embarked on transition to a market-based economy.[16]

Russia also took a big bang approach to privatization. All citizens received vouchers, which they could use to bid in auctions for state property or to obtain owner-operated small enterprises. The process was successful in privatizing quickly; 70 percent of state assets were privatized in 1992–1994. However, although the process was based on the egalitarian principle that state assets belonged to all and should be returned to all in equal proportions, in practice voucher privatization was unfair. Many voucher owners were poorly informed and enterprise managers had no incentive to provide accurate assessment of assets' value. The auctions of valuable resource-related assets were particularly biased in favor of preferred bidders, for example, by holding them on location in an inaccessible site whose nearest airport might be closed down to prevent unwanted competition in the auction. The inequity was exacerbated in the run-up to the 1996 presidential election when shareholdings that had been kept by the state were exchanged for loans, and in the depth of the transitional recession the buyers were the newly rich, referred to as the "oligarchs."[17] Defenders of Russia's privatization argue that in the chaotic circumstances of the first half of the 1990s any privatization process would be imperfect, but that Russia benefited from creating clear property rights quickly.[18] This was, however, at the cost of condoning massive corruption and shady practices, and the mood would be seized in the 2000 presidential election by Vladimir Putin, who promised a more autocratic style than Yeltsin's and who cowed the oligarchs, often by semilegal means.

The dissolution of the USSR, combined with the end of communism in Eastern Europe and in Mongolia, the dissolution of Yugoslavia, and the introduction of reforms in China and Vietnam meant that more than thirty countries were in transition from central planning to a market-based economy. They were adopting different strategies and appeared to provide a natural experiment in how to establish a well-functioning market economy. By the end of the 1990s dozens of econometric studies had sought to establish patterns of success and failure.

An explicit aim of many of these studies was to establish a connection between policies and performance. Many economists believed that rapid reform would yield the greatest benefits. Market-determined prices combined with clear ownership rights should lead to the most efficient allocation of resources, while ownership reform without price reform would lead to misallocation and price reform without ownership reform would lead to rent-seeking by those able to grab the benefits. The cross-country analysis did not yield a clear answer because the pace of reform, distance from Western Europe, and years spent under central planning were all positively related to output performance, but these three explanatory variables are highly correlated, which makes it difficult, if not impossible, to separate their independent influence. Thus, performance could be explained by rapid reform, or by geography or by history.

Anecdotal evidence could be used either way. In the 1990s the Eastern European countries performed better than the former Soviet republics, with a shorter period of negative growth followed in most cases by sustained growth.[19] They were also, together with the three Baltic countries, more successful in establishing democracy and legal systems. Whether this was due to wise policymakers, to the lure of EU membership, or to living memories of pre-Communist regimes is unclear. Among the Eastern European countries or within the Commonwealth of Independent States (CIS), that is, the twelve former Soviet republics other than the Baltics, there was no clear pattern. Among the CIS the best output performance in the 1990s was by Uzbekistan, a slow reformer. In the first decade of the twenty-first century the CIS countries performed better. That was largely driven by the success of energy-rich countries such as Russia, Kazakhstan, and Azerbaijan, although Anders Åslund (2007) has argued that superior long-run performance was also related to more extensive economic reforms in the decade after the end of central planning.

Despite the difficulty of drawing simple lessons about the best approach to transition from central planning to a market-determined economy, some conclusions did emerge from econometric studies of the formerly centrally planned economies.[20] The dissolution of the Yugoslav and Soviet federations was accompanied by interstate and civil wars, and war-torn countries performed particularly badly in the 1990s. All of the transition economies experienced periods of high inflation as they adopted market prices. This was especially true of countries at war, who used the printing presses to finance their war efforts, and of those former Soviet republics who continued to use the ruble without a good mechanism to control monetary policy, but in the aftermath of the planned economy all countries suffered from a shortfall of public revenue to meet ongoing demands for public expenditure. High inflation obscures movement of relative prices and hence the ability of the market economy to function well, and this negative relationship is clear from the cross-country studies that show high inflation to be strongly associated with poor output performance over the 1990s. The relationship is not a linear one: single-digit inflation was not noticeably harmful in the economies in transition from central planning; but the negative impact becomes apparent when prices were increasing by more than 13 or 14 percent annually, while once hyperinflation (conventionally defined as prices rising by more than 50 percent per month) occurs variations in the rate of increase are not significant.[21] These two negative influences, war and inflation, were often inter-related, and could be seen as symptomatic of a deeper failure to establish a well-functioning state in countries such as Tajikistan, Moldova, or Georgia from both a political and an economic perspective.

Reform in China and Vietnam

China's reforms began in December 1978 as an experiment with the household responsibility system in agriculture. Under this system instead of the rural commune acting as a single collective farm, individual households were given responsibility for specific plots of land, from which they had to produce crops to meet the plan target but could keep any output above the target. This change in incentive structure led to an immediate and dramatic increase in output.[22] The situation of farmers was further improved by changes in the official prices of farm products relative to nonfarm products. Between 1979 and 1983 China enjoyed rapid agriculture-led growth.

As rural families' spending power increased they demanded utensils, construction materials, and other simple manufactures that the planned economy supplied inadequately. The gap was filled by local businesses, known as township and village enterprises (TVEs). The TVEs employed local labor, which could be released by the more productive farm sector without causing food shortages, and mobilized local savings, which had nowhere else to go in light of the repressed financial sector. The ownership structure was opaque in a system where private enterprise was not recognized, but the TVEs were allowed to flourish; as Deng Xiaoping had pointed out earlier, it did not matter what you called something as long as it produced a desired outcome.

The second strand of China's reforms was the open door policy. Under Mao Zedong China had been largely closed to the global economy, selling some raw materials in return for essential imports but not allowing any foreign investment. The open door policy adopted in June 1979 permitted establishment of joint ventures between foreign investors and domestic partners, created special economic zones, and gradually loosened the state monopoly on foreign trade. This had little initial impact, but foreign trade began to take off after 1983.

In Hong Kong rising wages, an appreciating real exchange rate, and land scarcity were making local manufacturing of labor-intensive products less competitive on world markets. The solution was to ship sewing machines and other equipment across the border into southern China, where millions of literate unskilled workers were willing to work for much lower wages. The institutional arrangement was typically a joint venture between a Hong Kong entrepreneur and a TVE. For many TVEs the opportunity to supply global markets was a welcome solution to the problem of a limited local market. China's coastal provinces, especially areas of Guangdong Province adjacent to Hong Kong, boomed. Local authorities in areas with easy shipping, which was essential both to bring in inputs and to ship out the manufactured goods, competed for joint ventures, and the central government gradually eased restrictions on foreign investors, especially in 1986 (Pomfret, 1991). The combination of Chinese labor with Hong Kong management and exporting expertise was a winner that had plenty of scope for all partners to benefit.

The downside was that the boom fueled inflation. Without a well-functioning financial sector, the government had to resort to crude credit controls to cool the overheating economy, and in 1987–1988, after almost a decade of sustained growth, the economy faltered.

Labor market liberalization, which meant that students did not automatically obtain jobs when they graduated, further contributed to discontent. The massive, but inchoate student demonstrations in the first half of 1989 had other origins, such as opposition to corruption and support for a more transparent system of justice and perhaps for greater democracy. The Communist power-brokers responded by dismissing the reformist leader Zhao Ziyang and using force to end the protests at Tiananmen Square on 4 June 1989—ironically the same day as quasi-free elections in Poland began the unraveling of communism in Eastern Europe. One lesson learned by the Chinese leadership was that continued economic prosperity was an important means of forestalling opposition. After a brief internal debate, the leadership resumed economic reforms in 1992, including the financial sector reforms that would permit a more nuanced macroeconomic policy. However, the Communist Party's monopoly on power remains inviolate.

Vietnam entered on a reform path in 1986, called *doi moi*. In general outline this resembled China's path, combining agrarian reform and an open door policy with political control by the Communist Party. Although there was no counterpart to Hong Kong, Vietnam had an advantage in that, although much of the country had been devastated by war, the southern half of the country had until 1975 been a market economy and connections with the Vietnamese diaspora were strong. Vietnam flourished in the decades following reform, although unlike China there was high inflation in the early years and the pace of growth was less stellar.

An important reason for the difference was the less draconian enforcement in Vietnam. China allowed the TVE sector to grow rapidly without reducing the size of the planned sector—a process dubbed "growing out of the plan" by Barry Naughton.[23] This dual economy combined the benefits of growth and stability, but it was only sustainable as long as people did not arbitrage between the artificial prices in the planned economy and the market-driven prices in the nonplanned economy, for example, by selling the underpriced fuel or materials that reduced the losses of the state-owned enterprises to a TVE at their market value. Although state enterprise managers caught doing this are severely punished, often by death, the potential returns from such arbitrage are high, so it exists; this is one reason behind China having the highest rate of executions in the world. Such penalties have been unacceptable elsewhere, including Vietnam.

An even more striking contrast was between, on the one hand, China and Vietnam and, on the other hand, the formerly Communist countries of Eastern Europe and the CIS. Market-based reforms in China and Vietnam were followed by high growth rates, immediately in China and with a short lag in Vietnam, in sharp contrast to reform in Eastern Europe and the former Soviet Union where reforms were everywhere followed by a substantial recession. Some commentators (e.g., Roland, 2000) have ascribed this to too-rapid change in Eastern Europe and more gradual reforms in Asia, but the contrast applies to both rapid and slow reformers in Eastern Europe and the CIS. Moreover, in key respects the Chinese reforms were not gradual; four-fifths of the population lived in rural areas and the rapid spread of the household responsibility system after 1978 essentially terminated the old collective farm system where these people lived and worked, while the open door policy was also a dramatic reversal of earlier closed economy policies. The reforms continue to take a long time to complete their impact because the process of releasing hundreds of millions of workers from low-productivity farming to higher-productivity factory employment is lengthy, but their introduction was a major shock to the economy.

Economic structure explains why China and Vietnam enjoyed a smooth transition from central planning. Their comparative advantage was self-evident and strong; the process was one of transferring rural workers into production of labor-intensive manufactured goods for sale on the world market, and this process had already been charted by the new industrializing economies of East Asia. By contrast, while many of the old state enterprises in Eastern Europe and the Soviet Union were hopelessly uncompetitive, it was not obvious where these economies' comparative advantage would lie in a market setting. Destruction of employment in state enterprises with antiquated capital and product lines was unavoidable, but the creation of jobs in new activities was slow. In China, there was hardly any need for job destruction as the economy grew out of the plan; the state-owned industrial enterprises survived, perhaps transforming themselves over time, while millions of workers left agriculture willingly in search of more economically rewarding jobs in the new factories producing for export.

Conclusions

The fall of the Berlin Wall and the dissolution of the Soviet Union were dramatic symbols of the end of communism in Europe. In reality the economic decline that underpinned the collapse had been a gradual process already visible in the 1970s. Even more than in the ISI regimes described in Chapter 5, centrally planned economies appeared impervious to piecemeal reform and were only ended by revolutionary change. In Eastern Europe, the Soviet Union, and Mongolia the end of central planning coincided with the collapse of Communist regimes, but the large Asian Communist countries, China and Vietnam, shifted their economies from central planning to decentralized market-based economies while avoiding major political change.

Nevertheless, the radical economic and political change in Eastern Europe, the former Soviet Union, and Mongolia and the more evolutionary change in China and Vietnam share a common basic feature. All of these economies, whatever the pathways, were far more market-oriented by 2000 than two decades earlier. Nobody would have predicted such a dramatic change in 1980, and yet the change was so great and so widespread that by the end of the century the few small Communist countries that avoided economic and political change, for example, North Korea and Cuba, appeared as minor backward-looking anachronisms.

By the end of the twentieth century central planning was completely discredited, but it was not rejected in favor of unregulated capitalism. Another common feature of the economies making the transition from central planning is that all have shed the resource allocation ideology of planning but maintained a commitment to equality. Even the most radical converts to capitalism embraced the need for the welfare state and continued public provision of education and basic health care. If standards of social service provision slipped in some countries during the transition owing to resource constraints or poor governance, this was seen as a failing to be corrected.

CHAPTER 8

The End of the Third World

✦

The Cold War vision of a battle of systems between the capitalist First World and communist Second World, with a distinctive impoverished Third World as a bystander (and also part of the winner's prize), was already a doubtful description of reality by the 1970s when the newly industrializing economies (NIEs) shed the "less-developed country" label. The end of central planning and economic success of some of the world's most populous countries following market-oriented reforms made such divisions anachronistic. By the turn of the century India, Brazil, Mexico, and Indonesia as well as China and (perhaps) Russia were enjoying sustained growth.

Even more than in the old industrialized countries of Europe and countries settled by Europeans, the new industrializing countries of the late twentieth century embodied a variety of economic and political systems, albeit all with a central core of a market-driven economy. The differences can be classified by continent. The high-performing Asian economies followed the Japanese and NIE model of growth led by specialization in labor-intensive manufactured goods, with the Indian variant of specialization in labor-intensive services. In Latin America market-based capitalist economies had a long history and the principal need was to change the nature of government intervention from the microeconomic resource allocation focus of ISI to a focus on macroeconomic stability, investment in infrastructure, and provision of social policies with benefits accessible to all. In Africa, the picture is less positive, with few governments succeeding in establishing well-functioning modern economies. Nevertheless, it is important to bear in mind that continental generalizations have exceptions: Botswana is a success by any global ranking, while Haiti and Tajikistan have as disastrous a record as any failed state in Africa.

The High-Performing Asian Economies

The largest geopolitical shift in the second half of the twentieth century was the emergence (or reemergence) of Asia as a major pole in the world economy. The process began with Japan's post-1945 reconstruction and rapid catch-up growth. The driver was manufactured exports, which were initially low cost and low quality, but Japan moved up the quality ladder until by the 1980s it was an established high-income country producing high-quality goods. Hong Kong starting in the 1950s and Taiwan, South Korea, and Singapore in the 1960s followed a similar path. Their success encouraged the next generation (Malaysia, Thailand, and Indonesia) to abandon import-substitution in favor of manufactured export expansion. The reformed Chinese and Vietnamese economies became a major part of this development in the 1980s.

Because the East Asian model involves specialization in labor-intensive goods, its adoption has generally led to greater income equality, albeit as some successful entrepreneurs have become very rich, especially in Hong Kong. In Taiwan and South Korea the transfer of labor from agriculture to industry in the 1960s and early 1970s may have increased the well-being of those workers, but more dramatically starting in the early 1970s wages for all unskilled workers began a continuous rise. Higher living standards were reflected in better housing, better nutrition, and access to an ever-increasing range of affordable consumer goods. The pace of change was even faster in second-generation industrializers such as Thailand, the world's fastest-growing economy between 1982 and 1996. In China hundreds of millions of people crossed the international poverty line (a dollar a day at purchasing power parity) in the decade and a half after the adoption of reforms in 1978 and 1979.

Rapid industrialization was often associated with urbanization and widening regional income differences. Unlike in ISI countries where rural-urban migration created underemployment and slums, the migrants in East Asia were responding to high urban wages arising from excess demand for unskilled workers. The dynamic manufacturing sector clustered around major port cities, which offered low transport costs to overseas markets and agglomeration benefits in the form of better financial and other support services or denser markets for skilled workers and managers.[1] Negative consequences such as the legendary traffic jams and pollution in Bangkok in the 1990s were symptoms of success as car ownership spread at record rates; the negative effects were reversible, as country after country responded to congestion by building urban rail or other transport systems.

Financial sector development was a key component of growth. Initial adoption of the outward-oriented model required little financial support as labor-intensive manufacturing did not involve large setup costs and multinational enterprises or foreign buying houses would provide working capital and trade finance. Economic growth created increased demand for banking and other services from established businesses or cash-constrained potential entrepreneurs and from households with increasing incomes and high propensity to save. The nature of financial sectors varied considerably, from the big-firm-connected banks in Japan and South Korea to the crony financial capitalism of Suharto's Indonesia to the deregulated financial system of Thailand in the 1990s. In several countries rapid financial expansion and poor oversight led to over-risky lending and eventually to financial crises. Japan illustrated the problem in the late 1980s, but the most dramatic crisis followed Thailand's currency collapse in July 1997. The Asian crisis spread to involve banks in South Korea, Indonesia, and, to a lesser extent, Malaysia which ended up with extensive nonperforming loans. The tightening of credit and loss of wealth (e.g., associated with real estate whose value collapsed when bubbles burst) fueled a reduction in aggregate demand that led to major recessions in the most-affected countries, with important political consequences in Indonesia and Thailand.[2] Nevertheless, despite the short-term hardship in the worst-affected countries, the 1997–1998 Asian crisis had uneven impact, with little negative effect on economies with sound financial systems (Hong Kong, Singapore, Taiwan) or with regulated capital markets (China), and even the worst-hit economies resumed economic growth by 2000.

Do high-performing Asian economies have welfare states? Singaporean leaders assert the importance of Asian values, which they contrast with Western countries' state welfare, which weakens family bonds, diminishes incentives to work, and places a drain on the public budget. Peter Lindert (2006, 255–256) reports that in 1990 East Asian countries did spend significantly less on social transfers than South American countries or Turkey or Israel, but he claims that this share is increasing and that by 2020 Taiwan, South Korea, and even Singapore will have welfare states.

Asian values of paternalism and community-minded elders are sometimes invoked to justify forms of governance that are for the people but not by the people. South Korea and Taiwan started on their reform paths with military dictatorships, and post-1945 Japan, Malaysia, and Singapore all hold elections in which a dominant party wins without alteration of government (until 2009 in Japan) and with a sometimes pliant judiciary. Nevertheless, the trend is toward more competitive democracies and more independent judiciaries. This is clearly the case in the earlier industrializers such as Japan, South Korea, and Taiwan, and spectacularly so in Indonesia after 1998, although there has been backsliding in Thailand in the first decade of the twenty-first century.

During the 1990s East Asian trade patterns, which had previously been overwhelmingly between individual exporters and markets outside the region, began to be increasingly intra-regional as domestic demand within Asia became significant and, more importantly, as firms established regional value chains to benefit from differing comparative advantage; for example, the most labor-intensive activities may be carried out in Vietnam or China, more sophisticated processes in Thailand, and capital-intensive activities in Japan. This regionalization of trade has led to increasing political cooperation at the regional level and a blossoming of trade agreements aimed at reducing the costs of trade within Asia.[3]

For several decades Asian miracles were confined to East Asia. Myanmar, South Asia, and Southwest Asia were resistant to reform. After the dissolution of the Soviet Union, the Central Asian countries were among the least reformed successor states.[4] Episodes of reform and growth in Sri Lanka were not sustained, and despite talk of reform in India, Bangladesh, and Pakistan, there was little fundamental change in the economic strategies of these countries.

The most dramatic change came after India's reforms in 1991. The need for reform had been accepted by many economists and some policymakers as early as the late 1960s, but each attempt at reform met resistance. By the 1980s the cost of maintaining "sick enterprises," that is, plants that should have downsized or closed but were subsidized to prevent job loss, was placing an unbearable burden on the public purse, and serious systemic reform of the ISI system was implemented.[5] In essence, India's accelerated growth followed the Asian model of deregulating key markets and allowing greater responsiveness to price signals, and as in East Asia reforms were followed by a large increase in openness to the world economy. However, instead of exporting labor-intensive manufactures, India exported labor-intensive services such as back-office administration, call centers, and sometimes computer work. As in China, this generated rising incomes, rural- urban migration, and, after a time lag, domestic openings for more skilled workers and entrepreneurs.

The Transformation of Latin America

Similar shifts toward greater outward orientation occurred in the largest economies in Latin America. The catalyst was the trauma of the 1982 debt crisis, following which the highly indebted countries had to reduce their trade deficits which had been funded by borrowing or even create trade surpluses to rebuild their external creditworthiness. This was virtually impossible with an import-substituting industrialization strategy which over the decades had cut imports back to the bare bones while making exporting unattractive. Nevertheless, dismantling the protection offered to import-competing producers and deregulating key markets encountered strong opposition.

In Latin America the 1980s were viewed as a lost decade, as countries saw living standards stagnate in the aftermath of the 1982 debt crisis. The 1990s was a decade of recovery and reform, but several countries did not maintain the reforms. Argentina introduced a radical stabilization program tying the peso to the U.S. dollar, but when the country faced economic hardship in 2001, reform was abandoned in favor of populism. Ecuador went through a similar path, while Venezuela and Bolivia moved straight to populism. The long-term prospects for these countries are bleak, although resource wealth can enable autocratic regimes to remain in power without reform (as in Saudi Arabia, Libya, Russia, Venezuela, and elsewhere).[6]

The two most highly indebted countries in 1982 both succeeded with economic reform—Mexico in 1986 and Brazil in the early 1990s. Mexico created external anchors by joining the WTO in 1986 and opening negotiations with the United States and Canada to establish the North American Free Trade Area. Brazil went through several cycles of reform followed by reaction, each of which was associated with monetary problems and disagreements with creditors, until the debt crisis finally wound down in 1994 and reforms stuck. Both countries began to realize their potential by the turn of the century. Mexico had rising oil output as world prices began to climb after 1998. Brazil's was a more clear-cut case study of the costs of import substitution and benefits of reform as farm exports surged under the new policies and as firms in the manufacturing sector, such as aircraft manufacturer Embraer, became competitive in world markets.

Systemic reforms to transform an economy based on import-substitution require at least a decade before the benefits are truly apparent; hence the tortuous reform process in India from 1969 until 1991 and the even longer (and still incomplete) reform of the Egyptian economy since 1974. Successful reformers such as Mexico or Brazil (or Australia after 1983) stay the course, but others have not. In Mexico tying the reforms to external institutions that stood for market-based resource allocation made reversal difficult. In Brazil (and Australia) reform eventually became bipartisan and crucial steps were taken by leaders whose background was in labor unions.[7]

Successful reform in Latin America focused on efficiency, and the continent continues to be distinguished by high levels of inequality. However, steps are being taken to establish a more effective welfare state in countries where successful reforms have been followed by left-leaning governments that maintained the efficiency-enhancing reforms. Chile in the two decades following the overthrow of Pinochet in 1988–1989 had socialist governments that, especially under the 2006–2010 presidency of Michelle Bachelet, pursued an active state investment policy of building homes for poor people and crèches for poor children, and providing extensive free health care. After the Workers Party victory in Brazil's 2002 election, President Luiz Inácio Lula da Silva maintained the liberalization of the economy, but focused on improving the country's social policies, for example, by the Fome Zero (Zero Hunger) program and the Bolsa Família under which poor families receive cash contingent upon sending their children to school and keeping their vaccination records up to date.

The Challenge of Failed States

Reforms have often failed because of organized opposition, but elsewhere it is a case of the state being too impotent to implement good management, let alone policy reform. Thus, although many countries in the Third World category in the 1960s have become middle-income countries, some remain mired in poverty and economic stagnation. These are mostly in sub-Saharan Africa, but also include countries in the Western Hemisphere (Haiti), in Asia (Nepal, Laos, Tajikistan), and in Europe (Albania, Moldova).

The legacy of colonialism in Africa is difficult to assess because it is hard to know what the alternative would have been.[8] The colonial state itself was authoritarian and paternalistic, created by Europeans for their own purposes. To varying degrees the imperial powers constructed infrastructure, with the primary emphasis on facilitating export of natural resources, and began a process of economic modernization. The colonial revenue system was typically based on agricultural products and raw materials, whose prices fluctuated in world markets. Administration was through a network of government offices whose human and physical resources varied greatly from region to region, and the military and police forces usually had European officers. International borders had often been determined at European conferences, in which the statesmen had little knowledge of or concern for geographical, linguistic, or other boundaries.[9]

Decolonization proved disastrous almost everywhere because little or no provision had been made for nation-building or leaving institutions appropriate to an independent state, and in particular investment in indigenous human capital was generally low. The situation was exacerbated by the suddenness and speed of decolonization in Africa, in contrast to most decolonization in Asia. Once begun, and in the face of opposition to the concept of colonialism by the United Nations, the United States, and the USSR, the process of unraveling of the European empires was unstoppable, even though some delayed and some departed with unseemly haste. Ghana became independent in 1957, and by 1968 all but Rhodesia, Southwest Africa, Djibouti, and the Portuguese colonies had become independent.[10] The most sudden was the Belgian Congo; in 1955 the Bilsen Report recommended planning for independence in thirty years' time, but in January 1960 the Belgian government announced that the date for independence would be 30 June 1960. Portugal held on to its colonies the longest, but this was by force with little planning for future independence; independence came when rebel forces took power in the face of political collapse in Portugal.[11]

The lack of leadership and administrative capacity was exacerbated by the absence of national solidarity. Many colonial boundaries in Africa were lines drawn on a map by politicians in Europe and, when the imperial police and troops left, intertribal power struggles broke out, often spilling over into repression or civil war. As a further ingredient, the new independent states of Africa were at the center of Cold War competition between the United States and the USSR; although the competition was between economic systems, external intervention was dominated by military assistance that turned the continent into a heavily armed place and often the superpower not supporting the government would foment armed opposition.

Irrespective of whether postindependence governments were nominally socialist (e.g., Zambia) or capitalist (e.g., Nigeria), the state was captured by elites who then used the power of the state to accumulate wealth. When elections were held, voters looked to political leaders to deliver material benefits to their region, rather than to implement policies for the national good.[12] Such politics led to bidding wars, which were unstable, and by the end of the 1960s most rulers had formally established one-party states. Political competition was restricted to competition within the elite, and regimes were increasingly characterized by sycophancy and cronyism.

The development orthodoxy of import-substituting industrialization put a further strain on governance. New governments promised economic modernization and prosperity now that the rapacious imperialists had left, but their small domestic markets were particularly ill-suited to autarchic development. Economic disappointment encouraged presidents to hold on to power and protect their clients' economic interests, increasingly using repression to stifle opposition. The African variant of ISI often consisted of little more than a continuation of colonial policies of squeezing as much out of the primary product sector as possible and channeling the proceeds to the urban elite, who may or, more often, may not invest in manufacturing. The urban bias was inefficient, because it discouraged investment in agriculture where many African countries' comparative advantage lay, and inequitable, because it pillaged the rural poor to the benefit of the better-off urban dwellers.[13] In resource-rich countries the power struggle often centered on control over the resource rents; the institutional breakdown associated with a "resource curse" was most apparent in countries like Nigeria or Sierra Leone, although the example of diamond-rich Botswana showed that resources could be a boon.[14]

One of the better organized institutions was often the army, which became a source of instability when the control of the imperial power was loosened. A week after the Belgian Congo became independent, the army mutinied on 6 July 1960, triggering Belgian military intervention (Kabongo, 1988). In British East Africa discontent among the troops was, at the request of the new political leaders, put down by British armed forces in 1964. French military interventions continued much longer in West and Central Africa. In the Congo, General Mobutu twice overthrew the government; after the 1965 coup he assumed absolute power and ruled until 1996. By the second half of the 1960s, in many sub-Saharan African countries civilian regimes were unable to muster sufficient support to avoid military takeovers. In Uganda, after Prime Minister Milton Obote dismissed his former ally and the current army head Idi Amin on corruption charges in October 1970, Amin seized power, accusing Obote of corruption. During the 1970s and 1980s, about a third of sub-Saharan African countries' heads of state came from the armed forces (Bates, 2008, 21).

The regulated economy became increasingly inefficient, but economic reform was stifled by the leadership because the elite could live well, and had much to fear from any change that would install a popular government. African ISI regimes emphasized control, based on a closed economy and regulated markets. Foreign exchange earnings from primary product exports were controlled directly in the case of point resources (e.g., oil, minerals, diamonds) or through state marketing boards for crops such as cotton, coffee, cocoa, sugar, or sisal. Those with access to the scarce foreign exchange were able to purchase imports cheaply with the overvalued domestic currency; a particular symptom of the distorted markets in Africa was the large black market premium on foreign currency. In the more kleptocratic regimes, the foreign currency went into ostentatious consumption or to offshore bank accounts. When there was investment in import-substituting industries, the producers were protected by tariffs or other import restrictions, and with a small domestic market they often enjoyed substantial monopoly power. When the domestic economy was squeezed dry, many countries turned to international capital markets or aid agencies rather than undertaking economic and political reform.[15]

There was an occasional exception, notably Botswana where parliamentary democracy, freedom of speech, and a free media survived and the economy flourished. The norm, however, was increasing repression. Even in countries not under military leaders, militarization took place. Leaders kept tight control over the ministry of the interior, and in most sub-Saharan African countries policing was a national, not a local, function. Leaders often maintained special military forces organized for internal repression rather than for defense against external threats. In response, militias were formed by opposition groups, and the state lost its monopoly of violence in increasingly armed societies.

As in Latin America, the 1980s were widely seen as a lost decade for Africa characterized by economic crises, which many considered to have been exacerbated by structural adjustment programs imposed by the World Bank and IMF. Although the external institutions were a convenient scapegoat, the real culprit—as in Latin America—was failure to reform the ISI development strategy. Relative to economic capacity the debt crisis was even worse in Africa than in Latin America, although the amounts involved were smaller, and the prospects of the heavily indebted poor countries ever repaying their debts were slim.[16] There was, however, growing discontent, especially in the rural sector where most Africans lived and worked. The deleterious impact of ISI policies was exacerbated by population pressure leading to competition over land, for example, between pastoralists and farmers, and made even worse by drought in semi-arid countries around the northern African desert. Many Africans became increasingly discontented with their own governments. About fifteen countries were in a state of civil war in the early 1990s (Bates, 2008, 4). A less violent channel for discontent was the holding of constitutional conferences in a dozen or so countries in 1990–1991, which led to elections. In the "Second Liberation" dictators were displaced and democracy emerged in several countries, in a much-changed international context.

The end of communism in Eastern Europe and the USSR provided a shock to sub-Saharan Africa. Soviet advisors and assistance were pulled out, and Cuban soldiers and professional staff (e.g., in Ethiopia and Angola) were also withdrawn when Soviet sustenance ended. Without communist support the war in Mozambique wound down. Communist-supported regimes changed their spots, most notably Benin, which held elections in 1991 and over the next fifteen years experienced three peaceful changes of government following national elections. Zambia also held its first multiparty elections, in 1991, when the postindependence president Kenneth Kaunda lost power after twenty-seven years of rule. The apartheid regime in South Africa, no longer having a credible bogey, released Nelson Mandela, setting in motion a chain of events that would replace apartheid with a democratic regime with majority rule. On the other hand, in countries such as Togo, Gabon, and Kenya the rulers fought back, fixing elections to retain power and killing opponents. Without the Cold War, the world ignored home-grown strife such as genocide in Burundi and Rwanda and the breakdown of Zaire/Congo.

More than any other region, Africa in the second half of the twentieth century illustrated the importance of good institutions for economic growth and prosperity, although unfortunately this was demonstrated primarily by the negative consequences of poor institutions.[17]
A market economy cannot function well without the rule of law and
protection of property rights to ensure that private ownership cannot
arbitrarily be reversed by force. The power of the state derives from its
monopoly on legitimate force to administer the law. Political order results when rulers "choose to employ the means of coercion to protect
the creation of wealth rather than to prey upon it and when private citizens choose to set weapons aside and devote their time instead to the
production of wealth and to the enjoyment of leisure" (Bates, 2008, 5).
Almost everywhere in sub-Saharan Africa after the wave of independence between 1957 and 1968, rulers captured the state and used its
means of coercion to steal their country's wealth, ultimately driving
others to turn to military means and creating a climate of fear and uncertainty. The variation across countries highlights a facet of the relationship between democracy or autocracy and economic performance;
the postindependence leadership tailored institutions to cement their
own hold on power, but the individual leadership mattered, with, for
example, Botswana being lucky and Congo/Zaire cursed.

By the turn of the century several African countries were enjoying
more rapid, and sustainable, economic growth than at any time since
independence, and these were the countries that had improved governance with checks on power and improved rule of law. Despite the improved economic conditions and prospects of many sub-Saharan countries, others remain in the hands of corrupt autocrats or worse still
without any functioning government. Power in countries like Somalia
is localized and comes out of the barrel of a gun, with terrible consequences for the countries' citizens and sometimes, as in the case of Somalia's incapacity to control its pirates, for the global community.

Global concern, whether humanitarian or self-interested fears about
political instability, may be addressed to countries that have failed to
share the global prosperity, but what is to be done? Economic aid can
have a positive impact, but it can also be ineffective if the policy environment is growth-unfriendly.[18]

Conclusions

By 2000 there was no longer serious debate about the desirable economic system. The advantages of the market mechanism as an engine of material prosperity, able to match the availability of goods and services with people's demands and to balance present and future consumption, had been demonstrated both by the success of an increasing number of market-based economies at all income levels and by the failure of central planning and ISI to provide satisfactory long-run outcomes. Nevertheless, all countries moving toward a more market-based resource allocation system showed concern about the distributional consequences of capitalism, and no country did so without taking steps to ensure greater equality than would result from an unregulated market economy.

There was a widely held consensus that governments have a part to play, not just in the minimalist roles recognized by Adam Smith and nineteenth-century liberals (providing law and order, national defense, and other public goods such as roads and bridges) and in addressing market failures such as abuse of monopoly power, but also to promote equality of opportunity and outcome. Approaches to the latter aim vary both philosophically (e.g., the United States places more emphasis on equality of opportunity, Australia on equality of outcome) and practically in the design of support for the unemployed or the elderly. Active debates continue about the balance between market forces and state intervention and over the relative merits of the many varieties of capitalism. Nevertheless, the idea that the state must bear substantial responsibility for providing a social safety net and universal access to some level of schooling and health care was widely accepted by the start of the twenty-first century.

Part of the backdrop to the achievement of growth with equity has been establishment of an ever more tightly integrated global economy. Critics of globalization have been concerned about the loss of control over people's economic lives, as their livelihood can be threatened by events thousands of miles away and beyond their own government's control. Such concerns must be counterbalanced by the benefits from innovations or entrepreneurship in distant countries and from the division of labor; millions of mobile phone users far beyond Finland and Canada benefited from the innovations of Nokia and Blackberry, while the real prices of clothing, toys, bags, and many other goods (in terms of the time that people need to work in order to earn sufficient money to buy them) have been drastically reduced by the integration of China and other labor-abundant countries into the global economy. A challenge in the twenty-first century will be to develop appropriate rules for governance of the global economy, as well as meeting new challenges with global implications such as proliferation of nuclear weapons, global warming, and sustaining common resources such as the ocean fisheries.

CHAPTER 9

From the Age of Equality to the Age of Fraternity

✦

The century 1815–1914 was the Age of Liberty when successful nations minimized restrictions on individual choice and on actions that might limit operation of the market economy (e.g., guilds or despotic regimes were an anachronism in Europe by 1919 even though the aristocracy continued to use their titles). The European economies and their offshoots enjoyed unprecedented economic prosperity. By the early 1900s the absence of widespread absolute poverty was taken for granted in these countries, and the failure to share the fruits of prosperity equitably was increasingly challenged both by a better organized working class and by reformers among the more well-to-do.

The twentieth century was the Age of Equality as the high-income countries struggled with how to balance the high and rising output unleashed by the industrial revolution with a fair distribution of that output, where "fair" is a vague but commonly understood term encompassing some degree of equality of opportunity and of outcome. The most dramatic challenges came in the poorer industrialized countries. Communist ideology was nurtured in Germany and became government ideology in Russia after 1917. Latecomers such as Italy, Germany, and Japan turned in the 1920s and 1930s to fascism as a collaborative approach to sharing prosperity among the people and promoting national grandeur. After the defeat and discrediting of fascism, the choice became polarized after 1945 between the centrally planned economy of communism and a moderated market-based capitalism.

In the older industrialized countries such as Britain and France and especially in the United States, which was largely settled by people seeking to escape from state-sponsored repression, capitalism flourished, and the challenge from widening inequality was met in a more evolutionary way by providing greater equality of opportunity and outcomes. Within high-income countries economic inequality peaked in the first decade of the twentieth century. Between 1918 and 1939 the liberal democracies had difficulty mediating between demands for greater equality and the requirements of an unfettered market economy (or the self-interest of the elite). Since then, more equitable outcomes have been achieved by policies that may be collectively termed the welfare state. A high degree of individual freedom and say in political decision-making were combined with a welfare state providing insurance against income-threatening events such as disability, old age, unemployment, or sickness and some degree of equality of opportunity through subsidized schooling and health care for children.

The concept of a middle way—in Britain espoused by Harold Macmillan in the 1950s and embodied in the 1965 National Plan, in France's indicative planning, or in Germany's social market economy—was an illusion. Western European "planning" differed fundamentally from the central planning of the communist countries of Eastern Europe. Even in the most "reformed" centrally planned economies, such as Hungary's or the workers' self-managed economy of Yugoslavia, capital was allocated by the state.

The 1970s were a watershed leading to a reevaluation of the trade-off between the pursuit of equality and the needs of a market economy based on material incentives. The outcome was that governments in the wealthiest market economies abjured punitive taxes on the rich or heavy-handed regulation, while maintaining some redistribution through the taxation system and key elements of the welfare state (social insurance, a safety net, health and education for all). The final victory in 1989–1991 went to a mix of liberty and equality rather than to the totalitarianism of fascism or communism.[1]

Global convergence is more problematic. The pre-1914 era of globalization saw the creation of global empires ruled from the capitals of Europe and the United States. These empires crumbled after 1945, and in many new independent countries modernizing regimes came to power. They universally adopted development strategies based on import-substituting industrialization, limiting economic freedom with the aim of achieving faster economic growth. Such policies led to short-term growth acceleration, but during the long boom of the 1950s and 1960s living standards in most developing countries fell further behind those of the rich nations. Despite the similarities of development strategy across the low- and middle-income countries, there was a fundamental divide between centrally planned economies such as China, North Korea and North Vietnam, and Cuba, and those where nonstate actors played a role in capital formation. Directing financial capital to steel or fertilizers or other import-competing industries through the price mechanism or even by state banks was not the same as allocating physical materials and labor to building steel mills and fertilizer factories. The nonaligned movement led by India, Indonesia, and Yugoslavia was as much an illusion as the middle way. By the 1970s the Yugoslav economy was in terminal decline, Indonesia had reverted to being an unabashed market economy, and India was passing (but not yet implementing effectively) market-oriented economic reforms.

In the final quarter of the twentieth century, the battle between economic systems was definitively lost by central planning. The winner was not nineteenth-century capitalism with its concepts of unconstrained economic and political liberty, but a market-based economic system modified by extensive government intervention to promote equality of opportunity and outcome. There were many varieties of capitalism by 2000, but all shared the fundamental feature that goods and services and especially investment of capital were allocated primarily by the price mechanism rather than by government officials.

The twentieth century witnessed the biggest increase in global production of any century in history. A crucial element in the rejection of central planning was the greater economic efficiency of the market economy in meeting consumers' demands and in fostering sustained long-term growth. The growth advantage over both communism and fascism lay in the greater technological dynamism and superior allocation of capital in a competitive setting with market-driven rewards. In a peacetime economy where basic needs have been met, the allocation decisions are too complex, successful new technologies too hard to identify, and consumers too unpredictable for planners to be able to match the decentralized market system. The rewards amassed by individual entrepreneurs such as Bill Gates or Jorma Ollila are large, but so have been the benefits from products developed by Microsoft or Nokia, the like of which no centrally planned economy ever dreamed up. The connection between reward and contribution is more controversial when it comes to the financial sector, but it is important to bear in mind that risk-taking financial intermediation has been crucial to the dynamism of market economies.

The process of striking a balance between liberty and equality was long and costly. Nevertheless, despite widespread poverty and authoritarian regimes, the end of the twentieth century was a time for hope. The rapid economic growth in parts of Asia, especially China since 1979 and India since 1991, has led to more people loosening the shackles of poverty than ever before and to a diminution of global inequality.[2] In the 1990s in every continent large countries such as Brazil, Indonesia, Poland, and South Africa made the transition away from authoritarian rule and over-regulated (or perversely regulated) economies. Average income levels were higher than ever before and global inequality and poverty were falling. There were, of course, disputes over international institutions and regulation of the global economy, but a substantial consensus on the desirability of a market-based global economy.

The End of History?

The defeat of communism was heralded by Francis Fukuyama as the end of history; liberal democracy faced no serious ideological competitors: "What we may be witnessing is not just the end of the Cold War, or the passing of a particular period of post-war history, but the end of history as such: that is, the end point of mankind's ideological evolution and the universalization of Western liberal democracy as the final form of human government (Fukuyama, 1989)." In the economic sphere, the end of the Cold War signaled an end of history insofar as the market-based economy faced no serious ideological competitors. China's social market economy or Islamic banking laws are little more than fig leaves for market-driven economies in countries whose governments inherited an anti-capitalist ideology. In Europe, the German concept of a social market economy, set out by Ludwig Erhard, the architect of West Germany's post-1948 recovery, differs from the social market economy of China's post-Deng leadership, but the choice of words to reflect a balance between efficiency and equality indicates a common view of the good economic system at the start of the twenty-first century.[3] The victory of the market as the basis for all economies does not spell the end of government intervention or the end of disputes over how the fruits of the market economy should be divided, but it is not Cold War conflict between the distinct and antagonistic economic systems of capitalism and communism.

The winner in the Cold War was not unregulated capitalism of the kind opposed by communists (and fascists) in the first half of the 1900s, but regulated capitalism where the market is agreed to be the best resource allocation mechanism but the government plays a moderating role to improve equality of opportunity and to provide a safety net against some unfair outcomes. The many varieties of capitalism in the early twenty-first century include some very unequal systems with regimes that are little more than kleptocracies in which the ruler or an elite cream off the benefits. Nevertheless, universal standards have been emerging. UN or ILO conventions set standards for the rights of children, the elderly, the handicapped, and other groups deserving protection from pure market forces; these standards are acknowledged by all, even if they are not always implemented.

Robert Kagan (2008) has challenged Fukuyama's view that liberal democracy has triumphed decisively, predicting that "the global competition between democratic and autocratic governments will become a dominant feature of the twenty-first century world"; as autocracies he lists Russia and China, as well as radical Islam, which is "the most dramatic refutation of the convergence paradigm." A problem with this view lies in the difficulty of identifying real democracies or autocracies. If media dominance is the criterion, there was little difference between Russian elections and Italian elections in 2008. In Russia there was not much doubt about Putin's popularity and that any candidate with his support would win, just as in Thailand in 2007 Thaksin's surrogate won a democratic election, the result of which the opposition Democratic Party overturned in 2008 by extra-democratic means. If alternation of power were the key, then Singapore or Malaysia or Botswana would be labeled autocracies despite their regular elections and extensive civil liberties. The most populous Islamic country, Indonesia, moved from an autocracy to a lively democracy at the turn of the century, and other large middle-income countries such as Brazil, Russia, or South Africa were markedly more democratic at the start of the twenty-first century than a decade or two earlier. India, the world's largest democracy, remained more robustly free than ever.

Liberal democracy was stronger at the end of the twentieth century than ever before because the market economy delivered economic prosperity based on individual choices and the political system supported aspirations for individual liberty while satisfying concerns about equality through "welfare state" measures. It will always be under threat because autocratic leaders or entrenched elites have a predilection for opposing limits on terms of office or other measures that make an alternation of power likely. The economic appeal of fascism and of authoritarian regimes since 1945 lies in the widely held belief that a strong leader can take the decisive steps needed to promote economic growth or recovery from a negative economic shock, whereas parliaments are riven by factionalism and the need to compromise. This popular belief can be readily supported by examples, but it is a false generalization. The empirical literature from the period when consistent economic growth data exist reaches the opposite conclusion that transition from nondemocracy or autocratic presidential regimes to parliamentary democracy is associated with growth-promoting policies and better long-run economic outcomes.[4]

The popular view is usually based on anecdotal evidence, such as comparing reform in China and India during the 1980s or the success of Lee Kwan Yew's Singapore. Beneficial economic reforms have certainly been introduced by autocratic leaders, but the general point is that in autocracies or one-party democracies the individual leader matters more and outcomes are more varied than in democracies with effective legislatures: growth may on average be lower in autocracies, but the variance is higher. Thus, preferring a strong leader is risky:

what if Deng Xiaoping had not prevailed over Hua Guofeng in the struggle to succeed Mao Zedong in China? Moreover an undemocratic liberalizer may be displaced by hardliners, for example, because Khrushchev in the Soviet Union or Zhao Ziyang in China were considered too liberal by others in the narrow leadership group they were replaced and their policies reversed. A good undemocratic leader who survives may lose touch over time, or become unstable with age; autocrats have the power to overrule anybody, including their past selves.[5] The fundamental problem is that there is no legitimate way to change the ruler. Even in quasi-democratic settings, the wrong person may get the credit due to time lags and subsequently be hard to remove from power.[6]

Parliamentary democracies can make major policy changes (e.g., the United Kingdom in 1979, the United States in 1981, or India in 1991), although the capacity for bold change may be underappreciated if the shift is bipartisan and not associated with a single leader (e.g., Australia's sweeping reforms by Hawke and Keating in 1983 were retained by Howard and Costello and after the early 1990s underpinned fifteen years of the highest economic growth among OECD member countries). The benefits of reform typically take more than a decade before they are appreciated; the major reforms in the new industrialized economies of South Korea, Taiwan, and Singapore occurred in the early and mid-1960s, but their achievement was not widely recognized until the late 1970s. In democratic settings, reform needs to survive the election cycle; reforms were reversed in India and in Australia in the 1970s and in Brazil in the 1980s because opposition parties could win elections by pointing to the early negative effects of reform.[7]

In the early twenty-first century the welfare state is under challenge from many sides, but these are challenges for reform and not existential challenges. Budgetary issues have already been mentioned in Chapter 6; these debates concern the extent to which the state supports education and health care or the generosity of safety nets and are not about basic principles. In the high-income countries one of the most fundamental structural issues is how to deal with aging populations. The welfare states established during the twentieth century included state pensions as a fundamental pillar, with eligibility typically around

65 and perhaps younger for women. Universal pensions were popular because every taxpayer expected to benefit eventually, and debates over eligibility have encountered strong opposition to change. Failure to age-index pension eligibility to life expectancy has, however, left systems open to mushrooming claims as a rapidly increasing number of people live beyond the pensionable age and live longer as pensioners.[8] In order to contain costs, many countries have allowed the level of state pensions to fall relative to average living standards, emphasizing the safety net aspect of state support for the elderly, with minimal state pensions and basic health care, while people desiring better living standards and health care after they cease to work full time must take out insurance or rely on their own savings. The transition to a more general view of the state's role as providing a safety net against inequality of outcomes whether due to illness, disability, involuntary unemployment, or old age, rather than as provider of specific benefits such as health, education, pensions, or insurance against loss of income due to circumstances beyond an individual's control will, however, be difficult; people receiving specific benefits will resist their termination (e.g., because of a stigma attached to being in poverty which does not apply to being disabled, as well as due to expectation of financial loss from reclassification), and generous state pensions or state-supported health care are seen by many voters as entitlements.

The twentieth century was an age of extremism in which extremism took a beating. The hierarchical empires of the Habsburgs, Hohenzollerns, Ottomans, and the Qing dynasty that governed large areas in 1900 had disappeared by 1919; in some countries, notably the United Kingdom, the king and aristocracy retained their titles, but their power had long been diminished. Both defenders of privilege and advocates of unfettered market forces were routed between 1919 and 1945. Those who saw salvation in a charismatic national leader also had their hopes dashed by 1945, after which "fascist" became a term of abuse (and misuse). Doctrinaire communists excused the excesses of Stalin, Mao, and other autocrats in the name of creating a better society, but by 1989 the faulty economic foundations of that belief had been exposed. Even milder extremists such as Thatcher or Reagan were successful only up to a point, and their retrogressive attacks on policies to promote equality were rejected within a decade of their losing power.

In economics, victory over extremism did not go to a compromise between planning and the market, as envisioned in the "middle way" of the early 1960s, but to the market system modified by policies to promote an agreed degree of equality of opportunity and outcome. The allocative efficiency of the price system is widely recognized, while the inequality resulting from unfettered market forces is unacceptable. In politics the pattern was toward systems in which individuals' rights were protected and people had a say in choosing their government; there are, of course, many examples in the early twenty-first century of nondemocratic regimes, civil rights abuse, and miscarriage of justice, but far fewer than ever before.[9] Even half a century earlier, a female German chancellor or a black president of the United States or of South Africa would have been unimaginable.

The victory of market-based economic systems and of liberal democracy does not mean the end of political or economic evolution. The future political challenge for liberal democracies will be less about warding off the threat from authoritarianism, and more about rising to new challenges beyond liberty and equality. The issue is not new: the failed economic systems of communism and fascism both promoted fraternity, whether on the basis of the new man and internationalism or on the basis of national cohesion. A strength of the market system has been that pursuit of selfish economic interests can lead to socially desirable outcomes, but can that paradoxical strength cater to provision of public as well as private goods?

The Age of Fraternity

The French revolutionary slogan of *Liberté, Egalité, Fraternité* is too simple a characterization, but with the spread of market-based economies and concomitant increase in participatory political systems, the focus in the twenty-first century will surely be on invoking ways of living in harmony both within and among countries. Margaret Thatcher's aphorism that "There is no such thing a society" was conclusively rejected by voters in the late twentieth century who wanted governments that would provide more than a setting for rampant individualism. With an increasingly integrated global economy, the emergence of issues such as global warming that can only be resolved by international cooperation, and the existence of weapons of mass destruction that can pose global threats, there will be increasing pressures in the twenty-first century to improve the institutions of global society.

In the twentieth century, the idea of a global community was secondary to national interests. Despite high hopes of a brave new world after 1945, reflected in the inspiring preamble to the Charter of the United Nations, the world split into two opposing camps. The UN was successful in contributing to preventing the Cold War from becoming a hot war and many UN agencies did good work, but overall the UN failed to inspire in the second half of the twentieth century. The fundamental principle of UN action in practice was to recognize national sovereignty and to discourage interference in other member countries' affairs unless a member egregiously broke UN rules (e.g., Iraq's 1990 invasion of Kuwait).

The nation-state is not dead and nationalism remains a potent force, easily aroused in most countries. Nevertheless, the trend is toward diffusion of political authority beyond the nation-state. In economic matters the benefits of different levels of government have long been obvious as local authorities provide public goods such as rubbish collection, street lighting, or public parks. The creation of multiple levels of decision-making is enshrined in the constitutions of federal nations such as the United States, Germany, or India, and the funding and incentives of fiscal federalism have long been analyzed and debated. The creation of a supranational arrangement with significant powers is best illustrated by the European Union, although this has had unpredicted consequences of strengthening subnational regions' self-government as in Catalonia or Scotland, and the role of the nation-state has been eroded from both directions. At the global level the enforcement powers of the United Nations and other multilateral institutions are weak, but the desirability of abiding by international rules (e.g., of the WTO) are increasingly recognized by economically weak and strong nations alike.[10]

In contrast to the preceding century, the twentieth century, especially between 1914 and 1945, was characterized by hugely destructive wars in Europe and in Asia in which millions were killed by ever more destructive weaponry. The Cold War did not turn into open war between the superpowers in large part because of mutual fear of the destructive power of nuclear weapons. Proliferation of weapons of mass destruction, as the technology becomes better known and more easily reproducible, will encourage a new approach to global governance in the twenty-first century. Even the strongest nation-state cannot be immune to violent reactions to its foreign policies reaching domestic targets, a truth brutally brought home on 11 September 2001.

Bradford and Linn contrast the old global economic order, in which the nation-state is the point of departure and sovereignty and national interest are the key principles driving a unilateral and assertive foreign policy, with the new order's starting point that we live in a global society, where interdependency and recognition of common interests are the key principles to be pursued in reciprocal relations and with mutual respect across borders:

> Under the Old Order the rules of national power politics prevail, as competing blocs and fixed alliances strive for predominance, with "hard power" if necessary. Instead, the New Order operates on the basis of a new multilateralism, which builds on the prevalence of global networks in all spheres of life and multiple coalitions across borders, where bargaining for compromise and the tools of "soft power" prevail. (Bradford and Linn, 2009, 2)

Bradford and Linn claim the old order broadly reflects the principles underlying the foreign policy agenda of the 2001–2009 Bush administration and John McCain's 2008 presidential platform, while the new order approximates those underpinning the platform of Barack Obama's 2008 presidential campaign and of his administration's foreign policy stance. Key elements of the old order are attributed to the foreign policy approach of Russia under Putin, while new order principles can be ascribed to the European Union. The two approaches reflect the difference between twentieth-century principles of foreign policy and principles appropriate to twenty-first century realities. The drivers of change that necessitate moving from the old order to the new order include the changing global demographic and economic balance, emerging global threats, and the need for a more effective global governance system.

The twenty-first century will be the Age of Fraternity in the sense that fraternity will be an important aspect of the century. Examples of nonfraternal behavior during the first decade of the century do not negate this view. In the twentieth century the first decade was a period of great inequality, and economic conditions for many people would get even worse in the following decades. Nevertheless, the situation in 1900 contained the seeds that would make the upcoming century the Age of Equality. By 2000 the nature of the regime that would balance the prosperity of the Age of Liberty with the egalitarianism of the Age of Equality was generally recognized. In this market-based global system many areas of international interaction require supranational solutions, and meeting these challenges is likely to dominate the century's history even if there are many deviations along the way.

If fraternity is conceived in terms of living together, there are several dimensions in which global action may be called for.[11] Scott Barrett (2007) analyzes a wide range of more or less likely global problems that require concerted action, such as infectious disease, nuclear proliferation, global warming, or the threat from asteroids; none of these respect national borders. Global commons issues, such as depletion of the oceans or the atmosphere by overfishing or damage to the ozone layer, are classic cases of global public goods.[12] Privately beneficial actions are socially destructive and national policies are inadequate to address the negative externalities. Steps such as the Law of the Sea or the conservation of fish stocks are in the right direction, but have so far been cautious and are unlikely to be adequate.[13]

Sometimes such issues can be resolved regionally. River basins often involve conflicts over water use, which can be settled by the riparian states, sometimes even delegating authority to a supranational body, but in the knowledge that each of the few riparian states has a strong say in how that body operates. Cross-border pollution can also be solved bilaterally (e.g., acid rain from the United States destroying maple trees in Québec) or regionally (e.g., haze from forest burning in

Indonesia damaging health in Malaysia and Singapore), although it is often difficult to agree on reducing the activity with negative externalities or compensating those who suffer.

Global warming illustrates the need for and difficulty in coordinating international action. In the absence of a binding global agreement, major polluters are unwilling to restrict their own behavior, while poor countries that see themselves as victims of rich countries' past pollution rather than part of the problem demand financial aid in order to meet global standards.[14] Technology and market forces may help to alleviate the problem, for example, if there is sufficient demand for electric cars that major producers supply them at reasonable prices and a network of recharge facilities is constructed while service stations for cars using fossil fuels become scarcer. To some extent such a market-driven response happened at the start of the 2000s with natural gas, as high oil prices encouraged massive investment in LNG infrastructure (liquefaction plants near the gas fields, specialized LNG ships, and regasification plants near the markets) to increase the availability of natural gas, which is less polluting than coal or oil. With respect to global warming, however, a market-driven response is unlikely to happen to sufficient degree and at sufficient speed to prevent dangerous accumulation of carbon in the atmosphere without offering substantial new incentives. However, national taxation of carbon emissions or introduction of cap-and-trade measures will be less effective, and politically difficult to achieve, in the absence of global agreement and credible commitments. The economic problem lies in the incentive for countries to free-ride and let others bear the costs of abatement. The political problem, besides monitoring and enforcement of commitments, is that when agreements are being negotiated voters and politicians may find it easy to criticize the burden on their own population relative to that on another population and to use this as an excuse for inaction.[15]

A humanitarian argument for aid to poor countries was recognized in the post-1945 world, but official development assistance was largely hijacked by geopolitical motives or subverted by domestic pressure groups. Aid went to political allies or clients rather than to the neediest poor countries, for example, U.S. aid to Israel, USSR aid to Cuba, and European countries' aid to former colonies; the only major exceptions were the Scandinavian countries and the Netherlands. A large proportion of aid accrued to national suppliers in the donor countries, either through formal tying requirements or by sourcing technical assistance to donor-country consultants and travel to domestic airlines, and some of the aid that ended up in the recipient country went into the pockets of officials or politicians or accrued to middlemen rather than benefiting the poor. Overall, the record of promoting development and alleviating poverty through foreign aid was unimpressive in the 1960s and 1970s, and aid/GDP ratios in most donor countries fell during the 1980s. When aid revived in the 1990s, it was associated with greater recognition of global community and of the costs of failed states.

Fraternity may include joint responsibility for people in failed and repressive states, although this requires agreement about the line beyond which a government is unacceptable. The world cheered Tanzania's deposition of Idi Amin and Vietnam's ouster of Pol Pot, but opinions diverge when the Great Powers take action, such as China in Tibet, the Soviet Union in Afghanistan, or the United States in Iraq. The job of acting as global or regional policeman, whether to dislodge unacceptable regimes or to provide humanitarian aid when the government prevents it, requires institutional arrangements to provide legitimacy to intervention.

The recognition of universal rights is one of several developments challenging the future of the nation state. The creation of a global communications network and the increasingly unimpeded movement of capital create a global community and economy with less scope for the nation-state.[16] Natural disasters, disease and famine, or environmental concerns are increasingly being taken by the global community as arguments for intervention in nation-states. Even the terms "fragile" or "failed" state suggest justification for a global policeman to intervene, especially if the failed state provides a haven for international criminals.[17]

The concept of a global community has been given content by the expanding authority of the International Criminal Court (ICC), which was established in 2002 by the Rome Statute. The idea that the world should take responsibility if nations fail to protect their own population was first promoted at the United Nations in 1999 by Secretary-General Kofi Annan, citing conflicts in Angola, Kosovo, Sierra Leone, and East Timor. The "right to protect" concept gained momentum with the African Union's endorsement in 2000, a unique example of Africa taking the lead in recent global norm-setting, which defused concerns that it would become a tool of neo-imperialism only to be authorized against regimes opposing the established powers. At a 2005 summit in New York, the world's leaders unanimously approved the principle that intervention in a state's internal affairs is justified in the event of genocide, crimes against humanity, and other atrocities if that state is unable or unwilling to protect its own people. The Secretary-General's 2009 report, *Implementing the Responsibility to Protect,* identified three pillars: the state's primary responsibility to protect its population, the international community's responsibility to engage in capacity-building to help states to uphold their obligations, and the international community's responsibility to intervene when a state is manifestly failing to protect its population. The three pillars represent a softening of the original responsibility to protect (R2P) concept, with foreign intervention reduced to a last resort, but R2P still represents a fundamental reframing of the UN's concept of sovereignty as a responsibility rather than an inalienable privilege of national governments.[18] The fuzziness about when R2P applies permits some discretion about when action is justified; for example, Russia claimed that its 2008 war with Georgia was justified by the need to protect residents of South Ossetia. The option of requiring UN approval for international action raises the issue of why the five permanent members of the Security Council should have veto power.[19] Some proponents of R2P worry that Russia or China will use their veto to protect authoritarian clients, but such doubts seem extreme as, for example, China, despite close economic ties to Sudan, agreed in 2007 to UN peacekeepers operating in Darfur. Neither China nor Russia opposed UN action in Libya in 2011.

Even the most tendentious issue between nation-states, the delimitation of boundaries, is being increasingly settled by peaceful means; for example, in 2009 the International Court of Justice delimited the maritime boundary between Romania and Ukraine, allowing the two states to allocate concession blocks for gas exploration. The UN Commission for the Limits of the Continental Shelf has since 2009 monitored claims to exclusive economic zones, many of which overlap, for example, in the Gulf of Guinea, the Bay of Bengal, the South Atlantic around the Falkland/Malvinas Islands, and the Atlantic Ocean off northeast South America. In other disputed maritime areas with economic potential, joint development initiatives have been agreed, for example, in 2008 between China and Japan for the maritime areas around the Chunxiao gas field and in 2009 between Angola and Congo and between Brunei and Malaysia; this solution is based on the view that natural resources in border areas are to be shared rather than divided by a frontier.

Conclusions

Cataclysmic events like the industrial revolution and the French and U.S. political revolutions of the second half of the 1700s have long-lasting effects which develop their own dynamics. By 1914 the new economic system's influence was felt worldwide, but it had firm roots in only a small part of the globe, and elements of the old regime remained even in the most industrialized countries. The industrialized countries were able to dominate the world and to impose their views (or at least the views of their capitalist elites), including advocacy of liberty and opposition to autocratic government. By 1919 capitalism had decisively triumphed over precapitalist systems, even though elements of the latter remained around the world.

By the early 1900s opposition to the unequal distribution of the benefits from industrialization had become a powerful force in the industrialized countries, although responses to demands for greater equality took many decades to take effect. The most extreme response was rejection of a market-based economic system in favor of central planning, which was intended to improve the allocation of resources to produce high living standards with equal distribution. Central planning failed in this quest because the leadership became concerned with their own position rather than the general good and more fundamentally because central planners could not allocate resources as well as the market, especially when it came to capital formation and hence long-term prosperity. The market economies fared poorly in responding to the systemic challenge until they recognized the need to provide some measure of equality of opportunity and outcome; after 1945 such a commitment was universal in the established market economies. Governments recognized that they should not only support freedom to pursue wealth and happiness, but also freedom from poverty, ill health, and ignorance. In this respect the twentieth century was the Age of Equality, even though much inequality remained at the end of the century.

The need to incorporate public policies to promote equality was universally accepted by governments of the leading market economies after 1945 and was a prerequisite to victory over communism. That victory is not, however, the end of history. Debates about the balance between allocative efficiency and distributional equality remain and evolve. For example, as human capital is increasingly recognized as important for both national economic performance and individual earning power, the extent to which the state should provide and subsidize access to higher education has become a major political issue in many countries. Increasing labor mobility raises issues such as the rights of immigrants to social services and the limits to double taxation. Some of these issues will be settled by the nation-state, despite the international implications (e.g., need for global standards of tertiary education qualifications as in the so-called Bologna Process). Others require cooperation, at least among subgroups of countries, for example, to prevent tax competition among similar economies from leading to a race to the bottom.

In the twenty-first century new challenges such as global warming, the threat of piracy, and the right to protection all demand global solutions. War is an increasingly unacceptable method of conflict resolution, especially between major powers. The century must become the Age of Fraternity . . . and history moves on.

Glossary and Abbreviations

BIS   Bank of International Settlements; international organization of central bankers, established in 1930 and based in Geneva

Bolshevik   Communist faction headed by Lenin that came to power after the October 1917 Russian Revolution

BOP   Balance of payments; the BOP is a statement of all international transactions by a country's residents. By the principles of double-entry book-keeping the BOP must balance; any purchase of a good or service involves an equal and opposite-signed transfer of the means of payment. However, a distinction is made between autonomous and accommodating items; when a country's autonomous expenditures exceed its autonomous revenues it is said to have a BOP deficit. The accommodating item is a decrease or increase in reserves.

Bretton Woods institutions   The IMF and the IBRD; agreed upon at a 1944 conference in Bretton Woods, New Hampshire, and established in 1945 with headquarters in Washington, D.C.

CIS   Commonwealth of Independent States; successor organization to the USSR bringing together twelve former Soviet republics, other than the three Baltic states

consumer surplus   The difference between what a consumer would be willing to pay for a good or service and what that consumer actually has to pay

current account   The part of the BOP covering transactions with implications only for the current period, for example, imports and exports of goods and services, interest payments and workers' remittances, and gifts. The capital or financial account of the BOP contains transactions that add to or subtract from a country's external wealth, for example, purchase or sale of financial assets or foreign direct investment.

Dawes Plan   1924 agreement to reschedule German reparations

EFTA   European Free Trade Association; established in 1960 as a free trade area approach to European integration. By 1995 five of the original seven members had switched to the EU, leaving only Norway and Switzerland plus two newer members, Iceland and Liechtenstein, in EFTA.

ERP   European Recovery Program; announced in 1947, implemented between 1948 and 1952; also known as the Marshall Plan

EU   European Union; earlier known as the European Community; formed by the 1957 Treaty of Rome

exchange controls   Limits on the amount of foreign currency that can be taken into a country or of domestic currency that can be taken abroad

FIFA   Fédération Internationale de Football Association (the governing body of soccer worldwide)

GATT/WTO   1947 General Agreement on Tariffs and Trade, superseded in 1995 by the World Trade Organization; based in Geneva

GDP, GNP   Gross domestic product, gross national product; GDP is the amount of final goods and services produced within an economy, and GNP is the amount produced by a country's residents. The two will normally be similar, but can diverge if there are significant earnings from or payments to workers outside their home country or to foreign capital. In the national accounts total output must equal aggregate demand and total income.

GDR   German Democratic Republic (East Germany)

HPAEs   The high-performing Asian economies (World Bank, 1993). They include Hong Kong, Singapore, South Korea, Taiwan, Indonesia, Malaysia, Thailand, China, and, sometimes, Japan.

IBRD   International Bank for Reconstruction and Development. The World Bank Group includes the IBRD and four affiliated agencies created between 1956 and 1988: the International Development Association (IDA), which provides grants and interest-free loans to the poorest countries; the International Finance Corporation (IFC), which supports private sector development; the Multilateral Investment Guarantee Agency (MIGA); and the International Centre for Settlement of Investment Disputes (ICSID).

ICANN   Internet Corporation for Assigned Names and Numbers

IMF   International Monetary Fund

Impossible Trinity   Also known as the "trilemma"; a country cannot simultaneously have a fixed exchange rate, international capital mobility, and an independent monetary policy because only one interest rate is consistent with the fixed exchange rate given the trade balance and capital flows.

IOC   International Olympics Committee

ISI   Import-substituting industrialization

kulaks   Rich peasants in Russia

leveraging   Debt relative to equity (e.g., a highly leveraged company has high debt relative to the capital invested by its owners)

LIBOR   London Interbank Offered Rate on dollar-denominated assets.

LNG   Liquefied natural gas

Marshall Plan   *See* ERP.

MFN   The most-favored nation clause in international trade treaties requires each signatory to accord other signatories the same treatment as the most-favored trading partner receives in any trade transaction. In the WTO, the MFN clause requires trade policies to be nondiscriminatory between all WTO members.

moral hazard   People with insurance may take greater risks than they would do without insurance because they know they are protected against the full loss.

NAFTA   North American Free Trade Agreement (signed by Canada, Mexico, and the United States in 1992; entered into effect 1 January 1994)

NATO   North Atlantic Treaty Organization

NEP   New Economic Policy of the Soviet Union, introduced in 1921

NIEs   Newly industrializing economies; originally the newly industrializing countries (OECD, 1979)

nomenklatura   High Communist Party officials and other members of the elite in the Soviet Union

OEEC   Organization for European Economic Cooperation; originally established in association with the Marshall Plan (see ERP) and rebadged as the Organisation for Economic Co-operation and Development (OECD) in 1961; based in Paris

OPEC   Organization of the Petroleum Exporting Countries

Phillips Curve   Graphical representation of the trade-off between inflation and unemployment (Phillips, 1958)

Progressive era   Period of economic, political, and social reform in the United States between the mid-1890s and early 1920s

public goods   Goods or services that are nonexcludable (i.e., anybody can benefit whether or not they contributed to the supply) and nonexhaustible (i.e., one person's consumption of a public good does not prevent others' consumption). Examples include lighthouses and national defense. A partial public good, such as an uncongested bridge, may be transformed into a private good available only to those who pay but often is not.

purchasing power parity   The exchange rate that equates the price of a basket of identical traded goods and services in two countries

R2P   Responsibility to protect

real interest rate   The nominal interest rate minus the rate of inflation

real wages   The nominal wage adjusted for inflation

specie-flow mechanism   The automatic BOP adjustment mechanism under a pure gold standard. A BOP surplus involves an inflow of gold, which the government converts into national currency, and the increased currency pushes up domestic prices, making exports less competitive and imports more attractive; this process continues until the BOP surplus is eliminated. A BOP deficit involves an outflow of gold and decrease in prices, making exports more competitive and imports less attractive.

transaction costs   Costs incurred in making an economic exchange or participating in a market, above and beyond the price of the good or service being exchanged. Transaction costs include search and information costs, bargaining and contract costs, and monitoring and enforcement costs. The importance of transaction costs in explaining economic and political institutions has been emphasized by Nobel laureates Douglass North and Oliver Williamson. See Allen (1991), North (1990), and the collection edited by Williamson and Masten (1995).

TVE   Township and village enterprise (in China)

USSR   Union of Soviet Socialist Republics, also known as the Soviet Union

zero-sum game   A situation in which the gains made by winners exactly equal the losses suffered by losers. Contrast a positive-sum game, in which all participants can potentially become better off, and a negative-sum game, in which the aggregate losses outweigh the aggregate gains.

Notes

Introduction

1. The estimates, collated by Maddison (2006, 32, table I-5a), should be viewed as approximations but the orders of magnitude are indisputable. Kinsella (1992) provides more details about life expectancy changes in high-income countries, one of the most dramatic of which is the widening gap between male and female life expectancy from two or three years in 1900 to five to nine years in 1990. In high-income countries, age-specific mortality rates are now very low at all ages up to 50; the gender gap is primarily because death rates are significantly lower for women than for men at ages above 60 (i.e., the chances of reaching 50 to 60 are the same for men and women, but having reached 60, women live longer than men).

2. As with most generalizations, there has to be a caveat. Napoleon was also humbled by the Russian army, which relied on numbers and good generalship (and "General Winter"). Despite its economic backwardness, Russia remained a major European power until its naval weakness was exposed by Japan in 1904 and its soldiers were devastatingly defeated by a modern German army in the 1914–1917 war. Guerrilla warfare or insurgencies are a different matter; Britain was humiliated in Afghanistan in 1842, and all occupying powers suffered a similar fate at some point.

3. Before the 1200s China or the Islamic world had been more significant, and in the thirteenth century the *pax mongolica* following Genghis Khan's establishment of the largest land empire in history permitted long-distance trade between East Asia and Europe. Findlay and O'Rourke (2007) identify major shocks that contributed to Europe's rise in the second millennium from backwater to dominance. Trade with Asia brought goods, new technologies, and bacilli to Europe, whose economy had retrogressed from the Roman era until the tenth century, had begun to recover in the eleventh and twelfth centuries, and flourished in the 1200s and early 1300s. The first big shock to the European economy was the arrival of the plague in 1347; the Black Death wiped out a third of the population, which was the beginning of the end for feudalism as landowners competed for

scarce labor and saw the start of major labor-saving technical change in farming and in the processing of farm products. The second major shock followed the voyages of discovery in the fifteenth century; the biggest immediate effect was the inflow of precious metals from the Americas; the initial beneficiary was Spain, but the increase in aggregate demand stimulated economic activity in other regions, such as France, the Netherlands, and England, which challenged Spain's supremacy, and Spain slipped into relative decline in the seventeenth and eighteenth centuries. These shocks created fertile ground for the industrial revolution, but in themselves did not lead to long-term accelerated growth in European living standards or a major increase in intercontinental trade; before the 1700s trade with Asia was limited to a few luxuries (spices, silk, and so forth) passing through a handful of European trading posts.

4. Although major Enlightenment philosophers were German or French, Mokyr (2010) argues that Britain went furthest in protecting individual liberty and applying experimentation, mathematics, and observation to practical problems and hence hosted the industrial revolution.

5. Thomas Malthus, in his 1798 *Essay on the Principle of Population,* argued that whereas population grows at a geometric rate, food production only grows arithmetically, so that over time the increase in food output will be inadequate to feed the increasing number of individuals. When the number of mouths to feed runs too far ahead of available food, diseases, famines, and wars will reduce population size and reestablish the necessary balance between resources and population; sexual passion is too strong for voluntary limitations to have much impact on population growth. Such cycles could be observed historically, but Malthus underestimated the potential for technological improvements to increase agricultural yields and the impact that economic prosperity and education would have on population growth.

6. Tracing relative income levels becomes less reliable the further back we go. Maddison (2006) reckons that Europe began to move ahead of China in the 1300s, but the gap really widened after 1820. World per capita incomes were more or less the same at the start and the end of the first millennium of the modern era, and from 1000 to 1820 world per capita income increased by 50 percent. Between 1820 and the end of the second millennium, global per capita income increased 8.5 times; and although led by Europe and areas settled by Europeans, incomes more than tripled on every continent. This was achieved with a substantial reduction in hours worked and in workplace dangers, although Ramey and Francis (2009) argue that in the twentieth-century United States there was little change in the average number of leisure hours, with only 14- through 24-year-olds (more of whom were students) and those over 65 working less in 2000 than in 1900.

7. By 1900, women had the vote in some local jurisdictions and in the self-governing colonies of New Zealand (since 1893) and South Australia (since 1894). In Australia, white women gained the vote in 1901–1902 but aboriginal women had to wait more than sixty more years. The first European country to allow women to vote in national elections was Finland, in 1906, which elected the first female member of parliament in 1907. In the United States, women could vote in four states in 1900, but only after the Nineteenth Amendment to the Constitution in 1920 could they vote in national elections.

8. Aristocrats still held the reins of power in many countries in 1900. The British prime minister was the Marquis of Salisbury. The German chancellor, Viktor Chlodwig, was Prince of Hohenlohe-Schillingsfürst and Duke of Ratibor. The Japanese prime minister, Field Marshall Prince Yamagata Aritomo, was of samurai stock. Only the French and U.S. republics had leaders not born to rule. Little more than a century later, the German chancellor was the daughter of a rural pastor, the French president was the son of a Hungarian refugee, and the U.S. president had an African father.

9. The crude view is represented by Proudhon's slogan "Property is Theft!" Marx recognized that redistribution at low productivity levels would create equality of poverty and lead to struggles over access to resources; opponents who failed to recognize capitalism's historical role in raising productivity to a level at which socialism was feasible were derided as utopian socialists. The *Communist Manifesto* provides an enthusiastic statement of the benefits of capitalism and most of Marx's subsequent writing is on capitalism, whose contradiction lay in the fact that, the more successful it is in generating economic growth, the more it will generate class conflict and its eventual overthrow. Thus, he expected the revolution to occur in an advanced capitalist economy, as Germany was becoming at the time of Marx's death in 1883, and would not have foreseen it occurring in a relatively backward economy such as Russia's.

10. The first fish and chip shop opened in Oldham, near Manchester, in 1863; by 1900 almost every street in working-class towns had a pub and a chip shop. Blackpool, a sleepy town before the railway arrived in 1846, was by 1914 the biggest seaside resort in Europe, based on vacationing factory workers and offering a large variety of entertainment; in 1879 Blackpool became the first town in the world to install electric street lighting, followed by tramways and roller coasters, a winter gardens in 1875, an opera house in 1889 as well as many other theaters, and the Blackpool Tower in 1894 (taking only five years to respond to Eiffel's innovative structure in Paris). The first professional football league was founded in 1888 by twelve clubs, six from Lancashire and three from the West Midlands, and the first champions were from Preston, the industrial town stigmatized for

its grim conditions by Charles Dickens in *Hard Times*. Although bicycles had been around since the 1860s, the biggest bicycle craze occurred during the 1890s following the invention of the "safety bicycle" with its chain-drive transmission and of the first practical inflatable air-filled bicycle tire, by a Scotsman named Dunlop in 1888.

11. Also striking was the age distribution of the British workforce in 1900, with around a tenth of boys aged 10–14 in full-time employment (the minimum school-leaving age was 12) and two-fifths of men over 75 still working (Lindsay, 2003, 136).

12. Despite the manifest success of the new industrializing economies' reforms, other countries were slow to copy them, as vested interests created by interventionist economic policies resisted change. The recycling of petrodollars after 1973 provided a temporary lifeline as governments borrowed money to ease their economic problems, but this was a short-term solution that collapsed in 1982 when the major debtors defaulted on their repayments. The governments that introduced outward-oriented policies more decisively were autocracies such as China or Indonesia, and those in situations where there had been a major regime change, as in Eastern Europe after 1989.

13. In the distorted mirror of the late Cold War, Nicolae Ceauşescu, Romania's leader after 1965, became a hero in the West for resisting Soviet influence and not participating in the invasion of Czechoslovakia, even though Ceauşescu was one of the most repressive and least reformist leaders in Eastern Europe.

1. The Age of Liberty

1. The argument is usually framed in terms of the vast wealth accumulated by British agents in India. Eric Williams (1944) argued that profits from the transatlantic slave trade also played a major part.

2. The separation of saving from investing by intermediaries is central to the Keynesian model, in which investment demand (I) is autonomous, determined by entrepreneurs' animal spirits, and savings (S) is the part of income (Y) that is not consumed. By national income accounting identities, aggregate income, which is consumed or saved $(Y = C + S)$, must equal aggregate demand, which can be for consumption or investment goods $(Y = C + I)$. If consumption is a stable function of income, $C = a + bY$, then $Y = a + bY + I$, which can be rearranged as $Y = a/(1 - b) + [1/(1 - b)]I$. Any shift in I changes Y by a larger amount, with the multiplier equal to 1 divided by the marginal propensity to save out of income; for example, if people save a quarter of their incomes, then $1/(1 - b) = 4$, and a

$1 million drop in investment demand leads to a $4 million drop in aggregate demand and in output. Taxes and imports will affect the size of the multiplier, but do not change the basic mechanism.

3. Manias and crises predate the industrial revolution (Kindleberger, 2000), but greater availability of credit enabled risk-takers to leverage their exposure to risk. Sometimes the debt was desirable as in the text example of a bank backing firms' purchases of the steam engine, but sometimes it was not, for example, when people bought shares in imaginary railways in the bubble before Britain's 1847 financial crash.

4. The traditional textile industries before the industrial revolution had been wool in England and linen in Ireland, but cotton fibers were better suited to machine production than either wool or flax. An important point is that Britain's advantage lay in the activities of spinning and weaving; it did not matter that cotton was not grown in Lancashire. Lancashire mills could undercut any other textile producers in the world in terms of turning the cotton fiber into yarn or cloth, even allowing for the cost of shipping cotton from Egypt or the United States.

5. This begs the prior question of why some countries have good institutions and policies while others do not. Resource wealth can be a curse as often as it is a boon because resource abundance may lead to competition for rents, state capture, lack of investment in education, and other negative consequences. Simple arguments that geography is destiny, with tropical or landlocked countries disadvantaged, have to explain the successes of Singapore or Switzerland. Also, despite arguments for the benefits of large size (to reap scale economies) or small size (for social coherence), there is no correlation between country size and economic prosperity.

6. As with many technical breakthroughs, there were discrete improvements. The optical telegraph (or semaphore line) was perfected in 1791 to relay military evidence from French frontiers to Paris. Following the discovery of electromagnetism, the electrical telegraph was developed in the 1830s and 1840s and the first trans-Atlantic cable was completed in 1866. The first commercial telephone services were established in the United States (New Haven, Connecticut) in 1878 and in England (London) in 1879. Guglielmo Marconi invented wireless radio transmission in 1895 and sent the first trans-Atlantic radio message in 1901. The importance of the telegraph was not just in providing information about markets, but also in coordinating shipping so that less time was spent in port and cargoes could be aggregated from several ports; Lew and Cater (2006) provide evidence for 1870–1910. Radio and telephone played a similar role in the twentieth century.

7. Falling food prices, and perhaps even more the absence of high price spikes or famines, were an important component of improved living standards for the working classes in Western Europe. O'Rourke and Williamson (2002a) argue that globalization began in 1820 when intercontinental prices started to converge and the volume of intercontinental trade began to grow more rapidly—by almost 4 percent per annum over the century 1800–1899 or the longer period 1800–1992, compared with around 1 percent per annum from 1500 to 1799 (O'Rourke and Williamson, 2002b, table 1). That is not to deny antecedents following the European voyages of discoveries in the 1490s and early 1500s or Chinese trade with the Americas and Europe via Manila after 1571 (Flynn and Giráldez, 2004), but orders of magnitude, the range of goods traded, and the impact on domestic economies through internationally determined goods and factor prices were all much greater in the 1800s.

8. Although the literature has focused on the rise of protectionism in Europe after the 1870s, Jeffrey Williamson (2006, 109–143) points out that tariff increases were greater elsewhere. Almost all of the countries in the Americas, as well as Australia and New Zealand, increased their tariffs in the half-century before 1914, initially as a revenue source but later to prevent deindustrialization or to shelter infant industries.

9. The first major step in agricultural mechanization, the development of the mechanical reaper, began in the 1830s and had been widely adopted by North American grain farmers by the 1860s. Mechanization did not occur in the labor-abundant conditions in Russia, but railway construction drastically reduced the cost of shipping grain from the Russian Empire to Western Europe.

10. Although serfdom had been abolished by Prussia in 1806, many of the eastern landowners *(Junkers)* still saw themselves as heirs of the Teutonic Knights who had conquered the eastern German lands in the Middle Ages. Gerschenkron (1943) provides the classic account of this interpretation of German economic history between the 1870s and 1939. Ferguson (1998) disputes the consensus view of German militarism.

11. Even when political change did take place, China and Thailand were unfortunate in not having a modernizing regime assume power in conditions of domestic peace. After the 1911 revolution overthrew the Chinese emperor, China was split first by feuding warlords and later by the rise of the Communist Party and by Japanese invasion; not until 1949 did a modernizing regime exercise power over the mainland territory. Thailand's absolute monarchy was ended in 1932, but the constitutional regime fell under the sway of a fascist leadership in the 1930s and an unstable succession of military-backed regimes after 1945.

12. In the period 1870–1913, other things equal, bilateral trade flows were twice as large if the two partners belonged to the same empire (Mitchener and Weidenmier, 2008). This finding could be due to a lowering of trade costs through use of a common language, currency union, or other shared institutions, rather than a "zero-sum" division of trade.

13. Although notionally on the victorious side in the 1914–1918 war, Japan felt it had not benefited in the peace treaty and held a grudge against the Western powers, which was not helped when those powers refused to include a commitment to racial equality in the Charter of the League of Nations.

14. Jeffrey Williamson (2006) argues that the huge decline in trade costs over the 1800s reduced the wedge between the price paid by importers and that received by exporters to such an extent that every part of the world experienced improved terms of trade (i.e., paid less in exports for a given quantity of imports), even if structural change wiped out some import-competing activities.

15. There was a perception that the periphery lost, and groups like the Indian weavers who could not compete with industrially produced cotton textiles were devastated, but some groups in the periphery benefited from the new export opportunities and imported consumer goods. Japan benefited materially from the gains from trade associated with specialization by comparative advantage (Bernhofen and Brown, 2005), although there and elsewhere it is difficult to weigh the material gains against the costs and benefits of the destruction of traditional social relations. Many regions of the world suffered horrendously from effects such as the introduction of diseases and the violence of colonial regimes. See, for example, Hochschild (1998) on the extreme case of the Belgian Congo.

16. The BOP is a statement of all international transactions by a country's residents and must, by the principles of double-entry bookkeeping, balance; any purchase of a good or service involves an equal and oppositely signed transfer of the means of payment. We can, however, distinguish between autonomous and accommodating items and define a BOP deficit when the accommodating items involve an undesired reduction of net foreign assets in order to cover, for example, a trade deficit, or a BOP surplus when undesired accumulation of foreign assets occurs. In modern national accounting, BOP deficits and surpluses are associated with the running down and accumulation, respectively, of foreign reserves.

17. Reparation payments in silver were sold by Germany, depressing the price of silver and indirectly contributing to gold's relative attractiveness as a stable means of exchange and store of value. Bordo (1999) and Flandreau (2004) provide deeper analysis on the establishment and operation of the gold standard. López-Córdova and Meissner (2003) provide evidence of a positive impact of gold standard membership on bilateral trade.

18. Although there is a debate over the extent to which a country's adherence to the gold standard provided a "Good Housekeeping" seal of approval to potential foreign investors (Bordo and Rockoff, 1996; Flandreau and Zumer, 2004), exchange rate stability reduced the risk of international lending because the nominal return in Argentinean or Canadian currency was the nominal return in sterling or francs. When investors were concerned about exchange rate risk, as after 1914, capital flows were reduced. It should also be pointed out that the international financial system became more complex. Paris challenged London as the leading financial sector in the 1850s and 1860s (until it was occupied by Prussian troops in 1871) and again in the years before 1914 (Kindleberger, 2000, 186–187). Many secondary centers initially used intermediaries in London or Paris but, as bilateral financial transactions became more important, direct links between, say, Italy and Argentina were created.

19. Maddison (2006 [2001], 99) estimates that in 1914 the stock of foreign capital held by the main European investing countries was valued at more than $40 billion, about half of which was in the Americas and Australasia. However, French ($5.3 billion out of $8.6 billion) and German ($3.0 billion out of $5.6 billion) foreign investment was more concentrated in Europe than was Britain's ($1.1 billion out of $18.3 billion).

20. Agrarian discontent driven by a bad harvest in 1835 and expensive credit in 1836–1837 provided the stimulus for the 1837 rebellion in Upper Canada (present-day Ontario). The rebellion was a major event in Canadian history, because it was followed by the Durham Report, which acknowledged legitimate concerns about the nature of government in colonial Canada and led toward responsible government in 1848 and to confederation and the creation of the Dominion of Canada in 1867.

21. The vulnerable who were last in to manias were referred to as "ladies and clergymen" in Britain and "widows and orphans" in the United States. The equivalent groups in the United States in 2007–2009 included people with subprime mortgages who lost their homes and would-be retirees with equity-backed pensions.

22. The push factor was so strong during the potato famine that Ireland's population in the early twenty-first century is still less than the island's 1845 peak of 8.5 million. Episodes such as the post-1848 migrations from Germany were driven by political repression or religious dissent, but noneconomic considerations had a bigger impact on the composition of migrants than on aggregate flows.

23. Arthur Lewis (1978, 15), in describing this migration, refers to the "unlimited supply of Indians and Chinese willing to travel anywhere to work on

plantations for a shilling a day." Huff and Caggiano (2007) analyze migration to Burma, Malaya, and Thailand as a major component of Asian globalization in 1880–1939.

24. The forced transport of African workers to plantations in the Americas was largely an eighteenth-century phenomenon, but the existence and continued profitability of slavery in the United States until the 1860s was related to the value of cotton in the global economy.

25. Even before 1900 there were some limitations on capitalists' behavior. The slave trade was abolished, factory acts limited working hours and set rules on working conditions, and child labor was outlawed. However, these measures were driven by humanitarian rather than egalitarian motives, and by later standards were minimalist, for example, in definitions of child labor.

26. Before 1914 such opposition was manifested in street violence rather than in legislation. U.S. immigration restrictions became increasingly rigorous with the 1917 literacy test, 1924 Emergency Quota Act, 1924 Immigration Act, and 1929 National Origins Act.

27. Lindert (2000) provides a more nuanced view of income inequality in the two best-documented cases, concluding that in Britain the inequality trend may have flattened between 1867 and 1914 and that the inequality peak in the United States may have occurred anywhere from the late 1800s to 1939 depending on how one measures it. Shanahan (1995) provides a detailed study of the 1905–1915 inequality peak in a colonial outpost. In their study of the share of the highest 1 percent of incomes in twenty-two countries, Atkinson, Piketty, and Saez (2011) report a sharp decline in top incomes during the first half of the twentieth century due to wars and economic depression which destroyed income from capital.

28. Typically real wages remained flat as long as labor was being released from agriculture without significantly impacting on total agricultural output, or more precisely as long as the marginal product of farmworkers was below a subsistence wage (Lewis, 1954). In Britain this lasted until at least 1820 (Feinstein, 1998). Robert Allen (2001) argues that in Europe it is difficult to spot any clear movement in real wages until 1870, after which most countries enjoyed substantial increases. Wages were higher in Australia, the United States, Canada, and Argentina, but the rate of increase in wages was highest in countries of emigration; between 1870 and 1913 real wages increased by 1 percent in Australia and by 47 percent in the United States, but by 112 percent in Italy, 193 percent in Norway, and 250 percent in Sweden (J. Williamson, 1995).

29. The brick terrace houses or tenements that have now disappeared from European cities under slum clearance schemes were a substantial improvement over many laborers' preindustrial housing. The existence of discretionary spending

beyond the basic needs of food, clothing, and housing was evident in the rapid expansion of commercial leisure activities such as spectator sports whose main patrons were industrial workers. In the United States the National League was formed in 1876 by baseball clubs from eight industrial cities: Chicago, Philadelphia, Boston, Hartford, New York, St. Louis, Cincinnati, and Louisville. English football was exported across Europe, where it became a popular spectator sport in the industrial and port cities (e.g., the first Italian championship in 1898 was between teams from Genoa and Turin); the leading Argentine team was River Plate (not Rio de la Plata), and one of the top Italian teams is AC Milan (not Milano).

2. War and Depression

1. The treaty obligations were only part of the story; some were honored but others were not. Germany guaranteed to support Austria-Hungary if it punished Serbia and if Russia came to Serbia's aid. However, Germany had recognized Belgian neutrality, which it chose to ignore in order to make a more decisive attack on France. The Ottoman Empire had a secret treaty with Germany and the Ottoman leadership respected the treaty obligations when they perceived benefits from attacking Russia. Similarly Japan honored its alliance with Britain, declaring war on Germany in August 1914 and strengthening its position in the Pacific by occupying the German treaty port of Qingdao and seizing German Pacific island colonies (the Mariana, Caroline, and Marshall islands). Italy and Romania had alliances with Germany that were ignored when France and Britain offered territorial inducements to fight on their side.

2. The British dominions entered the war immediately. As Canadian prime minister Robert Borden said, "When Great Britain is at war, Canada is at war, and there is no difference at all." Germany's Asian and African colonies were soon occupied: Samoa by New Zealand, New Guinea by Australia, and Southwest Africa by South Africa.

3. Russia's 1914 offensive failed miserably; more than 250,000 men were killed, even though Germany's focus was on the western front. By the middle of 1915 Russian Poland, Lithuania, and most of Latvia were occupied by the German army. The military situation improved in 1916 when Russia achieved victories over Austrian armies and held off Turkish forces in Transcaucasia, but the diversion of industrial output to military use and crises in food supply led to food riots and mutiny, which forced the emperor to abdicate in February 1917. Blaming the imperial family and poor leadership for military defeats, the provisional government hoped to pursue the war more effectively and undertook a new of-

fensive in June, but the hopes of social transformation and an end to the war that the February revolution had unleashed led to soldiers deserting en masse. In April 1917 Germany provided safe passage for the return to Russia from Switzerland of Lenin, who led the Bolshevik revolution. The Central Powers responded to the Bolsheviks' appeal for peace by agreeing to an armistice; when the Russian leaders tried to delay matters in the hope of revolutions occurring in Central Europe, Germany resumed its invasion of Russia, pushing further east in five days of February 1918 than it had in the previous three years. Russia was forced to sign the Treaty of Brest-Litovsk on 3 March 1918, which ceded Finland, Poland, the Baltic provinces, Ukraine, and Transcaucasia to the Central Powers—a third of the old empire's population, a third of its agricultural land, and three-quarters of its industries.

4. Italy and Romania suffered major military defeats, but at war's end they received their reward of territory from the dismembered Austro-Hungarian Empire. Bulgaria, with promises of territorial gain at the expense of Serbia and Greece, joined the German side and was more successful militarily, at least until the final months of the war, but lost large swathes of territory to Greece and Yugoslavia in the peace. Greece, having made substantial territorial gains since becoming independent in 1830, was more cautious, but, under military threat from Bulgaria and Austria-Hungary, joined the French and British in 1917.

5. The influenza epidemics of 1918–1919 killed 50 million to 100 million people worldwide (Barry, 2005, 58), more than any previous epidemic, including the Black Death. The flu was spread by troop movements and by long distance trade, and affected most of the world. In India 17 million died. In Western Samoa about a quarter of the population died. The epidemic, unlike most flu epidemics, was particularly hard on people aged 20–40; death was rapid, and even among survivors there were long-term negative effects. Based on 1960 and 1980 U.S. census data, Almond (2006) found that the age cohort in utero during the pandemic had reduced educational attainment, higher rates of physical disability, lower incomes and socioeconomic status, and higher transfer receipts than other cohorts. Fetal health is crucial for human development and has been enhanced by the absence of pandemics since 1919.

6. About 9 million military personnel died: Germany 2.0 million, Russia 1.8 million, France 1.3 million, Austria-Hungary 1.1 million, Turkey 0.8 million, United Kingdom 0.7 million, Italy 0.6 million, Serbia 0.3 million, Rumania 0.3 million, British Empire 0.2 million, United States 0.1 million (Broadberry and Harrison, 2005, 27). The impact on the gender and age distribution of populations, especially the massive loss of French males born in the final decades of the nineteenth century is documented by Jay Winter (in Wall and Winter, 1988, 9–42).

7. The share of government spending in national income increased between 1913 and 1918 from 10 percent to 54 percent in France, from 10 percent to 50 percent in Germany, from 8 percent to 35 percent in the United Kingdom, and from 2 percent to 17 percent in the United States (Broadberry and Harrison, 2005, 15). Peacock and Wiseman (1967) argue that this initiated a permanent upward shift, but their hypothesis is disputed.

8. France and Germany mobilized about four-fifths of males aged 15–49, Italy and Austria-Hungary slightly less, the United Kingdom about half, New Zealand two-fifths, Australia and Canada about a third, and the United States under a fifth. Conscription was unpopular in many places, especially as the war dragged on; in Québec City demonstrators were killed during the 1918 Easter weekend. There were several mutinies by troops unwilling to continue fighting, notably in the French army in 1917 after disastrous loss of life, by Muslim troops of the Indian army in Singapore in 1915 unwilling to fight against a coalition that included the Ottoman Empire, and by German sailors ordered to set sail on what they saw as a suicide mission in the final month of war.

9. Despite the precision, no serious scheme envisaged full payment of this amount. However, the uncertainty added to the problems, especially for France, which was relying on reparations for funds to repay its creditors (Schuker, 1976).

10. Keynes (1919) was an articulate opponent of bleeding the German economy through reparations. Politically he failed to recognize France's need for reparations to repay its own war debts and the thirst for revenge after France had been forced to pay reparations to Germany in 1871 (Schuker, 1976). Intellectually Keynes's statement of the transfer problem was too extreme; as Ohlin (1929) pointed out, the net impact depended on the elasticities of demand and supply for German exports and imports.

11. France needed reparations to repay its wartime debts, whereas Britain had financed a larger part of its war costs by taxation. By October 1919 the United States had lent $4.2 billion to Britain, $2.75 billion to France, and $1.6 billion to Italy; Britain had lent $2.54 billion to France and $2.3 billion to Italy; and France had lent $1.8 billion to other allies, mainly Russia.

12. The Progressives' main targets were political and social rather than economic, and they worked to institutionalize reform in constitutional amendments. Political reforms, aimed at reducing the power of political bosses and dealmakers, included replacing the state legislatures' appointment of senators by popular elections (the Seventeenth Amendment in 1913) and giving women the right to vote in federal elections (the Nineteenth Amendment in 1920). The role of the state in protecting individual liberties led to "liberal" being associated in the United States with supporters of government intervention. Social measures

regulated work safety and child labor, as well as prohibition of alcoholic beverages (the Eighteenth Amendment in 1919, repealed in 1933) and attempts to limit trafficking of women for prostitution (the 1910 White Slave Trade Act, better known as the Mann Act).

13. Sales of electric refrigerators, which had been invented earlier, took off in the 1920s, for example, Frigidaire's refrigerator production topped 2.5 million by 1932 and climbed to more than 6 million by 1941 when Frigidaire boasted the world's largest refrigerator plant and more than 20,000 employees in the United States and abroad. Efficient and widely owned refrigerators stimulated further inventions; Clarence Birdseye's 1925 patent for fast-freezing marked the beginning of the modern frozen foods industry. The first practical self-contained portable electric vacuum cleaner was patented by James Murray Spangler in 1908. After William Hoover, who was the husband of Spangler's cousin, became president of their company, which he renamed the Hoover Company in 1922, improvements were made in the design of the vacuum cleaner and new sales strategies were tested. Innovative marketing techniques (e.g., stores that became dealerships for the company received a commission for each vacuum cleaner sold, and customers were offered a free ten-day trial period to test the vacuum cleaner) contributed to the Hoover Company becoming the largest vacuum cleaner manufacturer in the world. The Swedish company Electrolux independently developed vacuum cleaners that won markets in Germany and elsewhere and were produced in the United States after 1931. Electric washing machines were also invented in the early 1900s, and sales in the United States reached 913,000 units in 1928. The first laundromat opened in Fort Worth, Texas, in 1934.

14. In Britain, for example, "over the interwar period, new furniture became the most important category of household expenditure on durable goods" (Scott, 2009, 210). This reflected rising living standards for a large part of the population, but because of lower female wages or differing social pressures the major labor-saving household appliances spread slowly before 1950. There was some technical change in the furniture industry, for example, use of electric power and of new materials such as laminates, and the marketing techniques had elements similar to U.S. practice, for example, more than two-thirds of sales were on a hire-purchase credit arrangement and advertising was innovative, but the impact on GDP was much less significant.

15. Hungary remained a kingdom, but because the Habsburg monarch, Charles I, was unacceptable, no king ruled and Horthy was regent. Thus, landlocked Hungary was a kingdom without a king ruled by an admiral without a fleet.

16. From Benito Mussolini *Le Fascisme* (Paris 1933, 19), cited by Mazower (1998, 16).

17. When Japanese troops moved across the Korea-Russia border in 1938, they were forced to retreat by the superior Soviet artillery, and in 1939 Japan was defeated by the USSR in a major tank battle on the China-Mongolia border. As a consequence, Japan turned south rather than north in its search for further conquests, ultimately clashing with the British and French empires and with U.S. naval power.

18. Politically, Phibun had many fascist traits. His personalized regime was progressive, ending the absolute monarchy and promoting popular support through propaganda, and xenophobic, blaming ethnic Chinese for Thailand's economic problems. His economic program was, however, not clearly articulated, beyond encouraging self-sufficiency through buy-Thai campaigns. Despite an attempt to prosecute him for war crimes, Phibun remained popular and returned to power from 1948 to 1957 as a Cold War ally of the West.

19. Kindleberger (2000, 134–135) argues that it is virtually impossible to say where the global crisis began because so many potential causes exist, but it was not just of U.S. origin.

20. The Dust Bowl refers to the impact of severe dust storms causing major ecological damage to prairie lands in the United States and Canada from 1930 to 1936. The Dust Bowl was the result of severe drought following decades of extensive farming without concern for soil erosion; with no natural anchors to keep the soil in place, it turned to dust and blew eastward and southward in large dark clouds, leaving millions of acres of farmland infertile. The Dust Bowl primarily affected areas of Oklahoma, Texas, New Mexico, Colorado, and Kansas, from which hundreds of thousands of people were forced to migrate to California and other states to find work picking fruit and other crops at low wages, a situation dramatized in John Steinbeck's novel *The Grapes of Wrath*.

21. In 1932, only 1.5 percent of all government spending was on relief, averaging about $1.67 per citizen, and only a quarter of unemployed families received any relief. Cities, which had to bear the brunt of the relief efforts, faced bankruptcy; by 1932 Chicago was dismissing firemen, policemen, and teachers, some of whom had not been paid in eight months. Breadlines and Hoovervilles (encampments for the homeless) appeared across the United States. Schools, with budgets shrinking, shortened both the school day and the school year. Resistance to protest occasionally turned violent; in 1932 four hunger marchers were shot and killed when a thousand soldiers accompanied by tanks and machine guns evicted veterans living in a camp in Washington, D.C.

22. Here we abstract from income on foreign assets or remittances from workers overseas, which are both part of gross national product (GNP) but not of gross domestic product (GDP), and from depreciation, which is the difference between gross and net product (or income).

23. This view associated with Friedrich von Hayek (1931) relates the decline in investment or bank credit to the nature of financial capitalism, rather than being unexplained shocks in 1929. Their opposing approaches are expounded by Keynes and von Hayek in the *Fear the Boom and Bust* rap contest created by John Papola and Russ Roberts at http://www.econstories.tv/home.html (downloaded 20 March 2010).

24. Schattschneider (1935) provides a detailed analysis of the congressional progress of the Smoot-Hawley tariff. Meltzer (1976) argues that the Smoot-Hawley tariff exacerbated the depression, while Temin (1989) plays down its impact. Jones (1934) highlights the speed and severity of retaliation, and McDonald, O'Brien, and Callahan (1997) analyze the Canadian response.

25. Canada, the country most affected by U.S. tariff increases, used imperial preferences as a tool to penalize U.S. exporters. U.S. exports to Canada fell from $1,000 million in 1929 to $210 million in 1933 (Pomfret, 2001, 396). Jones (1934, 76) referred to the "mutilation of the billion dollar market that was Canada . . . as the most deplorable and the most costly single fruit of the Hawley-Smoot tariff."

26. After the U.S. economy ran into trouble in 1928 and 1929, Germany's problems were exacerbated by the reduction in capital inflows from U.S. banks, which it had been receiving under the Dawes Plan. The Young Plan of autumn 1928 to reschedule German reparations became a dead letter, although it was significant in calling for establishment of a Bank of International Settlements (BIS) to coordinate reparation payments. The BIS opened in Basel, Switzerland, and is today the international organization of central banks that "fosters international monetary and financial cooperation and serves as a bank for central banks" (www.bis.org).

27. Brown (1956) was the first to document and effectively publicize the quantitatively minor importance of Keynesian macroeconomic policies in the New Deal. Temin and Wigmore (1990) argue that Roosevelt's inauguration was a turning point not because of what the government did in the way of deficit spending but due to perceptions of a regime change. Eggertsson (2008) provides a formal test of whether changes in expectations about the government's commitment to a balanced budget or to maintaining the gold standard contributed to the end of the depression.

28. The fall in output was especially pronounced in durable goods, reflecting a running down of accumulated inventories. The 1937 recession is also blamed on premature easing of fiscal policy (by spending cuts and tax increases) or tightening of monetary policy.

29. An interest-free marriage loan was available to a woman who had been employed for six months prior to marriage and surrendered her job after marriage.

In 1933 there were 200,000 more marriages than in 1932, and 378,000 marriage loans worth 206 million marks had been made by the start of 1935 (Abelshauser, 1998, 127). The loans reduced unemployment by pulling women out of the workforce and by increasing aggregate demand.

30. This is disputed by Adam Tooze, who argues that "rearmament was the overriding and determining force impelling economic policy from the earliest stage" of Nazi rule, although on the same page he accepts that the increased supply of material for the military was eased by the simultaneous growth in output: "Putting to work 6 million unemployed provided for the needs of the Wehrmacht, whilst allowing consumption and civilian investment to be increased as well" (Tooze, 2006, 659).

31. This aspect is emphasized by both Overy (1982) and Cohn (1992).

32. Some historians (e.g., Mason, 1977) contend that the working class was never really bought off, and it was in the face of increasing discontent among the workers that Hitler went to war in order to rouse national fervor and justify more coercive methods in the workplace.

33. This helps to explain why both communist and liberal regimes felt compelled to resist the fascist countries. Soviet communism was never overtly expansionist in the same way as Germany or Japan in the 1930s. Eastern Europe fell under Soviet control as a result of war and a historic need for a barrier against European aggression, but the expectation was that other countries would adopt communism by revolution (as happened in China, Korea, Vietnam, and Cuba). Only in the death throes of the Brezhnev regime, boosted by an oil windfall, did the Soviet Union try to expand militarily by invading Afghanistan.

34. Entering the war on Germany's side in 1940 was in part a desperate throw of the dice by Mussolini, but also may have reflected a sense of picking the winner (as Italy had done in 1915). A consequence of this dénouement was that Italian fascism appeared to end in military defeat rather than economic failure, and the economic appeal of fascism remained strong among many Italians who remembered only that Mussolini made the trains run on time.

35. The period of greatest financial restriction was between the end of the Civil War (April 1939) and 1962. Reform efforts between 1962 and 1975 were limited and gradual; although new banks opened, the state limited competition by imposing interest rate regulations and by directing credit to favored enterprises, until privileged credit access was gradually reduced after the 1969 MATESA scandal. Liberalization in the 1970s coincided with a global recession that especially severely affected the tourism industry, and the banking system suffered many closures between 1977 and 1985, but the surviving banks emerged as strong European institutions.

36. It should also be stressed that, even though the years 1914 to 1945 saw major social and economic disruption and wartime destruction in Europe, economies were resilient and all the signs are of significant increases in European prosperity (Millward and Baten, 2010). Population increased from under 500 million in 1914 to almost 600 million in 1950, income per head increased by 25 percent, and average height (a measure of nutrition and health) increased by four centimeters. Rising standards of sanitation and housing boosted life expectancy, literacy and educational attainment continued to improve, and important social changes (e.g., rural-urban migration and gender roles) began or accelerated. Western Europe fell behind North America, but still belonged to the affluent "First World" and quickly rebuilt war-torn economies.

3. The Soviet Economic Model

1. Erlich (1960) is the classic study of the Soviet industrialization debate. A similar debate would be repeated many times in countries seeking rapid development (Pomfret, 1997, 20–29). In China in the 1950s and 1960s Mao Zedong followed the super-industrialization strategy of Preobrazhensky and Stalin, which Deng Xiaoping replaced in 1978 with a gradualist strategy using slogans similar to Bukharin's "Get Rich!" (see Chapter 5).

2. The main revenue source was the turnover tax, which was essentially a tax on consumer goods and which reduced demand for such goods while providing resources for investment in priority industries.

3. Use Δ to indicate "change in" a variable. Define Y as gross domestic product, which in a closed economy must be equal to total income and total expenditure and which is allocated between consumption, C, or investment goods, I, that is, $Y = C + I$. Savings (S) are defined as the part of Y that is not consumed: $S = Y - C$. Because $Y = C + I$ and $Y = C + S$, actual savings must equal actual investment. Ignoring depreciation, which would not change the model's qualitative conclusions, investment goods are the addition to the capital stock ($I = \Delta K$). This is a closed economy model, but with the assumption that productivity is technologically determined trade has no impact on growth.

4. In the late 1920s the model was developed by a Soviet planner named Fel'dman, and in the 1950s the same model was used by the Indian planner Mahalanobis. Note that the Harrod-Domar-Fel'dman growth model is a classic catch-up strategy in that it ignores the need for technical innovation, assuming that best technology can be adopted from more industrialized countries.

5. A World Cup semifinal spot in 1966 and a European championship final in the early 1960s constituted their total medal haul. In the other popular spectator sport, ice hockey, the Soviet team was never as good as Canada's best; despite giving the Canadians a fright in the first head-to-head meeting in 1972, the Soviets lost the series. Even in chess the Soviet grandmasters could not match the individual brilliance of Bobby Fischer, who won the world title in 1972.

6. This was no small achievement. Literacy rates had been very low in the Tsarist Empire, especially in the more rural regions. In the Turkmen Soviet Republic the literacy rate in the 1920s is believed to have been less than 5 percent, and the number of women who could read and write was about two dozen. Robert Allen (2003, 116–131) argues that a key condition for Soviet economic growth was the rapid fertility transition, which was largely a result of the massive increase of education for girls, unlike in, say, India. Allen projects Soviet population growth without the fertility decline to reach 1.1 billion in 1989; the actual value was less than 0.3 billion. He claims that, beyond the short run, rapid industrialization was not necessarily at the expense of consumption, but that this would not have been possible had Soviet population growth tracked that of India.

7. In the final years of the Soviet era the authorities recognized a category of "underprovisioned" households (i.e., with gross per capita monthly income less than 75 rubles); in the 1989 census 11 percent of households, mostly in Central Asia or the Caucasus, fell into this category (Atkinson and Micklewright, 1992, table U13, based on Goskomstat household survey data). Female participation rates in the labor force were very high, reflecting some gender equality but also a "double burden" on women who were often expected to do most of the household chores and child-rearing in addition to having a full-time job in the formal workforce. A striking feature of the Soviet Union and Eastern Europe was that, despite a commitment to gender equality, the leadership was without exception male.

8. Environmental degradation is also a feature of market economies, in which producers pay attention only to private costs. However, it can be and increasingly is addressed by pollution taxes, which bring private and social costs closer together, or by regulations in response to public outcry. The Soviet Union was home to the world's worst environmental disasters, such as the desiccation of the Aral Sea or the nuclear wastelands around Semipalatinsk, and also of the worst safety failures (e.g., frequent mining disasters as well as the 1986 Chernobyl nuclear power plant disaster).

9. The suppression of competition in the name of all working together for the benefit of the nation was also a fundamental flaw in the economics of fascism. This aspect was hidden in the relatively short peacetime experience of Nazism,

but before 1939 lack of economic dynamism was becoming visible in Italy where Mussolini had ruled since 1922, and in the post-1945 era it became evident in Franco's Spain despite various attempts at reform (Chapter 2).

10. The initial invasion was condemned by the United Nations, at a time when the USSR was boycotting the Security Council meetings in protest at refusal to allow the new communist regime to occupy China's UN seat. UN forces, predominantly supplied by the United States, repelled the invasion, but when the UN troops crossed the dividing line of the 38th parallel in October 1950, China intervened and pushed the UN and South Korean forces back from close to the Chinese border to near the 38th parallel, where a stalemate ensued from mid-1951 until armistice negotiations opened in July 1953. The Korean War was a proxy war insofar as the USSR supplied equipment but did not openly intervene, and it illustrated the limited value of nuclear weapons (which the United States considered using, but did not) in Cold War contests.

11. The extent to which the Soviet system was maintained by political repression was highlighted by Aleksandr Solzhenitsyn's *Gulag Archipelago,* which had been written between 1958 and 1968 but was first published in France in 1973 and in the USSR only in 1989.

4. Multilateralism and Welfare State in the First World

1. The share of workers with health insurance increased from a fifth in 1885 to a half in 1913, and the benefits were more generous. The number insured against workplace accidents increased from 3.7 million in 1886 to almost 30 million (94 percent of the workforce) in 1913. Spending on disability pensions increased from 5 million marks in 1894 to 167 million marks in 1913. The pension system was more limited because eligibility only came at age 70, which was well above the average life expectancy (Khoudour-Castéras, 2008).

2. Private sector welfare systems had been found to increase labor productivity and reduce the number of strikes, and hence were a rational profit-maximizing response to the emergence of large firms and powerful labor unions. The firm Siemens and Halske, for example, introduced many benefits for workers of which the most costly to the firm was a pension fund introduced in 1872, seventeen years before the state pension (Kastl and Moore, 2010).

3. The United States had virtually no social security measures, apart from some state-level industrial accident compensation laws, and ideas of social responsibility only began to spread in the 1920s. Before the 1935 Social Security Act most social insurance in the United States was in the form of self-help schemes.

4. The Beveridge report was far more inspirational than its title suggested. It declared war on the five giant evils of Want, Disease, Ignorance, Squalor, and Idleness and sold 800,000 copies. Churchill had been one of the sponsors of the 1906–1910 reforms, but his subsequent defection to the Conservative Party and history as the chancellor who returned Britain to the gold standard in 1925 and led the opposition to the 1926 General Strike disqualified him in the eyes of most voters as a politician capable of implementing Beveridge's vision.

5. Having the programs administered by the states was necessary to obtain support among Southern members of Congress, as was the exclusion of farm workers (Alston and Ferrie, 1993; Quadagno, 1984).

6. U.S. Secretary State of State George Marshall announced his plan for a European Recovery Program (ERP) in June 1947. By the time Marshall Aid ended in 1952, $13 billion had gone to sixteen countries, with few strings attached. These amounts were unprecedented, but the impact of the ERP was more far-reaching in that, through the Organization for European Economic Cooperation (OEEC) established in 1948 as a conduit for ERP funds, it promoted collaboration and integration among recipients and discouraged protectionism (and specifically quantitative restrictions on trade). The European governments provided a shopping list of goods that they would like the United States to supply, and the counterpart funds associated with sale of ERP goods in their economy could be used to purchase imports from other OEEC countries. The monetary arrangements were formalized in the European Payments Union in 1950, which partially overcame the problem of inconvertible currencies and enabled intra-European trade to flourish in the 1950s. The emphasis on market forces contributed to the USSR boycotting the ERP and forcing the Eastern European countries not to participate.

7. David Cook (2002) analyzes the post-1945 rapid growth in countries where physical capital had been destroyed by war. Japan's recovery without Marshall Aid suggests that the ERP was not the crucial element in Western European economic recovery.

8. Abramovitz (1986) stressed that convergence was not automatic and emphasised these three conditions. Nelson and Wright (1992) argue that technology transfer became much easier after 1945, in part because of the open global economy and growth of multinational corporations. Crafts (1995) provides catch-up evidence from Western Europe.

9. Another big contrast to 1919, and to the European-dominated League of Nations, was the low profile of Europe. Few European representatives were in San Francisco for the signing of the UN Charter and, at the first meeting of the UN General Assembly in London in January 1946, the French foreign minister

was moved "to note the extent to which Europe is absent" (quoted in Mazower, 2009, 151).

10. This is not to deny the ambiguity of the Charter or the evolution of the UN. A driving force at the San Francisco conference was the South African Prime Minister, Jan Smuts, who saw the UN as a commonwealth of like-minded (i.e. white) nations, but that vision would quickly be dispelled. In the first major UN debate South Africa's attempt to incorporate South West Africa (future Namibia) was defeated by a coalition mobilized by non-white politicians (Mazower, 2009), and with the influx of new members over the next two decades the UN became associated with self-determination and anti-colonialism. Despite references to combined efforts, the UN was explicitly dominated by the victorious Great Powers who held veto power in the Security Council, and hence could block any resolutions passed by the UN General Assembly. Nevertheless, many UN agencies were universal in their outreach and often played roles that no nations would accept, as in the work of the UN High Commission for Refugees (established in 1950). By the end of the century, the UN Development Programme (established in 1965) had become the world's largest disburser of economic aid.

11. British and U.S. drafters in the pre–Bretton Woods negotiations recognized the need for a vision to counter the fascist New Order in international economic relations promised by Hitler and that this vision would need to combine an open multilateral financial system with interventionist economic policies to manage national economies (Helleiner, 2010). In the face of strong opposition to economic commitments, the Bretton Woods agreement was sold to the U.S. Congress as essential for world peace (Mikesell, 1994, 44). Although Soviet delegates participated in the Bretton Woods conference, the USSR created its own bloc with Eastern European satellites, and the centrally planned economies stayed apart from the global economy until the 1970s.

12. The ITO Charter was signed by fifty-three countries in Havana in 1948, but several countries had reservations and when it was not ratified by the U.S. Congress the Charter, and the ITO, became a dead letter. The WTO and its predecessor (GATT) provided a widely accepted basis for international trade law and a framework for substantial tariff reductions, as well as regulating use of nontariff barriers to trade, and the WTO has a dispute settlement procedure for trade disputes. The basic GATT/WTO principles are that all members must be treated as well as the most-favored nation (i.e., nondiscrimination, with some exceptions for customs unions, free trade areas, etc), trade rules should be transparent, and tariffs are the preferred trade barrier. Countries bind tariffs (i.e., set maximum levels) that are negotiated in rounds of multilateral trade negotiations; since 1947 much of the reduction in tariffs and other trade restrictions came about through inter-

national negotiations. The average tariff levied on industrial goods has fallen from around 40 percent in 1947 to less than 4 percent today, and many nontariff barriers that could be used to offset this trade liberalization have been outlawed or tightly controlled. One indicator of success is that, while the original GATT was signed by twenty-three countries, by 2011 the WTO had 153 members.

13. Agricultural trade remained heavily regulated, especially in EFTA members Switzerland and Norway, and services trade was regulated everywhere. Non-tariff barriers were pervasive and would only be seriously reduced in the 1980s with the EU's Single Market program. An attempt at monetary integration in the 1970s failed dismally as all of the major currencies were floated in the early 1970s; monetary union would only get back on track in the 1990s, leading to the creation of the euro at the end of the century.

14. By providing home entertainment TVs threatened communal activities such as cinema-going and professional sporting events, although in the longer term TV and sport turned out to be a money-making match. Elections were won and lost by candidates' TV performance; e.g., in the United States Richard Nixon's five o'clock shadow and shifty appearance contributed to his loss of a close presidential election in 1960, and the consequences of political decisions could be highlighted by TV footage in a way that newspapers could not match, e.g., in coverage of the Vietnam War. Transistor radios and portable record-players liberated teenagers from their parents' control over the home radio or gramophone, so that the popular music revolution of the 1960s had wider impact than the more overtly revolutionary rock and roll music of the 1950s.

15. While downplaying the student revolt as "not serious," Judt describes the connection between universities and factories and offices "run from the top down with no input from below. Managers could discipline, humiliate or fire their staff at will. Employees were often accorded little respect, their opinions unheeded."

16. Social change with respect to sexual mores was reflected in many countries' repealing laws related to sexual behavior between consenting adults—in the words of Canadian prime minister Pierre Trudeau, getting the government out of the bedroom.

17. Noble concepts of all residents in an empire having a shared culture and citizenship were not threatening as long as the people outside the metropolitan area stayed in their place. Members of local elites or students might make it to London or Paris, but not until the late 1950s did unskilled workers exercise their rights as citizens and start to arrive in large numbers from present or former colonies in the West Indies, Africa, and Asia. Within colonies with large European populations tensions rose, notably in Algeria and Rhodesia, as the minority feared the consequence of the majority exercising democratic rights.

18. The essential structure is set out in Samuelson (1947). In the simplest two-input form, the inputs are substitutable, but at a diminishing marginal rate of substitution, that is, to keep a constant output level more and more units of an input must be added to compensate for a one-unit reduction of the other input. Output (Y) depends upon inputs: $Y = f(K, L)$, such that the first derivative with respect to either capital (K) or labor (L) is positive and the second derivative negative. Constant returns imply that per capita income (Y/L) depends on the capital/labor ratio (K/L), and the relationship is independent of the size of the labor force.

19. At the new interest rate and the existing wage rate, there is a single equilibrium value of K/L, associated through the production function with a single value of Y/L. The growth rate of the labor force, the capital stock, and output must be the same unless there is a shift in the production function such that more output can be produced with the same amount of inputs. Both the Harrod-Domar and neoclassical growth models are simplifications, assuming extremes of either no or perfect substitutability, but the models clarify why capital formation may drive growth in the short run and why productivity increases are key in the long run, with the difference between the long and short run depending on the speed with which techniques can be changed; the two simple models also suggest why centrally planned economies are relatively good in heavy industries where opportunities for substitution between labor and capital may be less than in light industries.

20. Barro and Sala-i-Martin (1995, table 10.8) provide summaries of growth accounting estimates. Mankiw, Romer, and Weil (1992) argue that the neoclassical model, augmented to include human capital (proxied by a measure of school enrollment) as well as physical capital, fits the international cross-country data for 1960–1985.

21. As a simple analogy, if you have to hammer in a nail you may look around for a suitable rock, but if you have many nails you will buy a hammer, and if you have thousands of nails you may try to invent a mechanical hammer. The relationship between increasing returns, capital formation, and growth was formalized by Young (1928), although his contribution was largely neglected for sixty years.

22. Joseph Schumpeter (1911) emphasized the role of entrepreneurs and the process of creative destruction whereby capitalism progresses through the replacement of old products and processes with new ones. Modern expositions include Romer (1994) and Aghion and Howitt (1998).

23. Business schools existed in many countries before 1945, but these offered low-prestige courses often related to bookkeeping. Harvard offered the first MBA

in 1910, but the University of Chicago's Executive MBA introduced in 1940 was a closer precursor of modern post-graduate in-career MBAs. The University of Western Ontario in 1950 and the University of Pretoria in 1951 offered the first MBA degrees outside the United States, and INSEAD near Paris offered the first European MBA in 1957. The popularity of MBAs surged in the 1960s and has kept growing. Popular interest in, and concern about, managerialism and advertising was reflected in sociological best sellers such as James Burnham's *The Managerial Revolution* (published in 1941) and Vance Packard's *The Hidden Persuaders* (published in 1957).

24. Open registry fleets (i.e., boats registered under flags of convenience such as Panama or Liberia) accounted for 5 percent of world shipping in 1950, 31 percent in 1980, and 49 percent in 2000; their operating costs are estimated to be 12 percent to 27 percent lower than those of traditional registry fleets (Hummels, 2009, 15).

25. The pioneer was the U.S. semiconductor industry in the late 1950s: Philco invested in automated production technologies to offset high U.S. labor costs and suffered disastrous losses due to the rapid obsolescence of its expensive equipment, while Fairchild set up a manufacturing plant in Hong Kong in 1961 to assemble U.S.-made components for reexport to the United States. Semiconductor technology involved four discrete steps: design required highly skilled labor and became concentrated in areas such as Silicon Valley in California, fabrication was capital-intensive, assembly could be automated (as Philco did) or was extremely labor intensive, and testing required expensive equipment. Fairchild's strategy was so successful that it was soon copied by other U.S. corporations, which located design and fabrication in the United States, sent the components to Mexico or Asia for assembly, and returned the finished product to the United States for testing and marketing. This was facilitated by the high value/weight ratio of silicon chips (and hence low transport costs) and by tariff reform, which exempted the U.S.-made components from import duties when the assembled product was imported into the United States.

26. Telex networks became widely accessible for North American and European businesses in the 1950s and 1960s, although the dedicated teleprinter tied to a pair of leased copper wires would be made functionally obsolete by the fax and later e-mail. Modern fax machines became feasible in the mid-1970s and first became popular in Japan, where they had a clearer advantage over the teleprinter because at the time it was faster to handwrite kanji than to type the characters. As their cost fell, by the mid-1980s fax machines were popular around the world. Electronic communication between users of a common mainframe dates from the 1960s, but the spread of desktop computers broadened the demand for e-mail and rapid acceptance of the World Wide Web in the mid-1990s.

27. Between 1957 and 1972, when jet engine usage became widespread, quality-adjusted real prices of aircraft fell by 13–17 percent per annum (Gordon, 1990). Quantum shifts in speed and cost of transatlantic flights in the 1960s followed the introduction of the Boeing 707, and in the 1970s longer distance travel was facilitated by introduction of three-engine wide-bodied jets and the Boeing 747. Changes in costs of flying mainly affected passenger traffic in the 1960s (including the growth of mass tourism), but after the mid-1970s the share by value of freight trade going by air increased rapidly (Hummels, 2007).

28. Eichengreen (2007) ascribes the rapid catch-up growth of continental Western Europe in 1945–1973 to cohesive institutions which limited wage demands so that a larger share of output could be invested; the welfare state was part of this social compact. Saint-Paul (2004) emphasizes the cost in terms of higher unemployment when people have access to unemployment insurance, and ascribes Europe's failure to continue to close the gap with U.S. incomes after 1973 to the disincentive effect of the pervasive welfare state.

29. British economists in the 1960s observed the changing balance of private and public economic power (Shonfield, 1965) and some even castigated British governments for their half-hearted attempts to emulate French and German governments' economic planning (Denton, Forsyth, and MacLennan, 1968), but this would be the high-water mark of belief in a middle way between central planning and capitalism described in the Introduction. In Britain the attraction of consumer choice was highlighted by the government's futile attempt to enforce the BBC's radio monopoly in the face of hugely popular offshore "pirate" radio stations; the episode ended with a humiliating government back-down.

30. Equal voting rights for women are implicit in the 1948 UN Universal Declaration of Human Rights, in which Article 21 states, "The will of the people shall be the basis of the authority of government; this will shall be expressed in periodic and genuine elections which shall be by universal and equal suffrage and shall be held by secret vote or by equivalent free voting procedures." In the high-income countries, except Switzerland, women had already gained the vote in the first half of the twentieth century, but few women were elected or held political office and many social and workplace restrictions remained in the 1950s and 1960s.

31. In 1970 the voting age was reduced to 18 in the United Kingdom, Germany and Canada (for non-federal elections already reduced to 19 in 1952 in British Columbia, and to 18 in Quebec in 1963 and Manitoba 1969), and to 19 in Austria. The voting age was reduced to 18 in 1971 in the Netherlands and the United States (by the Twenty-sixth Amendment to the Constitution—previous reductions in several states and in Guam in 1954 and American Samoa in 1965),

in 1972 in Finland and Sweden, in 1973 in Ireland and Australia, in 1974 in France and New Zealand, in 1975 in Italy (minimum voting age to elect the Senate remained at 25), in Denmark and Spain in 1978, in Belgium in 1981, in Switzerland in 1991 and in Austria in 1992 (from 19).

32. The dichotomy between "freedom from" and "freedom to" is common usage, but a crucial freedom established in the Age of Liberty was freedom from arbitrary state power. The invisible hand of the market needs the helping hand of a state that can enforce property rights, but it also needs to be free from the grabbing hand of an overpowerful and rapacious state (see the section titled The Challenge of Failed States in Chapter 8).

33. In 1950, according to the IMF's *International Financial Statistics,* the United States held gold reserves worth $22.8 billion and U.S. official liabilities amounted to $8.9 billion. In 1960 gold reserves had fallen to $17.8 billion and official liabilities had risen to $21.0 billion. By 1970 U.S. official liabilities were more than four times the size of the country's gold reserves.

34. The French franc became convertible for most current account transactions in 1958, the British pound and German mark in 1959, and the Italian lira in 1960.

35. During the 1960s the Phillips Curve trade-off between inflation and unemployment became a staple tool of macroeconomic policy analysis, supporting the conventional wisdom among economists of the time that they could fine-tune the economy by macropolicy, and perhaps even shift the Phillips Curve to the left by active labor market policies to better match labor with jobs and to reduce unemployment without increasing inflation. The stability of the Phillips Curve was questioned by Milton Friedman (1968), who argued that as workers anticipated inflation they would incorporate this into their wage demands and the Phillips Curve would shift to the right, that is, the unemployment-inflation trade-off would become more adverse.

36. Energy-conserving responses on the demand side, as factories introduced more energy-efficient technologies and consumers bought more fuel-efficient cars, also contributed to the fall in price, although as with the supply-responses, these took years to work their way through.

37. According to Nordhaus's estimates, the 1970s slowdown was comparable to the productivity slowdown at the start of the 1900s, which was a rebound from two decades of rapid productivity growth associated with new technologies (electricity, chemicals). Such "long cycles" related to new goods were documented by Nikolai Kondratieff in books and articles published in Russian in the 1920s and are sometimes referred to as Kondratieff cycles, but mainstream economics from the 1930s to 1960s focused on Keynesian analysis of short-term business cycles. Because he believed that capitalism was a stable system characterized by

self-correcting cycles, in contrast to the Marxist view that it was self-destructively unstable, Kondratieff ended up in one of Stalin's prisons, where he died. In the 1990s renewed technical change would be based on IT advances in the United States, and a speedup of productivity growth from 1.5 percent per annum in the mid-1970s to 2.5 percent in 1995–2000 and 23.5 percent in 2001–2004 (Baumol, Litan, and Schramm, 2007, 12).

38. Harbingers of the conservative reaction were common, but not sustained in the early and mid-1970s. Leaders such as Edward Heath in the United Kingdom, Valéry Giscard d'Estaing in France, Richard Nixon and Jimmy Carter in the United States, and Gough Whitlam in Australia started down the path of deregulation, but failed to sustain fundamental economic reform.

5. Decolonization and Cold War

1. Despite the strength of Communist parties in some European countries (e.g., France and Italy), they never came close to assuming power, and, despite market-oriented reforms in some Eastern European countries (notably Hungary), these never reached the stage of being system-threatening. The only near exception to this generalization was Yugoslavia, which left the Soviet bloc in 1948 and adopted its own system of workers' self-management, but this was far from being a market system.

2. This became known as the Prebisch-Singer thesis after two writers who provided evidence of secular decline in the terms of trade of primary product exporters and explained this by the higher income elasticity of demand for manufactured goods. Data from the 1950s and 1960s supported the hypothesis because primary product prices were at a peak in the early 1950s due to the Korean War commodity boom. Over longer periods aggregate trends are difficult to identify, and depend on which particular products are included. In the 1970s, when many commodity prices rose sharply, the opposite argument was made: the supply of primary products is limited, so their price relative to the price of manufactured goods must increase in the long run.

3. In 1919 Germany's colonies were ceded under a League of Nations mandate to the victorious powers (Britain, France, Belgium, Japan, and British dominions). Independence was not an option for Tanganyika, Cameroon, German New Guinea, and other colonies. The Russian Empire became a union of notionally equal Soviet republics, controlled from Moscow.

4. Sputnik 1, the first earth-orbiting artificial satellite, was launched by the Soviet Union on 4 October 1957, and Sputnik 2, launched on 3 November 1957,

carried the first living passenger into orbit, a dog named Laika (mission planners did not provide for the safe return of the spacecraft, making Laika the first space casualty). The second mission was dubbed "muttnik" by U.S. humorists, but U.S. policymakers were seriously embarrassed by the Project Vanguard satellite launched by the United States in December 1957; the rocket rose only four feet from the ground. The Space Race became a subsidiary competition of the Cold War. After Yuri Gagarin became the first human in space in April 1961, President Kennedy committed the United States to putting the first man on the moon before the end of the 1960s, which was achieved by Neil Armstrong in July 1969.

5. The modern concept of aid dates from the late 1940s when the high-income countries began to recognize that income disparities were a shared concern and that capital shortage was a key constraint on economic growth. Before that, assistance had typically involved humanitarian responses to natural calamities or support for colonies. The 1948 Economic Cooperation Act, creating the Marshall Plan (1948–1952) to provide financial assistance for the reconstruction of European economies, marked the start of U.S. aid, and the 1950 Act for International Development (creating the Point Four Program) provided U.S. technical help to agrarian nations; the various institutions were combined to form USAid in 1961. British aid dates from the 1950 Colombo Plan, signed by the United Kingdom, Australia, Canada, Ceylon, India, New Zealand, and Pakistan, which aimed at coordinating assistance from the United Kingdom and the wealthy dominions to the new independent Commonwealth countries of South Asia. Other European countries, notably Norway and other Scandinavian countries, began to allocate funds for development aid in the early 1950s.

6. In some cases foreign intervention was driven by business interests concerned about control over raw materials or fears of expropriation, as in the U.K.- and U.S.-backed overthrow of the Mossadegh government in Persia in 1953 or the U.S.-backed overthrow of Chile's Allende government in 1973, and the widespread influence of the United Fruit Company on Central American politics (e.g., in getting the United States to overthrow the Arbenz government in Guatemala in 1954).

7. Katanga's secession from the newly independent Belgian Congo in 1960 illustrated the interaction of Cold War, foreign business, and domestic interests. The leader of the mineral-rich breakaway province, Moshe Tshombe, was supported by Western mining interests. After national leader, Patrice Lumumba, sought support from the USSR, he was overthrown by a September 1960 coup. Western military forces under UN auspices then assisted in the forcible reunification of the country, and the secession formally ended in 1963. After a second coup in 1965, the leader of the 1960 coup, Joseph Mobutu, assumed absolute

power, and for thirty years ruled over one of the most corrupt regimes in the world.

8. The founding of development economics was a paper prepared by a Polish economist in London on the postwar reconstruction of Eastern and Southeastern Europe (Rosenstein-Rodan, 1943). The advice would not be used in that context, but the imagery of the need for a "Big Push" and other writers' emphasis on externalities that made uncoordinated approaches to economic development ineffective would strike a chord across the Third World, and with foreign aid donors. Similar imagery was evoked by the low-level equilibrium trap (Nelson, 1956; Leibenstein, 1957) in which developing countries languished and by the vicious and virtuous circles that characterized less- and more-developed economies (Nurkse, 1953; Myrdal, 1957).

9. Lewis (1955) and Rostow (1960) gave a much more nuanced treatment than this one-line summary suggests, but elements such as increased agricultural productivity and appropriate social and political change in Rostow's growth sequence and Lewis's treatment of education were largely ignored in the 1950s and 1960s. The main debate was over whether growth should be balanced to capture externalities or unbalanced, as in Rostow's emphasis on the historic role of a leading sector, to create the tensions that drive development, but the debate over the allocation of capital was secondary to the consensus on increasing the amount of investment.

10. This model of rural-urban migration in response to expected wage increases was developed by Harris and Todaro (1970). The visible counterpart was the emergence of large slums in cities as diverse as São Paolo, Mexico City, Dakar, Lagos, Calcutta, or Dhaka.

11. Estimates of the costs of trade barriers that focused on short-term resource misallocation costs (the so-called Corden triangles) often amounted to 1 percent of GNP or less, which seemed trivial compared with the obvious underperformance of ISI economies highlighted by Little, Scitovsky, and Scott (1970) and a succession of similar studies during the 1970s. Attempts to identify dynamic gains from trade have found many suspects, but it has been difficult to prove conclusive causality. Apart from the superior environment for project evaluation when domestic prices are more closely aligned to world prices, the suspects include access to high-quality imported inputs, improvements in productivity from having to compete in international markets, and awareness of global best practices.

12. Capital markets are imperfect for reasons other than financial repression. Pervasive market failures, such as information asymmetries between borrowers and lenders, may justify state intervention (Stiglitz, 1994). The test is whether restrictions on the financial sector improve or hamper the efficient working of

the economy in specific circumstances. The evidence from the ISI countries is that financial repression was detrimental to long-term prosperity. Financial deregulation was potentially beneficial, although that is not to argue that no regulations were needed. The next chapter argues that the challenge for policymakers in economies with nonrepressed financial sectors is how to protect small depositors while encouraging sufficient prudence in lending by financial institutions. Because financial reform involves discarding one set of regulations in favor of a different set of regulations whose precise nature is debated, for governments abandoning ISI strategies financial reform was much more difficult than trade reform, which only involved dismantling barriers. Mistakes were made, and the record of financial reform is littered with financial crises.

13. Indirectly, of course, the subsidies were supporting beneficiaries from the ISI strategy such as owners and workers in the protected capital-intensive industries. A futile debate in the 1960s raged over whether inflation was structural (due to the inefficient large farms and other structural weaknesses that required reform) or monetary (due to governments increasing the money supply too quickly), but the proximate causes of inflation were less important than the systemic reason for inflation in an ISI economy with loose macroeconomic control.

14. The Green Revolution illustrated how a small dose of intervention (money from nongovernmental organizations and the initiative of one man, Norman Borlaug, who won the 1990 Nobel Peace Prize) can overcome a major market failure. Individual farmers have little incentive to undertake the risky task of experimenting with new hybrid grains; especially if they are living close to subsistence, the risk of crop failure outweighs any future benefits. Yet such experimenting in international research centers in the Philippines (rice) and Mexico (wheat) produced high-yielding varieties that led to massive increases in farm output in the countries adopting them. National governments had a role to play in establishing research stations to adapt new varieties to local conditions, in providing extension services to spread the knowledge among often illiterate farmers, and in facilitating access to credit to buy seed and complementary inputs such as fertilizers.

15. Borrowing was not itself the issue. With negative real interest rates, the mid-1970s was a good time for astute borrowers. When the debt crisis erupted in 1982, South Korea was one of the five most indebted countries, with the highest foreign debt per capita, but it, like Taiwan, did not experience a repayment problem because the loans were invested in profitable foreign-exchange-earning projects.

16. Sixteen of these were Latin American countries, and the four largest debtors (Mexico, Brazil, Argentina, and Venezuela) owed $176 billion to foreign banks, of which $37 billion was owed to eight U.S. banks (Bankers Trust, Chemi-

cal New York, First Chicago, Manufacturers Hanover, BankAmerica, Chase Manhattan, Citicorp, and J. P. Morgan), equivalent to 147 percent of those banks' capital and reserves.

17. Coordination was essential to avoid opportunistic behavior by individual creditors. Banks that rolled over part of their outstanding loans to enable a country to continue to service its foreign debt while negotiating a discount on the amount outstanding had to be sure that the rollover money would not be grabbed by another creditor, leaving the debtor no better placed to generate future foreign exchange earnings. Time was necessary to allow the debtors to reorient their economies toward accruing foreign exchange to service debts and also for the banks to recognize that they had to take a serious loss. The average secondary market price of developing country debt in 1986 was around two-thirds of its face value; by 1989 this had dropped to a third, which was a more realistic basis for an eventual settlement. The Brady Plan involved individual national negotiations because the appropriate discount on sovereign debt would vary from borrower to borrower.

18. An important distinction is between solvency and liquidity problems. The Latin American countries were not insolvent, but the burden of meeting their current interest obligations was too large. Many smaller debtors, especially in sub-Saharan Africa, were unable to repay their debts and were technically bankrupt, which required a different approach, ultimately leading to debt forgiveness. Both of these processes could be helped by an honest broker to monitor each case and promote consistent outcomes; the IMF, which had lost its original role since the end of the fixed exchange rate system, stepped in as the principal monitor.

19. Panagariya (2008) highlights the real issue from the mid-1960s as declining productivity, with attempted reforms becoming more and more serious up to Rajiv Gandhi's reforms in 1985–1986 but always without follow-up. Mushrooming costs of supporting sick enterprises led to ever-larger government budget deficits, public debt, and in the 1980s foreign borrowing. In 1991, faced with unsustainable debt servicing requirements, India undertook serious reform of the licensing system and the economy was opened up. The ratio of trade (exports plus imports) to GDP tripled, from 16 percent in 1990 to 48 percent in 2007.

20. The GATT signatories extended MFN treatment to most nonmembers. This allowed free-riding by countries that could benefit from others' tariff reductions while not reducing their own tariffs, but meant that the countries at the negotiating table could reach agreement on matters of greatest concern to them, without major complaints from nonmembers; tariffs on most manufactures were slashed, but restrictions remained on farm products and on textiles, clothing, and footwear. This bargain was beneficial to the few low-income countries pursuing

export-oriented development strategies based on exporting a variety of labor-intensive manufactures, but less beneficial for food exporters, and even exporters of manufactures began to experience protectionist threats in the 1970s and 1980s. The outcome was to convince most countries to join GATT (or its successor, the WTO) and have a seat at the negotiating table rather than to lobby for special privileges through the UN system.

21. In deference to China's concerns about the status of Taiwan and Hong Kong, the term "newly industrializing economies" soon replaced "newly industrializing countries." The non-Asian newly industrializing countries experienced difficulties sustaining growth in the 1970s and 1980s, and the label became more narrowly applied to the high-performing Asian economies.

22. Myrdal's three-volume *Asian Drama* was considered a classic at the time, in the heyday of import-substitution policies. His belief that India represented the best prospects for economic prosperity in the final third of the twentieth century because of its large domestic market was widely shared. Myrdal won the Nobel Prize in Economics, proving that economists' predictions must always be taken with a grain of salt (remember that when reading the final chapter of this book!).

23. In variants of the developmental state model, proposed by Chalmers Johnson (1982) to capture Japan's economic success, Alice Amsden (1989) and Robert Wade (1990) popularized the view that government support was crucial in promoting new export sectors in South Korea and Taiwan. Other economists have argued that the important government role was to allow markets to direct resources so that entrepreneurs and workers can concentrate on "doing what comes naturally" (Riedel, 1988). The *East Asian Miracle* report by the World Bank (1993) summarizes the literature, but sits on every fence.

24. This view was popularized by Paul Krugman (1994), based on the research of Alwyn Young (1994; 1995).

25. Some authors traced South Korean and Taiwanese success to their history as Japanese colonies, when new industrial methods (Kim and Park, 2008) and agricultural technology were introduced, but as a simple explanation this fails to explain the failure of North Korea, which had been the more industrialized part of colonial Korea.

26. South Korea's per capita GDP, the lowest of the four, was $21,530 in 2008, compared with Uruguay's $8,260 and Argentina's $7,200 (World Bank, *World Development Indicators*). Fifty years earlier, Uruguay's per capita income had been seven times that of South Korea and Argentina's had been four and a half times larger than Korea's (Table 5.1).

27. The highest-profile restrictions were voluntary export agreements to restrict Japanese car imports; for example, in 1981 the United States negotiated a

limit of 1.68 million cars a year, while France and Italy had even more restrictive agreements. Such agreements were "voluntary," but concluded under the threat that without an agreement import quotas would be unilaterally imposed. The U.S. auto VER benefited Japanese carmakers as well as their U.S. competitors because restricting supply pushed up car prices, costing U.S. consumers about $1,000 per new car. To evade the restrictions on imports, Japanese companies built factories in the United States (even though, absent the VER, it may not have been the most efficient location) and U.S. consumers bought alternatives such as Korean cars and sport utility vehicles, which as "vans" were not covered by the agreement. In a similar vein, the high-income countries negotiated bilaterally with the new industrializing economies many orderly marketing arrangements, which protected U.S. or European producers from competing imports but hurt consumers and had other undesired side effects.

28. Some Western economists who had been on carefully guided tours of China did not even perceive any need for change. Joan Robinson, often tipped during her lifetime as a potential Nobel laureate, noted (Robinson, 1979, ix) that in 1978 "I do not think that anyone would deny that the Chinese method of organizing a highly labour-intensive agriculture is more successful than any in the so-called free world."

6. The Conservative Reaction in the West

1. The conservative reaction was a widespread phenomenon among the high-income countries. In the 1984 Canadian election Brian Mulroney's Progressive Conservatives won the biggest majority in Canadian history and formed the first majority conservative government in twenty-six years. After the 1984 New Zealand election, Finance Minister Roger Douglas introduced policies that included control of inflation by monetarist means, privatization, cutting farm subsidies and trade barriers, and which earned the name of Rogernomics. These measures were viewed by some of his party colleagues as a betrayal of Labour Party principles, but other leaders of nominally left-wing parties (Mitterrand in France, Gonzales in Spain, Craxi in Italy, Hawke in Australia) embraced market-oriented reforms after 1982.

2. Although they operated within the mainstream right-of-center party, both were perceived as political outsiders: Reagan from California and Thatcher from Lincolnshire.

3. This was ascribed to the fragmentation of trade unions in Britain that arose from a crafts tradition in which specialized workers got together. The national

Trades Union Congress was an umbrella organization without coercive powers over its members.

4. The 1970–1974 Conservative government under Edward Heath came to power on an election promise of "cutting inflation at a stroke," but failed to do so. After returning to power in the 1974 general election, the Labour governments lost by-elections and became a minority government in the second half of the decade, surviving only with support from other parties. The government embraced a monetarist approach to inflation in 1978, but too late to have an impact before the 1979 election, so the Thatcher government garnered all the credit for ending double-digit inflation.

5. In 1979, 55 percent of the United Kingdom housing stock was owner-occupied, and 32 percent was rented from local governments, 3 percent rented from housing associations, and 11 percent rented from private landlords, that is, almost three-quarters of the rental housing was "council houses." Initial disposals were simple sales at attractive prices to current tenants; 1.3 million homes were sold at discounts estimated to be between 30 percent and 70 percent. When it became clear that some tenants could not afford, or did not choose, to buy their housing, the council houses were transferred to various types of private-public not-for-profit organizations, reflecting a continued obligation of the state to provide housing for all but minimizing the government's financial burden.

6. The gains to shareholders in privatized firms and the profits made by some people from financial deregulation, combined with the high unemployment associated with the recession of the early 1980s and the destruction of trade union power, contributed far more to increasing inequality in the Thatcher era than any attack on the welfare state.

7. Public monopoly on telephone services or letter mail was justified by the natural monopoly argument of high fixed costs and by a social policy argument for universal service at a common price. When technical change drastically reduced the need for expensive fixed lines and exchanges, telephone services were ripe for privatization and deregulation, but the argument that rural communities might not be served by profit-maximizing private suppliers was raised and often hijacked by workers who preferred to remain public-sector employees rather than becoming part of a highly competitive industry.

8. The highest-profile example was the restriction of Japanese car imports to 1.68 million units in 1981. After several renewals of the "voluntary" export restraint agreements, they were eventually phased out. The VERs protected the Big Three U.S. producers, but reduced supply allowed all suppliers to increase prices. The indirect effects were to encourage imports of light trucks and sport utility

vehicles, and investment by foreign car companies in U.S. plants, while the domestic car firms came to rely on lobbying rather than increased efficiency to meet the competition (and Chrysler and General Motors in particular needed recurring government support).

9. On 3 August 1981 almost 13,000 air traffic controllers went on strike after months of negotiations with the federal government. The union's three major demands were a $10,000 across-the-board pay raise, a 32-hour workweek (down from 40), and a better retirement package. President Reagan declared the strike in violation of the law and gave workers 48 hours to return to their jobs. He fired the 11,350 controllers who had not returned to work after 48 hours, and to underline the message he declared a lifetime ban on rehiring the strikers (the ban was rescinded by President Clinton in 1993). The union and workers, believing they were negotiating from strength because of their monopoly in providing an essential service, underestimated the adverse public relations impact of the pay demand and the potential for automation of their jobs. The Federal Aviation Authority replaced the fired staff by less-skilled, lower-paid workers and in 1982 announced a twenty-year program costing $15–$20 billion to replace the system's aging computers, further automating air traffic control.

10. Evidence of the negative impact of means-tested pensions on labor supply was provided for Canada by Baker and Benjamin (1999), for the United Kingdom by Disney and Smith (2002), for the United States by French (2005) and Benitez-Silva and Heiland (2007), and globally by Gruber and Wise (2005). The shift away from means-testing has been incremental, but widespread; earnings tests for pensions were gradually relaxed in Canada from the mid-1970s and in the United Kingdom after 1989, and the earnings test for U.S. social security was eliminated in 2000 for people over 65.

11. The most obvious element was the highly indebted poor countries' initiative, aimed at debt forgiveness for insolvent poor countries (mainly in sub-Saharan Africa). There were also bailouts of countries suffering from financial crises during the 1990s, although these were divisive, as the Asian countries perceived a much less supportive attitude from the IMF and the Western economic powers during the 1997–1998 Asian crisis than was shown toward Argentina, Mexico, Turkey, or Russia when their economies were hit by debt or currency crises.

12. The logic is not watertight because the impact of interest ceilings on bank profits depends on the interest elasticity of supply of deposits and demand for loans.

13. The term euro-dollar refers to any dollars domiciled outside the United States. The market emerged to evade U.S. regulations and also to cater to depositors,

such as the USSR, wishing to hold dollars but fearful of the security of dollars held in the United States. The United Kingdom in the 1950s had a tightly regulated domestic monetary system but lightly regulated international banking and an unrivaled reputation for the protection of property rights.

14. For example, Orange County, California, declared bankruptcy on 6 December 1994 after losing $1.7 billion in an investment fund betting that interest rates would fall. Many cases were reported of "rogue traders" who were denounced for not following usual procedures after they made large losses for their employers (Pomfret, 2010, table 2); these same traders had often been lauded for making large profits through arcane and misunderstood speculation in a previous period, but senior bank managers were willing to turn a blind eye to the risk as long as the speculation was successful.

15. The excesses of New York and London in the 1980s were fictionalized by Tom Wolfe in *Bonfire of the Vanities* and by Alan Hollinghurst in *The Line of Beauty*.

16. Even small depositors might have concerns about whether the insurance institution had sufficient funds to meet all its obligations and, if not, whether the government would bail it out (as happened in the U.S. S&L crisis). This is an example of the more general problem of credibility in the face of potentially large financial crises. Policymakers want people to believe that they will be tough in a crisis in order to reduce moral hazard and over-risky behavior, but during a crisis governments come under pressure to be lenient (e.g., by bailing out banks with nonperforming loans) and are criticized for being tough (e.g., allowing Lehman Brothers to go bankrupt on 15 September 2008 increased the severity of the U.S. financial crisis). Kydland and Prescott (1977) is the classic analysis of time inconsistency in macroeconomic policy. Reinhart and Rogoff (2009) marshal eight centuries of evidence to show why this time it is not different; financial crises have similar underlying mechanisms and occur frequently.

17. The actual number depends upon how serious the financial sector's problem has to be before calling it a crisis. Eichengreen and Bordo (2002) identify 38 financial crises between 1945 and 1973, and 139 between 1973 and 1997. Caprio and Klingebiel (1997) identified 112 banking crises in 93 countries (and 51 borderline crises in 46 countries) between the late 1970s and 1997, with an average fiscal cost of about 12 percent of GDP. Laeven and Valencia (2008), excluding "crises" affecting isolated banks, identify 124 systemic banking crises from 1970 to 2007 and examine 42 of these in detail.

18. The 1998 bailout of Long-Term Capital Management (LTCM) orchestrated by the Reserve Bank of New York also provided a warning about the instability of the financial sector. LTCM partners included Myron Scholes and Robert

Merton, who had shared the 1997 Nobel Prize in Economics for their work in financial theory, and LTCM used sophisticated models to identify arbitrage opportunities, which could be realized by taking very large positions in order to realize small percentage gains. The model broke down in the face of financial market turmoil following the Asian crisis and Russia's debt default in August 1998. Thus, even with state-of-the-art theory and huge computing resources, risk management was inadequate in the face of low probability but high impact events—labeled a "black swan event" by Nassim Nicholas Taleb (2007). The LTCM bailout sent a signal that, if a financial institution were large enough, then it would receive public support if it faced failure.

19. The most determined cutters were Ireland after 1983 and the Netherlands after 1993. The most frequently cut social transfers were unemployment benefits. With aging populations all of the countries reconsidered their pension policies; on average the share of GDP going to the elderly through pensions and medical aid remained stable during the 1980s and 1990s, but the average hides big variations (large cuts in the Netherlands, New Zealand, Ireland, and Australia and increases in Austria, Greece, and Italy). Italy had especially generous support, offering early retirement at 55 and disability benefits that encouraged older workers to retire with a job-related disability; Italy is projected to have the oldest population in the OECD by the mid-twenty-first century, but with the oldest politicians in the OECD a proactive response is unlikely. By contrast, Japan and the United States, with weaker welfare states, have tended to keep workers employed at older ages than elsewhere.

20. The nature of the labor market was shifting in high-income countries. Higher skill levels meant that workers were better able to take care of themselves within a legal framework that specified employees' rights, rather than relying on a union to represent their interests. Industries that had provided fertile conditions for organizing labor and radical unionism were transformed, for example, the docks by containerization, steel by the emergence of mini mills, and autos by the move to smaller model runs.

21. These studies include Kim and Nelson (1999), Kahn, McConnell, and Perez-Quiros (2002), and Stock and Watson (2003).

22. Clarida, Gali, and Gertler (2000) argue that the Great Moderation was due to improved monetary policy, following the example of Paul Volker at the U.S. Federal Reserve. Fogli and Perri (2006) and Galí and Gambetti (2009) also give credit to macroeconomic policymakers, and Woodford (2009) relates the Great Moderation to improved macroeconomic theory. Sims and Zha (2006), however, find that switching macroeconomic policy regimes explains only a small part of the Great Moderation. The sharp downturn in the United States and Western Europe in

2008–2009, however, suggested limits to the extent that economic policymakers can forestall cycles when individuals make decisions based on limited information and processing capacity; this critique of macroeconomics, voiced by behavioral economists, is reminiscent of Hayek's critique of the inability of planners to process all of the information necessary for efficient microeconomic resource allocation.

23. Andolfatto and Gomme (2003) introduce learning into a dynamic stochastic general equilibrium model.

24. Those willing to take risks either as entrepreneurs or as lenders could become wealthy, and especially after financial crisis struck the U.S. and U.K. economies in 2007–2008 there was increased concern about income inequality fueled by the contrast between bankers who became rich on undeserved bonuses and their customers who failed to keep up mortgage payments and lost their homes. Nevertheless, as argued in the Preface, the increasing inequality of the 1990s and early 2000s was different in nature to that of the early 1900s; the rich were mostly self-made, benefiting from equality of opportunity and a (fairly) level playing field, and governments were worried and prepared to take measures to mitigate the increased inequality.

25. Ranciere, Tornell, and Westermann (2008) provide evidence of a positive relationship between crisis-prone economies and growth. In contrast to the pre-2007 literature on the Great Moderation, economists started to dust off the ideas of Schumpeter and Hayek about the benefits of instability in pruning weak firms during recessions so that the economy can better grow in boom periods; see Maurel and Schnabl (2011) and references therein, and Papola and Roberts (2010) for a rap treatment. Some studies, however, continued to find evidence of long-lasting negative effects from crises (e.g., Cerra and Saxena, 2008).

7. The Collapse of Central Planning

1. The description is by Bukharin's widow (Larina, 1993, 123–124), who was 21 at the time and whose husband would be executed four years later. According to Khrushchev, of the 1,966 delegates at the Seventeenth Congress 1,108 were subsequently arrested for counter-revolutionary crimes, and a mere 59 of the 1,966 made it to the Eighteenth Party Congress (Bullock, 1991, 542).

2. The car industry was a prime example of planners' obsession with scale economies and disregard for people's desire for variety. Elsewhere, notably Japan, car producers followed a more nuanced approach of realizing scale economies for engines or chassis while outsourcing many components to specialized suppliers and at the assembly stage offering a range of models and options. Producers

in market economies who did not match best practice ran into trouble, however large they were.

3. Ericson (1991) provides a concise analysis of the system characteristics and their consequences. Kornai (1992) provides a fuller analysis. R. Allen (2003) sees a major weakness in the predilection for upgrading existing factories rather than building new ones; similar pressure from large unionized labor forces in North America and Western Europe did not prevent firms from building new car factories or steel mills outside the rustbelts. Where planners saw waste, competition provided dynamism.

4. Concerns about avoiding waste and obtaining maximal use from equipment meant that the Soviet capital stock was rarely replaced until it physically wore out, unlike in market economies where capital is usually replaced when it becomes obsolete (i.e., technically superior equipment is available). In the 1960s, due to wartime destruction, the Soviet capital stock was on average about twenty years old, but by the 1980s the average was approaching thirty years, compared with around sixteen years in the United States (Pomfret, 2002).

5. Leonid Kantorovich shared the 1975 Nobel Prize in Economics for his contribution to the theory of the optimum allocation of resources.

6. It would get worse in the 1990s. Yugoslavia's rate of inflation hit 5×10^{15} percent over the time period 1 October 1993 to 24 January 1994.

7. Slovenia's more or less peaceful independence in 1991 permitted a more or less orderly transition to a market economy, but for the rest of Yugoslavia the contested dissolution dominated economic performance during the 1990s. The 1991–1995 war involving Serbia, Croatia, and Bosnia and Herzegovina was ended by the 1995 Dayton Agreement, but that failed to settle the internal problems of Bosnia and Herzegovina or the future of Kosovo. While Croatia and Macedonia could concentrate to some extent on economic matters after 1995, the 1999 NATO bombing campaign inflicted further damage on the Serbian economy.

8. The specific form of the collapse varied from country to country, e.g., coalescing around popular support for a respected dissident in Czechoslovakia and being managed by members of the Communist elite in Romania and Bulgaria, but in all cases the economic outcome was renunciation of central planning in favor of a market-based system.

9. The GDR became an economic showpiece of communism in the 1950s. In the 1930s the part of Germany that became the GDR had been the most productive region in continental Europe, with per capita income 27 percent higher than that in the part of Germany that became the Federal Republic (Sinn and Westermann, 2001, 5).

10. Monetary and economic union came into force on 1 July 1990 and political unification was completed on 3 October.

11. The velvet divorce under which the Czech Republic and Slovakia became separate countries in 1993 was partly driven by the Czechs wanting to reform quickly and the Slovaks wanting a more gradual process with subsidies for enterprises during the transition. In fact, both countries created market economies in time to be among the first wave of accessions to the European Union in 2004, and in many respects Slovakia had a better functioning economy by that time, reflected in its adoption of the euro in 2009 when such a step was still several years off for the Czech Republic.

12. The far higher than expected costs for East and West Germans provided a warning to South Koreans who were keen for the reunification of their country.

13. Gorbachev may have acquiesced in events in Eastern Europe in the hope that more popular regimes would stabilize the Soviet Union's western border and help to improve relations with rich Western European countries, or he may have miscalculated as events moved at breakneck speed in the second half of 1989. Within the USSR many date the erosion of central power to the ethnic riots between Azeris and Armenians, which became more frequent in 1988 and 1989, culminating on 20 January 1990 when Soviet troops entered Baku and killed more than a hundred people. Inter-republic conflict between Armenia and Azerbaijan over the disputed territory of Nagorno-Karabagh became more violent and the central government seemed powerless to restore peace. Estonia, Latvia, Lithuania, and Georgia declared independence in the first half of 1991, but this was not recognized by the Soviet authorities.

14. Yeltsin had publicly split with Gorbachev in 1987 and been demoted in the Communist hierarchy. After Yeltsin had been elected as Moscow delegate to the Congress of the People's Deputies in March 1989 and gained a seat on the Supreme Soviet of the Russian Soviet Republic, he was elected chairman of the Presidium of the Supreme Soviet in May 1990. The next month the Russian Congress adopted a declaration of sovereignty, and in July 1991 Yeltsin resigned from the Communist Party of the Soviet Union. When democratic presidential elections were held in June 1991, Yeltsin won 57 percent of the popular vote, compared with 16 percent for Nikolai Ryzhkov, the candidate supported by Gorbachev.

15. Economic reform lagged political reform in the final years of the Soviet Union. Gorbachev's economic reforms were substantial enough for many to date the end of central planning from his enterprise reforms of 1987–1988, but these reforms weakened the control of the central planners without creating an alternative resource allocation mechanism. By 1990–1991 the Soviet government was

supporting inefficient state enterprises by printing money, which led to triple-digit inflation and expansion of the unofficial economy.

16. The three Baltic countries took the opportunity to break away from the Russian sphere of influence, introducing national currencies and rapid reforms in preparation for applying for EU membership, which they attained with the first wave of Eastern European countries in 2004. The other twelve Soviet successor states formed the Commonwealth of Independent States, but this loose organization had little authority.

17. In the loans-for-shares scheme, some of the largest state industrial assets were leased through auctions for money lent to the government. Under the terms of the deals, if the Yeltsin government did not repay the loans by September 1996, the lender acquired title to the stock. The loans were not repaid, and the scheme effectively ended up being a fire-sale of valuable state assets to a few financial groups. Politically the scheme was a short-term success as, with the oligarchs' support, Yeltsin won an election he had been expected to lose to his Communist Party opponent. The scheme also eased short-term economic problems as the government ceased subsidizing the then-inefficient enterprises and their performance improved under new ownership.

18. Boycko, Shleifer, and Vishny (1995) provide a contemporary account by people involved in the privatization process. Shleifer and Treisman (2000) are less exuberant, with more emphasis on the problems. Åslund (2007) argues that despite their poor reputation the oligarchs actually improved the performance of the enterprises they owned.

19. The Southeastern European countries formed a third group whose performance was somewhere between that of the Eastern European countries who joined the EU in 2004 and that of the CIS countries.

20. The econometric literature is reviewed in Pomfret (2002, 90–93) and in World Bank (2002).

21. The idea of a threshold level above which inflation was seriously damaging to growth in low- and middle-income countries was popularized by Bruno and Easterly (1998). Their proposed threshold of 40 percent was, however, considered by many commentators to be too high. Christoffersen and Doyle (1998) estimated a threshold of 13–14 percent based on the experience of transition economies during the 1990s.

22. The important economic point is that incentives at the margin are what matter. On output up to the plan target households effectively paid 100 percent in tax, but beyond this output level the tax rate was zero. The response depends on the plan target being below realistically potential output and on the state not changing the rules when output increases (Pomfret, 2000).

23. This is the title of Naughton (1995). His more recent book (Naughton, 2007) provides the best account in English of the Chinese economy since 1949.

8. The End of the Third World

1. A large part of Asian growth was generated within 50 to 100 kilometers of Osaka, Yokohama, Seoul, Taipei, Tianjin, Shanghai, Hong Kong, Bangkok, Jakarta, Singapore, and Kuala Lumpur. Even when governments tried to restrict migration to the dynamic areas, it had little impact; in China tens of millions of migrant workers from interior provinces illegally moved to coastal areas in search of work, which they easily found. In countries where there were no restrictions, such as Thailand where movement from the poor northeast to Bangkok was facilitated by a good road system built in support of the United States' Vietnam War effort, the urban-rural migration and income gap were huge; Greater Bangkok, with an eighth of the national population, produced more than half of GDP in the 1990s.

2. Thailand in the mid-1990s was a thriving democracy with the most open media in Southeast Asia, but the 1997–1998 crisis paved the way for a populist party to gain power and this led to political disruption in the early 2000s. The Thai Rak Thai Party led by Thaksin Shinawatra won the 2001 election, but was ousted in a 2006 military coup d'état. When democracy was restored in 2007, Thaksin was not allowed to stand but the election was won by a party closely aligned to him. This government was displaced in 2008 after street protests in Bangkok. Civil disruption in support of or against the undemocratically constituted government continued through 2009 and 2010. In Indonesia, by contrast, the crisis led to the overthrow of the autocratic Suharto regime, and by the early 2000s Indonesia had become the most open democracy in Southeast Asia, albeit still with serious corruption problems.

3. National governments responded during the 1990s by simplifying border procedures and other measures to reduce the costs of international trade and hence make their country an attractive participant in regional value chains (Pomfret and Sourdin, 2009). A striking feature of East Asian economic relations after 2000 is the proliferation of regional trading agreements, whose content has little to do with preferential tariff provisions as in classical customs unions or free trade areas and is more to do with reducing the costs of international trade (Pomfret, 2011).

4. There was variation, but even the country with the best economic policies, the Kyrgyz Republic, failed to create institutions appropriate to a well-functioning

market economy, and all five countries established autocratic political systems with power concentrated in the hands of an unaccountable president (Pomfret, 2006). By 2010 there were signs that the Central Asian countries' economic and political systems may be evolving, with sensible use of Kazakhstan's oil-based prosperity and with the Kyrgyz Republic's shift to a more parliamentary system with constraints on presidential power, but the situation in the region remains fluid.

5. The architect of India's reforms was Finance Minister Manmohan Singh, whose Oxford PhD thesis on India's export performance (published as Singh, 1964) was supervised by Ian Little—and influenced Little, Scitovsky, and Scott (1970). Singh became India's prime minister in 2004. The performance of the reformed Indian economy is analyzed in Panagariya (2008).

6. In 2011 the limits to this model, a variant on the resource curse, were exposed in the Arab world, where autocratic regimes were overthrown in Tunisia and Egypt and popular uprisings occurred in many of the Gulf states. Populism is a vague term, used in the text to capture the phenomenon of a charismatic leader ruling with a mixture of short-term policies benefiting the majority (e.g., low prices for essential goods) and force to dispel opposition; over time, with deteriorating economic performance, the latter is likely to become dominant. Regimes built on a narrow clique, whether defined by family (Saudi Arabia) or religion (Iran) or a shared occupational background (Russia), have many of the same characteristics.

7. Fernando Henrique Cardoso, who had been Finance Minister when the Brazilian economy was finally stabilized under the Plano Real in 1993–1994, served two terms as president (1995–2003). In Cardoso's second term there was mounting opposition to reform, and in the 2002 elections his party's candidate lost by a landslide to the Workers Party candidate Luiz Inácio Lula da Silva.

8. Hopkins (2009) reviews the debate over the "reversal of fortune" hypothesis that sub-Saharan Africa was relatively rich in 1500 and became relatively poor as a result of European imperialism—or of specific forms of imperialism such as the slave trades. The hypothesis is related to an older literature that saw imperialism as a process of underdeveloping the colonial world, but in the context of the twenty-first century it is necessary to explain the divergent postindependence histories of the world's ex-colonies.

9. Ironically, the international boundaries, together with the colonial language of administration, were to prove resilient. Federal units that may have been better partitioned before independence, such as Nigeria or Sudan, became if anything more centralized after independence. Attempts to consolidate individual colonies into larger units shortly before independence, such as British East

Africa (Kenya, Tanganyika, and Uganda) or Central Africa (Rhodesia and Nyasaland) did not survive, but proposals for a federal nation, as in Uganda, went nowhere.

10. The process had started earlier in North Africa with the independence of Morocco and Tunisia in 1956, and the transfer of power to Sudanese leaders and the Suez crisis in which Egypt gained control over the Suez Canal in the same year contributed to the atmosphere of rapid decolonization. Rhodesia unilaterally declared independence in 1965, but the regime was not recognized internationally until 1980 when elections with universal suffrage were held.

11. By 1970 Portugal deployed 40,000 troops in Guinea-Bissau, 50,000 in Angola, and 50,000 in Mozambique, a situation that contributed to an officer corps revolt in Portugal in April 1974, and amid regime change in Portugal the colonies became independent in 1974–1975.

12. Easterly and Levine (1997) blame ethnic fragmentation for Africa's tragedy, but political scientists and historians have found both measurement of ethnic diversity and causality problematic (e.g., Hopkins, 2009; Bates, 2008, 9–10). In my argument, competition among regions could be competition among ethnic groups, and indeed the two are often difficult to separate, but divisions may also be based on religion or economic interests.

13. The folly of repressing agriculture had been highlighted in the early 1960s by the French agronomist René Dumont (1962). Reliance on state marketing monopolies to squeeze farmers by paying well below world prices for their crops and to channel the profits to the urban elite was analyzed by Robert Bates (1981). In the same year, the influential Berg Report (World Bank, 1981) provided extensive evidence of the failure of interventionist economic policies and advocated market-oriented reforms. The reversal of these policies has, however, been sporadic.

14. The modern resource curse literature was initiated by Sachs and Warner (1995). Collier and Hoeffler (2004) claim that resource wealth was a trigger for civil wars in Africa, but their econometric results have been challenged by Fearon (2005). For an application to Nigeria, see Sala-i-Martin and Subramanian (2003).

15. African leaders maintained control over the ministry of planning, not from commitment to planning and even less from a belief in communism, but because these ministries administered foreign aid. The World Bank in particular became frustrated by the frequency with which aid funds lined the pockets of the wealthy rather than helping the poor, and after the 1981 Berg Report tried to direct assistance to social projects and to bundle assistance so that costs of noncompliance were higher, but attempts to impose governance conditions were resisted. Outside the common currency areas of francophone Africa, leaders also

kept control over the central bank, often maintaining offshore accounts only accessible by the leader, most blatantly in the case of Zaire's President Mobutu.

16. The African countries generally faced a solvency problem, not a liquidity problem. Thus, resolving the debts by a negotiation between debtor and creditors to share the burden of overambitious lending in the 1970s was not an option. The heavily indebted poor countries needed debt forgiveness, but the creditor countries were worried about the moral hazard implications, so Africa's debt crises remained unresolved, leaving countries with limited access to international financial markets other than through multilateral institutions (the World Bank, IMF, African Development Bank, and so forth).

17. The literature on institutions and growth draws on the work of Douglass North. Easterly and Levine (2001) and Rodrik, Subramanian, and Trebbi (2006) provide econometric support for the primacy of institutions, although their conclusions are disputed (e.g., by Dollar and Kraay, 2003).

18. Debates about the effectiveness of aid and its relationship to the recipient's policy environment were triggered by Burnside and Dollar (2000). Easterly (2001) argues that debt forgiveness and further loans to heavily indebted countries are a waste of resources because the countries' existing debt problems are a result of poor policies and unless there is a change in policies, and probably also in regime, further external aid will have no positive impact on economic performance.

9. From the Age of Equality to the Age of Fraternity

1. Not all market economies are associated with great individual liberties, but all planned economies and all fascist economies inevitably subordinate individuals to the state. The richest market economies are all democracies, and in the middle-income countries of South America and East Asia, the trend in the final decades of the twentieth century was clearly away from authoritarian rule.

2. More people were brought out of poverty in the late twentieth century than ever before; the World Bank estimates that 1,815 million people were living on less than $1.25 a day (purchasing power parity at 2005 prices) in 1990, but by 2005 this number had fallen to 1,341 million. The aggregate change can be ascribed entirely to China, where the number fell from 683 million to 208 million, while the number in poverty rose slightly in South Asia and substantially (from 295 million to 357 million) in sub-Saharan Africa. If we are concerned with nations rather than individuals, the picture is less rosy; the distribution of income across nations became more unequal in the second half of the twentieth century

as the majority of African countries fell further and further behind the rest of the world.

3. The premier of Germany's most populous state, Jürgen Rüttgers, in the early years of the twenty-first century ruled in a coalition between his right-wing CDU (Erhard's party) and the centrist FDP under an agreement calling for "freedom before equality" and "private before state," but he had also written a book entitled *The Market Economy Must Remain Social*.

4. For a summary of this literature and further references, see the opening footnote in Andersen and Aslaksen (2008).

5. There are many examples from the Third World of liberation leaders who started well, or at least with good intentions, but once they had set off on a wrong track they could not be removed. Julius Nyerere of Tanzania appears to have been well intentioned, but misguided economic policies ruined his country; after twenty-four years in power, he did retire voluntarily from the presidency in 1985. Fidel Castro of Cuba, after establishing a regime that satisfied basic needs, became a caricature of a communist dictator, but only stepped down for health reasons after almost fifty years in power. Robert Mugabe of Zimbabwe ended white supremacist rule but became a monster and after thirty years clung tenaciously to power despite evidence that the majority of Zimbabwe's citizens wanted change.

6. Vladimir Putin benefited from the positive consequences of Boris Yeltsin's economic reforms, as well as being president from 2000 to 2008 during the energy boom, which was a huge economic windfall to Russia. Although Putin respected the two-term limit on his presidency, he remained popular and powerful after 2008.

7. Reforms are not automatic. In poor countries with crony capitalism, democracy may produce a vicious circle of nonreform if voters support parties promising more regulation in order to restrict opportunities for enrichment or vote for politicians promising to expropriate the rich; Di Tella and MacCulloch (2009) model vicious circles antithetical to the emergence of a robust market economy. Those in power may channel anti-capitalist emotions into support for regulations that create or protect rents accruing to politically connected firms or other groups (Parente and Prescott, 2000; Djankov et al., 2002).

8. There is a wider potential for intergenerational conflict as the proportion of the population in full-time work shrinks, with the possibility that the workers will revolt against the share of their product being used to support the consumption of the old. Additionally, there is potential for intragenerational conflict, as public-sector workers have managed to commit the state to generous job-related pensions out of future government revenue (as a way for politicians to reduce the

current cost of providing public services), while private sector employees have to fend for themselves.

9. In mainland Africa, the continent where undemocratic regimes appear most prevalent, in 1991 Mathieu Kérékou of Benin became the first leader to accept defeat in a free election. In the following two decades nine other leaders accepted electoral defeat and another dozen retired because of term limits. Out of fifty-three countries this is not a great record, but the direction of change seems clear.

10. The GATT/WTO succeeded because countries accepted that trade liberalization was desirable in others and that it was a positive-sum game requiring coordinated action to discourage opportunistic behavior in circumstances where unilateral tariff increases might bring national benefits at the cost of other countries. By contrast, the IMF's mandate to coordinate fixed exchange rates was abandoned in the early 1970s because national governments valued monetary policy independence higher than exchange rate predictability. Since the 1970s the IMF has regained significance because it has proven useful to have a multilateral institution that can act as lender of last resort to nations with international liquidity problems, as technical manager of sovereign debt resolution negotiations, and as coordinator of debt forgiveness for highly indebted poor countries. Whether the IMF will further evolve into a global central bank when the world considers adopting a global currency is a more distant issue, requiring institutional reforms in order for there to be sufficient trust in the impartiality of the guardian of global monetary policy.

11. I ignore less controversial areas in which coordination is desirable in a global economy, such as standard-setting or compatible national regulations. The World Customs Organization (WCO) provides benefits from setting common standards of commodity classification and customs documentation, which reduce trade costs for all; with 177 customs administrations as members, covering 98 percent of world trade, the WCO clearly provides a useful function without threatening national interests. The Internet Corporation for Assigned Names and Numbers (ICANN) has effectively, although not always without controversy, managed Internet domain name assignments, evolving from a U.S. government creation in 1998 to a multistakeholder association. Some national regulations can become burdensome in a global economy. Laws requiring use of domestically registered ships penalized traders from high-income countries. During the second half of the twentieth century international shipping was increasingly carried out in boats flying flags of convenience (e.g., registered in Panama or Liberia). The absence of a global anti-trust policy is relatively unimportant given the scarcity of global monopolies apart from in the peculiar, but increasingly profitable, international sports industry, where global organizations such as the International

Olympic Committee or the Fédération Internationale de Football Association—
both of which have more members than the United Nations and nontransparent
budgets that exceed some countries' GDP—operate largely outside normal business rules.

12. Public goods are defined as nonexcludable (i.e., anybody can benefit
whether or not they contributed to the supply) and nonexhaustible (i.e., one person's consumption of a public good does not prevent others' consumption). Because of the incentive to free-ride, market mechanisms typically lead to underprovision of public goods or underprovision of actions to mitigate public "bads."
Valuation of public goods is difficult because respondents will understate their
value if they think they have to pay and overstate their value if somebody else is
expected to pay. Provision of global public goods will be especially difficult in the
absence of shared values, to which national or local governments may appeal
when deciding how much of a public good to provide.

13. The UN Law of the Sea Convention, concluded in 1982 and entering into
force in 1994, defines the rights and responsibilities of nations in their use of
the world's oceans, establishing guidelines for businesses, the environment, and
the management of marine natural resources. It replaced the vaguer concept of the
freedom of the seas and filled an obvious need for codification of acceptable
practices. However, it still took almost half a century from the opening of negotiations at the UN in 1956 until entry into force, and the treaty was not ratified by
some countries; the United States recognized the treaty as a codification of cus-
tomary law, but refused to ratify the treaty because the rules for exploitation of
the ocean bed were considered insufficiently market-friendly (although the
Obama administration announced in 2009 that ratification would be a priority).

14. Agreement on carbon emissions and climate change is much harder than
on substances damaging the ozone layer because the countries most harmed by
ozone depletion, i.e., high-income countries in temperate zones, were the main
users of ozone-damaging substances. The Montréal Protocol on Substances that
Deplete the Ozone Layer, which entered into force in 1989 and has been ratified
by all UN members, mandated elimination of use of chlorofluorocarbons (CFCs)
by 1996 and of the less active hydrochlorofluorocarbons by 2013, and also established a multilateral fund to help developing countries phase out the use of
ozone-depleting substances. A similar alignment of costs and benefits does not
apply to climate change, which will most damage poor tropical countries, whereas
abatement and its costs must largely be borne by temperate-zone rich countries.
Moreover, a reasonable technological fix was available in replacing CFCs by
other materials, whereas there is no similarly straightforward fix for carbon
emissions.

15. Pearson (2011) reviews the issues associated with measuring the costs and benefits of climate change and finding an effective international solution to the policy challenges. Even with agreement that global warming is a problem, there is uncertainty about the size of the benefits from abatement measures, about the time horizon before net benefits would accrue, and about the costs of delaying action. A partial agreement may be ineffective due to carbon leakage; carbon-emitting activities may relocate to places not covered by the agreement, and, to the extent that the countries which do take steps succeed in reducing emissions, the cost of extra emissions from nonsignatories will be reduced.

16. Bobbitt (2002) argues that after the long war of 1914–1990, the nation-state faces a terminal challenge from the "market state," which supplies an environment in which individuals operate as they choose, and that, if a state does not provide an attractive framework, individuals will emigrate.

17. Refusal to extradite a terrorist leader, Osama bin Laden, triggered the U.S.-led invasion of Afghanistan in 2001. The activities of pirates operating from ports in Somalia in 2008 led the world's naval powers to collaborate in protecting shipping regardless of whether the warships encroached into Somali territorial waters.

18. During the second half of the twentieth century, respect for national sovereignty was a basic tenet. The UN laid down conditions for settling interstate disputes, but did not interfere within states unless requested by the national government—a distinction highlighted at its most heartless when the UN High Commission for Refugees helps the victims of civil war who flee their country but must ignore those people displaced within the country.

19. The UN itself must evolve in the Age of Fraternity. Alternative fora for high-level meetings such as the G7 largest market economies or APEC in the late twentieth century and more recently the self-selected G20 provoke complaints from those countries who are excluded. The UN is a natural monopoly, but it must strike a balance between the one-country-one-vote principle of the General Assembly and the disparity in weight between the largest and smallest countries. The veto power of the five permanent members of the Security Council has archaic roots in the world of 1945 and demands reform, but at least with the United States and China both represented at the highest UN level the biggest clash between established and rising powers in the early twenty-first century has better opportunities for peaceful resolution than in 1914.

References

Abelshauser, Werner (1998). Germany: Guns, Butter, and Economic Miracles. In *The Economics of World War II: Six Great Powers in International Comparison*, ed. Mark Harrison (Cambridge University Press, Cambridge, UK), 122–176.

Abramovitz, Moses (1986). Catching Up, Forging Ahead and Falling Behind, *Journal of Economic History 46*, 385–406.

Aghion, Philippe, and Peter Howitt (1998). *Endogenous Growth Theory* (MIT Press, Cambridge, MA).

Ahmed, Shaghil, Andrew Levin, and Beth Anne Wilson (2004). Recent US Macroeconomic Stability: Good Luck, Good Policies, or Good Practices? *Review of Economics and Statistics 86(3)*, 824–832.

Allen, Douglas (1991). What Are Transaction Costs? *Research in Law and Economics 14*, 1–18.

Allen, Robert (2001). The Great Divergence in European Wages and Prices from the Middle Ages to the First World War, *Explorations in Economic History 38*, 411–447.

Allen, Robert (2003). *Farm to Factory: A Reinterpretation of the Soviet Industrial Revolution* (Princeton University Press, Princeton, NJ).

Almond, Douglas (2006). Is the 1918 Pandemic Over? Long-Term Effects of In Utero Exposure in the Post-1940 U.S. Population, *Journal of Political Economy 114(4)*, 672–712.

Alston, Lee, and Joseph Ferrie (1993). Paternalism in Agricultural Labor Contracts in the U.S. South: Implications for the Growth of the Welfare State, *American Economic Review 83*, 852–876.

Amsden, Alice (1989). *Asia's Next Giant: South Korea and Late Industrialization* (Oxford University Press, New York).

Andersen, Jørgen Juel, and Silje Aslaksen (2008). Constitutions and the Resource Curse, *Journal of Development Economics 87*, 227–246.

Andolfatto, David, and Paul Gomme (2003). Monetary Policy Regimes and Beliefs, *International Economic Review 44(1)*, 1–30.

Arrow, Kenneth (1962). The Economic Implications of Learning by Doing, *Review of Economic Studies 29*, 155–173.

Åslund, Anders (2007). *How Capitalism Was Built: The Transformation of Central and Eastern Europe, Russia, and Central Asia* (Cambridge University Press, New York).

Atkinson, Anthony, and John Micklewright (1992). *Economic Transformation in Eastern Europe and the Distribution of Income* (Cambridge University Press, Cambridge, UK).

Atkinson, Anthony, Thomas Piketty, and Emmanuel Saez (2011). Top Incomes in the Long Run of History, *Journal of Economic Literature 49(1)*, 3–71.

Baker, Michael, and Dwayne Benjamin (1999). How Do Retirement Tests Affect the Labour Supply of Older Men? *Journal of Public Economics 72*, 27–51.

Barrett, Scott (2007). *Why Cooperate? The Incentive to Supply Global Public Goods* (Oxford University Press, Oxford, UK).

Barro, Robert, and Xavier Sala-i-Martin (1995). *Economic Growth* (McGraw Hill, New York).

Barry, John (2005). 1918 Revisited: Lessons and Suggestions for Further Inquiry. In *The Threat of Pandemic Influenza: Are We Ready?*, ed. Stacey Knobler, Alison Mack, Adel Mahmoud, and Stanley Lemon (National Academies Press, Washington, DC), 58–68.

Bates, Robert (1981). *Markets and States in Tropical Africa: The Political Basis of Agricultural Policy* (University of California Press, Berkeley).

Bates, Robert (2008). *When Things Fell Apart: State Failure in Late-Century Africa* (Cambridge University Press, New York).

Baumol, William, Robert Litan, and Carl Schramm (2007). *Good Capitalism, Bad Capitalism, and the Economics of Growth and Prosperity* (Yale University Press, New Haven, CT).

Benitez-Silva, Hugo, and Frank Heiland (2007). The Social Security Earnings Test and Work Incentives, *Journal of Policy Analysis and Management 26(3)*, 527–555.

Bernhofen, Daniel, and John Brown (2005). An Empirical Assessment of the Comparative Advantage Gains from Trade: Evidence from Japan, *American Economic Review 95(1)*, 208–225.

Beveridge, William (1942). *Social Insurance and Allied Services* (also known as the Beveridge Report) (His Majesty's Stationery Office, London).

Bhagwati, Jagdish (1966). *The Economics of Underdeveloped Countries* (McGraw-Hill, New York).

Bobbitt, Philip (2002). *The Shield of Achilles: War, Peace and the Course of History* (Penguin, London).

Bordo, Michael (1999). *The Gold Standard and Related Regimes* (Cambridge University Press, Cambridge, UK).

Bordo, Michael, and Hugh Rockoff (1996). The Gold Standard as a Good Housekeeping Seal of Approval, *Journal of Economic History 56*, 389–428.

Boycko, Maxim, Andrei Shleifer, and Robert Vishny (1995). *Privatizing Russia* (MIT Press, Cambridge, MA).

Bradford, Colin, and Johannes F. Linn (2009). Is the G-20 Summit a Step toward a New Global Economic Order? *Brookings Policy Brief Series 170*, September (available at http://www.brookings.edu/papers/2009/09_g20_bradford_linn.aspx) (accessed 21 April 2011).

Broadberry, Stephen, and Mark Harrison (2005). *The Economics of World War I* (Cambridge University Press, Cambridge, UK).

Broadberry, Stephen, and Kevin O'Rourke, eds. (2010). *The Cambridge Economic History of Modern Europe*, vol. 2, *1870 to the Present* (Cambridge University Press, Cambridge, UK).

Brown, E. Cary (1956). Fiscal Policy in the Thirties: A Reappraisal, *American Economic Review 46*, 857–879.

Bruno, Michael, and William Easterly (1998). Inflation Crises and Long-Run Growth, *Journal of Monetary Economics 41(1)*, 3–26.

Brunt, Liam (2006). Rediscovering Risk: Country Banks as Venture Capital Firms in the First Industrial Revolution, *Journal of Economic History 66(1)*, 74–102.

Bullock, Alan (1991). *Hitler and Stalin: Parallel Lives* (Knopf, New York).

Burnside, Craig, and David Dollar (2000). Aid, Policies, and Growth, *American Economic Review 90(4)*, 847–868.

Calvo-Gonzalez, Oscar (2007). American Military Interests and Economic Confidence in Spain under the Franco Dictatorship, *Journal of Economic History 67(3)*, 740–767.

Capgemini (2010). *World Wealth Report 2010* (available at http://www.capgemini.com/services-and-solutions/by-industry/financial-services/solutions/wealth/worldwealthreport/) (accessed 23 April 2011).

Caprio, Gerard, and Daniela Klingebiel (1997). Bank Insolvencies: Cross-Country Experience, *World Bank Annual Conference on Development Economics 1996* (World Bank, Washington, DC), 1–26.

Cerra, Valerie, and Sweta Chaman Saxena (2008). Growth Dynamics: The Myth of Economic Recovery, *American Economic Review 98(1)*, 439–457.

Christoffersen, Peter, and Peter Doyle (1998). From Inflation to Growth: Eight Years of Transition, *IMF Working Paper WP/98/100*, July (International Monetary Fund, Washington, DC).

Clarida, Richard, Jordi Gali, and Mark Gertler (2000). Monetary Policy Rules and Macroeconomic Stability: Evidence and Some Theory, *Quarterly Journal of Economics 115(1)*, 147–180.

Cline, William (1982). Can the East Asian Model of Development Be Generalized? *World Development 10*, 81–90.

Cline, William (1995). *International Debt Reexamined* (Institute for International Economics, Washington, DC).

Cohn, Raymond (1992). Fiscal Policy in Germany during the Great Depression, *Explorations in Economic History 29*, 318–342.

Collier, Paul, and Anke Hoeffler (2004). Greed and Grievance in Civil Wars, *Oxford Economic Papers 56(4)*, 53–95.

Cook, David (2002). World War II and Convergence, *Review of Economics and Statistics 84(1)*, 131–138.

Crafts, Nicholas (1995). The Golden Age of Economic Growth in Western Europe, 1950–73, *Economic History Review 48(3)*, 429–447.

Crafts, Nicholas, and Nick Woodward, eds. (1991). *The British Economy since 1945* (Clarendon Press, Oxford).

Credit Suisse (2010). *Global Wealth Report 2010*. Prepared by James Davies and Andrew Shorrocks, principal contributors to Davies (2008) (available at https://

emagazine.credit-suisse.com/app/shop/index.cfm?fuseaction=OpenShopDetail &aoid=291481&lang=EN) (accessed April 2011).

Curry, Timothy, and Lynn Shibut (2000). The Cost of the Savings and Loan Crisis: Truth and Consequences, *FDIC Banking Review 13(2)*, 26–35.

Davies, James, ed. (2008). *Personal Wealth from a Global Perspective* (Oxford University Press, for UNU-WIDER, Oxford, UK).

Davies, Robert (1998). *Soviet Economic Development from Lenin to Khrushchev* (Cambridge University Press, Cambridge, UK).

Davies, Robert, Mark Harrison, and Stephen Wheatcroft (1994). *The Economic Transformation of the Soviet Union, 1913–1945* (Cambridge University Press, Cambridge, UK).

Denton, Geoffrey, Murray Forsyth, and Malcolm MacLennan (1968). *Economic Planning and Polices in Britain, France, and Germany* (Allen and Unwin, London).

Disney, Richard, and Sarah Smith (2002). The Labour Supply Effect of the Abolition of the Earnings Rule for Older Workers in the United Kingdom, *Economic Journal 112*, C136–C152.

Di Tella, Raphael, and Robert MacCulloch (2009). Why Doesn't Capitalism Flow to Poor Countries? *Brookings Papers on Economic Activity 2009.1*, 285–321.

Djankov, Simeon, Rafael La Porta, Florencio Lopez-de-Silanes, and Andrei Shleifer (2002). The Regulation of Entry, *Quarterly Journal of Economics 117(1)*, 1–37.

Dobb, Maurice (1960). *Soviet Economic Development since 1917.* (Routledge & Kegan Paul, London). (Orig. pub. 1948.)

Dollar, David, and Aart Kraay (2003). Institutions, Trade, and Growth, *Journal of Monetary Economics 50(1)*, 133–162.

Domar, Evsey (1957). *Essays in the Theory of Economic Growth* (Oxford University Press, New York).

Dumont, René (1962). *L'Afrique noire est mal partie* (Editions du Seuil, Paris). English translation (1996). *False Start in Africa* (Deutsch, London).

Dyck, Alexander (1997). Privatization in Eastern Germany: Management Selection and Economic Transition, *American Economic Review 87*, 565–597.

Easterly, William (2001). *The Elusive Quest for Growth: Economists' Adventures and Misadventures in the Tropics* (MIT Press, Cambridge, MA).

Easterly, William, and Ross Levine (1997). Africa's Growth Tragedy: Policies and Ethnic Divisions, *Quarterly Journal of Economics 112(4),* 1203–1250.

Easterly, William, and Ross Levine (2001). It's Not Factor Accumulation: Stylized Facts and Growth Models, *World Bank Economic Review 15(2),* 177–219.

Edelman, Robert (1993). *Serious Fun: A History of Spectator Sports in the USSR* (Oxford University Press, New York).

Eggertsson, Gauti (2008). Great Expectations and the End of the Depression, *American Economic Review 98(4),* 1476–1516.

Eichengreen, Barry (1992). *Golden Fetters: The Gold Standard and the Great Depression* (Oxford University Press, New York).

Eichengreen, Barry (2007). *The European Economy since 1945: Coordinated Capitalism and Beyond* (Princeton University Press, Princeton, NJ).

Eichengreen, Barry, and Michael Bordo (2002). Crises Now and Then: What Lessons from the Last Era of Financial Globalization, *NBER Working Paper 8716* (National Bureau of Economic Research, Cambridge, MA).

Ericson, Richard (1991). The Classical Soviet-Type Economy: Nature of the System and Implications for Reform, *Journal of Economic Perspectives 5(4),* 11–27.

Erlich, Alexander (1960). *The Soviet Industrialization Debate* (Harvard University Press, Cambridge, MA).

Fearon, J. D. (2005). Primary Commodities Exports and Civil War, *Journal of Conflict Resolution 49(4),* 483–507.

Feinstein, Charles (1998). Pessimism Perpetuated: Real Wages and the Standard of Living in Britain during and after the Industrial Revolution, *Journal of Economic History 58,* 625–658.

Ferguson, Niall (1998). *The Pity of War: Explaining World War One* (Allen Lane / Penguin, London).

Findlay, Ronald, and Kevin O'Rourke (2007). *Power and Plenty: Trade, War, and the World Economy in the Second Millennium* (Princeton University Press, Princeton, NJ).

Fischer, Stanley (1992). Russia and the Soviet Union Then and Now, *NBER Working Paper 4077* (National Bureau of Economic Research, Cambridge, MA).

Flandreau, Marc (2004). *The Glitter of Gold: France, Bimetallism, and the Emergence of the International Gold Standard, 1848–1873* (Oxford University Press, Oxford, UK).

Flandreau, Marc, and Frédéric Zumer (2004). *The Making of Global Finance, 1880–1913* (OECD Development Centre, Paris).

Flynn, Dennis, and Arturo Giráldez (2004). Path Dependence, Time Lags, and the Birth of Globalisation: A Critique of O'Rourke and Williamson, *European Review of Economic History 8,* 81–108.

Fogli, Alessandra, and Fabrizio Perri (2006). The "Great Moderation" and the US External Imbalance, *NBER Working Paper 12708* (National Bureau of Economic Research, Cambridge, MA).

Ford, Henry, and Samuel Crowther (1922). *My Life and Work* (Garden City Publishing Company, Garden City, NY).

Foreman-Peck, James (1983). *A History of the World Economy: International Economic Relations since 1850* (Wheatsheaf Books, Hemel Hempstead, UK).

Frank, Robert (2007). *Richistan: A Journey through the American Wealth Boom and the Lives of the New Rich* (Crown Publishers / Random House, New York).

French, Eric (2005). The Effects of Health, Wealth, and Wages on Labour Supply and Retirement Behaviour, *Review of Economic Studies 72,* 395–427.

Frieden, Jeffrey (2007). *Global Capitalism: Its Fall and Rise in the Twentieth Century* (Norton, New York).

Friedman, Milton (1968). The Role of Monetary Policy, *American Economic Review, 58(1),* 1–17.

Friedman, Milton, and Anna Schwartz (1963). *A Monetary History of the United States, 1867–1960* (Princeton University Press, for the National Bureau of Economic Research, Princeton, NJ).

Fry, Maxwell (1988). *Money, Interest, and Banking in Economic Development* (Johns Hopkins University Press, Baltimore, MD).

Fukuyama, Francis (1989). The End of History? *The National Interest 16,* 3–18.

Fukuyama, Francis (1992). *The End of History and the Last Man* (Penguin, London).

Galí, Jordi, and Luca Gambetti (2009). On the Sources of the Great Moderation, *American Economic Journal Macroeconomics 1(1),* 26–57.

Gerschenkron, Alexander (1943). *Bread and Democracy in Germany* (University of California Press, Berkeley and Los Angeles).

Gerschenkron, Alexander (1962). *Economic Backwardness in Historical Perspective: A Book of Essays* (Belknap Press of Harvard University Press, Cambridge, MA).

Gordon, Robert (1990). *The Measurement of Durable Goods Prices* (University of Chicago Press, Chicago).

Gregory, Paul (1994). *Before Command: An Economic History of Russia from Emancipation to the First Five-Year Plan* (Princeton University Press, Princeton, NJ).

Gruber, Jonathan, and David Wise (2005). Social Security Programs and Retirement around the World: Introduction and Summary, *NBER Working Paper 11290* (National Bureau of Economic Research, Cambridge, MA).

Harris, John, and Michael Todaro (1970). Migration, Unemployment and Development: A Two-Sector Analysis, *American Economic Review 60(1),* 126–142.

Harrison, Mark (1998). *The Economics of World War II: Six Great Powers in International Comparison* (Cambridge University Press, Cambridge, UK).

Harrod, Roy (1948). *Towards a Dynamic Economics* (Macmillan, London).

Helleiner, Eric (2010). A Bretton Woods Moment? The 2007–2008 Crisis and the Future of Global Finance, *International Affairs 86(3),* 619–636.

Higgins, Matthew, and Jeffrey Williamson (1996). Asian Demography and Foreign Capital Dependence, *NBER Working Paper 5560* (National Bureau of Economic Research, Cambridge, MA).

Hochschild, Adam (1998). *King Leopold's Ghost* (Pan Macmillan, London).

Hopkins, A. G. (2009). The New Economic History of Africa, *Journal of African History 50(2),* 155–177.

Huff, Gregg, and Giovanni Caggiano (2007). Globalization, Immigration, and Lewisian Elastic Labor in Pre–World War II Southeast Asia, *Journal of Economic History 67(1),* 33–68.

Hummels, David (2007). Transport Costs and International Trade in the Second Era of Globalization, *Journal of Economic Perspectives 21,* 131–154.

Hummels, David (2009). Globalization and Freight Transport Costs in Maritime Shipping and Aviation, *OECD International Transport Forum Papers 3* (Organisation for Economic Co-operation and Development, Paris).

IMF, World Bank, EBRD, and OECD (1991). *A Study of the Soviet Economy*, 2 vols. (International Monetary Fund, Washington, DC).

Irwin, Douglas, and Randall Kroszner (1996). Log-Rolling and Economic Interests in the Passage of the Smoot-Hawley Tariff, *Carnegie-Rochester Series on Public Policy 45*, 173–200.

Johnson, Chalmers (1982). *MITI and the Japanese Miracle: The Growth of Industrial Policy, 1925–1975* (Stanford University Press, Stanford, CA).

Jones, Joseph (1934). *Tariff Retaliation: Repercussions of the Hawley-Smoot Bill* (Philadelphia, University of Pennsylvania Press).

Judt, Tony (2005). *Postwar: A History of Europe since 1945* (William Heinemann, London).

Kabongo, Ilunga (1988). The Catastrophe of Belgian Decolonization. In *Decolonization and African Independence: The Transfers of Power 1960–1980*, ed. Prosser Gifford and Roger Louis (Yale University Press, New Haven, CT), 381–400.

Kagan, Robert (2008). *The Return of History and the End of Dreams* (Knopf, New York).

Kahn, James, Margaret McConnell, and Gabriel Perez-Quiros (2002). On the Causes of the Increased Stability of the U.S. Economy, *Federal Reserve Bank of New York Economic Policy Review 8(1)*, 183–202.

Kastl, Jakub, and Lyndon Moore (2010). Wily Welfare Capitalist: Werner von Siemens and the Pension Plan, *Cliometrica 4(3)*, 321–348.

Kenwood, Albert G., and Alan Lougheed (1999). *The Growth of the International Economy, 1820–1990*, 4th ed. (Routledge, London).

Keynes, John Maynard (1919). *The Economic Consequences of the Peace* (Macmillan, London).

Khoudour-Castéras, David (2008). Welfare State and Labor Mobility: The Impact of Bismarck's Social Legislation on German Emigration before World War I, *Journal of Economic History 68(1)*, 211–243.

Kim, C. J., and C. Nelson (1999). Has the US Economy Become More Stable? *Review of Economics and Statistics 81(4)*, 608–616.

Kim, Duol, and Ki-Joo Park (2008). Colonialism and Industrialisation: Factory Labour Productivity of Colonial Korea, 1913–37, *Australian Economic History Review 48(1)*, 26–46.

Kindleberger, Charles (1951). Group Behavior and International Trade, *Journal of Political Economy 59*, 30–47.

Kindleberger, Charles (1975). The Rise of Free Trade in Western Europe, 1820–1875, *Journal of Economic History 35(1)*, 20–55.

Kindleberger, Charles (1986). *The World in Depression, 1929–1939*, revised and enlarged ed. (University of California Press, Berkeley, CA).

Kindleberger, Charles (2000). *Manias, Panics, and Crashes: A History of Financial Crises*, 4th ed. (John Wiley & Sons, New York).

Kinsella, Kevin (1992). Changes in Life Expectancy 1900–1990, *American Journal of Clinical Nutrition 55*, 1196S–1202S.

Kondratieff, Nikolai (1935). The Long Waves in Economic Life, *Review of Economics and Statistics 17(6)*, 105–115..

Kornai, Janos (1992). *The Socialist System: The Political Economy of Communism* (Princeton University Press, Princeton, NJ).

Krugman, Paul (1994). The Myth of Asia's Miracle, *Foreign Affairs 73*, November/December, 62–78.

Kydland, Finn, and Edward Prescott (1977). Rules Rather Than Discretion: The Inconsistency of Optimal Plans, *Journal of Political Economy 85*, 473–491.

Laeven, Luc, and Fabian Valencia (2008). Systemic Banking Crises: A New Database, *IMF Working Paper WP/08/224*, November (International Monetary Fund, Washington, DC).

Larina, Anna (1993). *This I Cannot Forget: The Memoirs of Nikolai Bukharin's Widow* (Norton, New York). Translation from the Russian version serialized in 1988 and published as a book in 1989.

Leibenstein, Harvey (1957). *Economic Backwardness and Economic Growth* (Wiley, New York).

Levinson, Mark (2006). *The Box: How the Shipping Container Made the World Smaller and the World Economy Bigger* (Princeton University Press, Princeton, NJ).

Lew, Byron, and Bruce Cater (2006). The Telegraph, Co-ordination of Tramp Shipping, and Growth in World Trade, 1870–1910, *European Review of Economic History 10,* 147–173.

Lewis, W. Arthur (1954). Economic Development with Unlimited Supplies of Labour, *Manchester School of Economic and Social Studies 22,* 139–191.

Lewis, W. Arthur (1955). *The Theory of Economic Growth* (Allen and Unwin, London).

Lewis, W. Arthur (1978). *The Evolution of the International Economic Order* (Princeton University Press, Princeton, NJ).

Lindert, Peter (2000). Three Centuries of Inequality in Britain and America. In *Handbook of Income Distribution,* vol. 1, ed. A. B. Atkinson and Francois Bourguignon (Elsevier Science, Amsterdam), 167–216.

Lindert, Peter (2004). *Growing Public: Social Spending and Economic Growth since the Eighteenth Century* (Cambridge University Press, Cambridge, UK).

Lindert, Peter (2006). What Is Happening to the Welfare State? In *The Global Economy in the 1990s: A Long-Run Perspective,* ed. Paul Rhode and Gianni Tonniolo (Cambridge University Press, Cambridge, UK), 234–262.

Lindsay, Craig (2003). A Century of Labour Market Change, *Labour Market Trends,* March, 133–144 (available at http://www.statistics.gov.uk/articles/labour_market_trends/century_labour_market_change_mar2003.pdf) (accessed 23 April 2011).

Little, Ian, and James Mirrlees (1969). *Manual of Industrial Analysis in Developing Countries,* vol. 2, *Social Cost Benefit Analysis* (Organisation for Economic Co-operation and Development, Paris).

Little, Ian, Tibor Scitovsky, and Maurice Scott (1970). *Industry and Trade in Some Developing Countries* (Oxford University Press, New York).

López-Córdova, J. Ernesto, and Christopher Meissner (2003). Exchange-Rate Regimes and International Trade: Evidence from the Classical Gold Standard Era, *American Economic Review 93(1),* 344–353.

Lucas, Robert (1988). On the Mechanics of Economic Development, *Journal of Monetary Economics 22,* 3–42.

Lucas, Robert (1993). Making a Miracle, *Econometrica 61(2)*, 251–272.

Lucas, Robert (2009). Trade and the Diffusion of the Industrial Revolution, *American Economic Journal: Macroeconomics 1(1)*, 1–25.

Maddison, Angus (1995). *Monitoring the World Economy, 1820–1992* (Organisation for Economic Co-operation and Development, Paris).

Maddison, Angus (2006). *The World Economy* (Organisation for Economic Co-operation and Development, Paris). Previously published by the OECD in two parts: vol. 1, *A Millennial Perspective* (2001), and vol. 2, *Historical Statistics* (2003).

Malthus, Thomas (1798). *An Essay on the Principle of Population* (J. Johnson, London).

Mankiw, Greg, David Romer, and David Weil (1992). A Contribution to the Empirics of Economic Growth, *Quarterly Journal of Economics 107*, 407–437.

Marshall, Alfred (1890). *Principles of Economics* (Macmillan, London).

Marx, Karl, and Friedrich Engels (1848). *Communist Manifesto* (London). (Orig. pub. in German as *Manifest der Kommunistischen Partei*.)

Mason, Timothy (1977). *Sozialpolitik im Dritten Reich. Arbeiterklasse und Volksgemeinschaft* (Westdeutscher Verlag, Wiesbaden). English translation (1993). *Social Policy in the Third Reich: The Working Class and the "National Community"* (Berg Publishers, Providence, RI).

Maurel, Mathilde, and Gunther Schnabl (2011). Keynesian and Austrian Perspectives on Crisis, Shock Adjustment, Exchange Rate Regime, and (Long-Term) Growth, *Working Papers on Global Financial Markets No.18*, Universities of Jena and Halle (available at http://www.gfinm.de/images/stories/workingpaper18 .pdf) (accessed 23 April 2011).

Mazower, Mark (1998). *Dark Continent: Europe's Twentieth Century* (Allen Lane, Penguin Press, London).

Mazower, Mark (2009). *No Enchanted Place: The End of Empire and the Ideological Origins of the United Nations* (Princeton University Press, Princeton, NJ).

McDonald, Judith, Anthony Patrick O'Brien, and Colleen Callahan (1997). Trade Wars: Canada's Reaction to the Smoot-Hawley Tariff, *Journal of Economic History 57(4)*, 802–826.

McKinnon, Ronald (1973). *Money and Capital in Economic Development* (The Brookings Institution, Washington, DC).

Meissner, Christopher (2002). A New World Order: Explaining the Emergence of the Classical Gold Standard, *NBER Working Paper 9233* (National Bureau of Economic Research, Cambridge, MA). Rev. version pub. in *Journal of International Economics 66(2)*, July 2005, 385–406.

Meltzer, Alan (1976). Monetary and Other Explanations of the Start of the Great Depression, *Journal of Monetary Economics 2*, 455–471.

Mikesell, Raymond (1994). The Bretton Woods Debates: A Memoir, *Essays in International Finance No. 192*, Princeton University Department of Economics, International Finance Section.

Mill, John Stuart (1859). *On Liberty* (John W. Parker and Son, London).

Millward, Robert, and Joerg Baten (2010). Population and Living Standards, 1914–1945. In *The Cambridge Economic History of Modern Europe*, vol. 2, *1870 to the Present*, ed. Stephen Broadberry and Kevin O'Rourke (Cambridge University Press, Cambridge, UK), 232–263.

Mingay, G. E. (1986). *The Transformation of Britain, 1830–1939* (Routledge and Kegan Paul, London).

Mitchell, B. R. (1983). *International Historical Statistics: The Americas and Australasia* (Macmillan, London).

Mitchell, B. R. (1992). *International Historical Statistics: Europe, 1750–1988*, 3rd ed. (Macmillan, Basingstoke).

Mitchener, Kris, and Marc Weidenmier (2008). Trade and Empire, *Economic Journal 118*, 1805–1834.

Mokyr, Joel (2002). *The Gifts of Athena* (Princeton University Press, Princeton, NJ).

Mokyr, Joel (2010). *The Enlightened Economy: An Economic History of Britain, 1700–1850* (Yale University Press, New Haven, CT).

Mouré, Kenneth (1991). *Managing the Franc Poincaré: Economic Understanding and Political Constraint in French Monetary Policy, 1928–1936* (Cambridge University Press, Cambridge, UK).

Mundell, Robert (2000). A Reconsideration of the Twentieth Century, *American Economic Review 90(3)*, 327–340.

Myrdal, Gunnar (1957). *Economic Theory and Underdeveloped Regions* (Duckworth, London).

Myrdal, Gunnar (1968). *Asian Drama: An Inquiry into the Poverty of Nations* (Pantheon Books, New York).

Naughton, Barry (1995). *Growing Out of the Plan: Chinese Economic Reform, 1978–1993* (Cambridge University Press, New York).

Naughton, Barry (2007). *The Chinese Economy: Transitions and Growth* (MIT Press, Cambridge, MA).

Nelson, Richard (1956). A Theory of the Low-level Equilibrium Trap, *American Economic Review 46*, 894–908.

Nordhaus, William (2004). Retrospective on the 1970s Productivity Slowdown, *NBER Working Paper 10950* (National Bureau of Economic Research, Cambridge, MA).

North, Douglass C. (1990). A Transactions Cost Theory of Politics, *Journal of Theoretical Politics 2(4)*, 355–367.

Nove, Alec (1972). *An Economic History of the USSR* (Penguin, Harmondsworth, UK). (Rev. ed. 1982; final ed. 1992.)

Nurkse, Ragnar (1953). *Problems of Capital Formation in Underdeveloped Countries* (Basil Blackwell, Oxford).

OECD (1979). *The Impact of the Newly Industrializing Countries on Production and Trade in Manufactures* (Organisation for Economic Co-operation and Development, Paris).

Ofer, Gur (1987). Soviet Economic Growth: 1928–1985, *Journal of Economic Literature 25(4)*, 1767–1833.

Ohlin, Bertil (1929). The Reparations Problem—A Discussion: I—Transfer Difficulties, Real and Imagined, *Economic Journal 39*, June, 172–82; II—Mr. Keynes' Views on the Transfer Problem—A Rejoinder, *Economic Journal 39*, September, 400–404.

O'Rourke, Kevin, and Jeffrey Williamson (2002a). When Did Globalisation Begin? *European Review of Economic History 6*, 23–50.

O'Rourke, Kevin, and Jeffrey Williamson (2002b). After Columbus: Explaining Europe's Overseas Trade Boom, *Journal of Economic History 62*, 417–456.

Overy, Richard (1982). *The Nazi Economic Recovery, 1932–1938* (Macmillan, London).

Panagariya, Arvind (2008). *India: The Emerging Giant* (Oxford University Press, New York).

Papola, John, and Russ Roberts (2010). *Fear the Boom and Bust: A Hayek vs. Keynes Rap Anthem* (available at http://www.youtube.com/user/EconStories) (accessed 1 February 2011).

Parente, Stephen, and Edward Prescott (2000). *Barriers to Riches* (MIT Press, Cambridge, MA).

Peacock, Alan, and Jack Wiseman (1967). *The Growth of Public Expenditure in the United Kingdom* (Allen and Unwin, London).

Pearson, Charles (2011). *Atmospheric Economics: A Global Warming Primer* (Cambridge University Press, Cambridge, UK).

Perkins, Dwight, and Thomas Rawski (2008). Forecasting China's Economic Growth to 2025. In *China's Great Economic Transformation,* ed. Loren Brandt and Thomas Rawski (Cambridge University Press, Cambridge UK), 829–886.

Phillips, A. W. H. (1958). The Relationship between Unemployment and the Rate of Change of Money Wage Rates in the United Kingdom, 1861–1957, *Economica 25,* 283–299.

Piketty, Thomas, and Emmanuel Saez (2007). How Progressive Is the U.S. Federal Tax System? A Historical and International Perspective, *Journal of Economic Perspectives 21,* 3–24.

Pomfret, Richard (1991). *Investing in China, 1979–89: Ten Years of the Open Door Policy* (Harvester Wheatsheaf, Hemel Hempstead, UK, and Iowa State University Press, Ames).

Pomfret, Richard (1997). *Development Economics* (Prentice Hall, Hemel Hempstead, UK).

Pomfret, Richard (2000). Agrarian Reform in Uzbekistan: Why Has the Chinese Model Failed to Deliver? *Economic Development and Cultural Change 48(2),* 269–284.

Pomfret, Richard (2001). *The Economics of Regional Trading Arrangements,* rev. ed. (Oxford University Press, Oxford, UK).

Pomfret, Richard (2002). *Constructing a Market Economy: Diverse Paths from Central Planning in Asia and Europe* (Edward Elgar, Cheltenham, UK).

Pomfret, Richard (2006). *The Central Asian Economies since Independence* (Princeton University Press, Princeton, NJ).

Pomfret, Richard (2010). The Financial Sector and the Future of Capitalism, *Economic Systems 34(1)*, 22–37.

Pomfret, Richard (2011). *Regionalism in East Asia: Why Has It Flourished since 2000 and How Far Will It Go?* (World Scientific Publishing Company, Singapore).

Pomfret, Richard, and Patricia Sourdin (2009). Have Asian Trade Agreements Reduced Trade Costs? *Journal of Asian Economics 20*, 255–268.

Pritchett, Lant (1997). Divergence, Big Time, *Journal of Economic Perspectives 11(3)*, 3–17.

Quadagno, Jill (1984). Welfare Capitalism and the Social Security Act of 1935, *American Sociological Review 49*, 632—647.

Ramey, Valerie, and Neville Francis (2009). A Century of Work and Leisure, *American Economic Journal: Macroeconomics, 1(2)*, 189–224.

Ranciere, Romain, Aaron Tornell, and Frank Westermann (2008). Systemic Crises and Growth, *Quarterly Journal of Economics 123(1)*, 359–406.

Reinhart, Carmen, and Kenneth Rogoff (2009). *This Time Is Different: Eight Centuries of Financial Folly* (Princeton University Press, Princeton, NJ).

Ricardo, David (1817). *On the Principles of Political Economy and Taxation* (John Murray, London).

Riedel, James (1988). Economic Development in East Asia: Doing What Comes Naturally? In *Achieving Industrialization in East Asia,* ed. Helen Hughes (Cambridge University Press, Sydney), 1–38.

Robinson, Joan (1979). *Aspects of Development and Underdevelopment* (Cambridge University Press, Cambridge, UK).

Rodrik, Dani, Arvind Subramanian, and Francesco Trebbi (2006). Institutions Rule: The Primacy of Institutions over Geography and Integration in Economic Development, *Journal of Economic Growth 9(2)*, 131–165.

Roland, Gérard (2000). *Transition and Economics: Politics, Markets, and Firms* (MIT Press, Cambridge, MA).

Romer, Paul (1986). Increasing Returns and Long-Run Growth, *Journal of Political Economy 94*, 1002–1037.

Romer, Paul (1994). New Goods, Old Theory, and the Welfare Costs of Trade Restrictions, *Journal of Development Economics 43(1)*, 5–38.

Rosenstein-Rodan, Paul (1943). Problems of Industrialization of Eastern and South-Eastern Europe, *Economic Journal 53*, 202–211.

Rostow, Walt (1960). *The Stages of Economic Growth* (Cambridge University Press, Cambridge, UK).

Rothkopf, David (2008). *Superclass: The Global Power Elite and the World They Are Making* (Farrar Straus and Giroux, New York).

Sachs, Jeffrey, and Andrew Warner (1995). Natural Resource Abundance and Economic Growth, *NBER Working Paper 5398* (National Bureau of Economic Research, Cambridge, MA).

Saint-Paul, Gilles (2004). Why Are European Countries Diverging in Their Unemployment Experience? *Journal of Economic Perspectives 18(4)*, 49–68.

Sala-i-Martin, Xavier, and Arvind Subramanian (2003). Addressing the Natural Resource Curse: An Illustration from Nigeria, *NBER Working Paper 9804* (National Bureau of Economic Research, Cambridge, MA).

Samuelson, Paul (1947). *Foundations of Economic Analysis* (Harvard University Press, Cambridge, MA).

Schattschneider, Elmer Eric (1935). *Politics, Pressures, and the Tariff: A Study of Free Private Enterprise in Pressure Politics, as Shown in the 1929–1930 Revision of the Tariff* (Prentice-Hall, New York).

Schuker, Stephen (1976). *The End of French Predominance in Europe: The Financial Crisis of 1924 and the Adoption of the Dawes Plan* (University of North Carolina Press, Chapel Hill, NC).

Schumpeter, Joseph (1911). *Theorie der Wirtschaftlichen Enwicklung* (Duncker & Humblot, Leipzig). English translation (1934). *The Theory of Economic Development* (Harvard University Press, Cambridge, MA).

Scott, Peter (2009). Mr. Drage, Mr. Everyman, and the Creation of a Mass Market for Domestic Furniture in Interwar Britain, *Economic History Review 62(4)*, 802–827.

Shanahan, Martin (1995). The Distribution of Personal Wealth in South Australia, 1905–1915, *Australian Economic History Review 35(2)*, 82–111.

Shaw, Edward (1973). *Financial Deepening in Economic Development* (Oxford University Press, New York).

Shleifer, Andrei, and Daniel Treisman (2000). *Without a Map: Political Tactics and Economic Reform in Russia* (MIT Press, Cambridge MA).

Shonfield, Andrew (1965). *Modern Capitalism: The Changing Balance of Public and Private Power* (Oxford University Press, Oxford).

Sims, Christopher, and Tao Zha (2006). Were There Regime Switches in US Monetary Policy? *American Economic Review 96(1)*, 54–81.

Singh, Manmohan (1964). *India's Export Trends and Prospects for Self-Sustained Growth* (Clarendon Press, Oxford).

Sinn, Hans-Werner, and Frank Westermann (2001). Two Mezzogiornos, *NBER Working Paper 8125* (National Bureau of Economic Research, Cambridge, MA).

Smith, Adam (1776). *An Inquiry into the Nature and Causes of the Wealth of Nations* (Strahan and Cadell, London).

Solow, Robert (1956). A Contribution to the Theory of Economic Growth, *Quarterly Journal of Economics 65*, 65–94.

Stiglitz, Joseph (1994). The Role of the State in Financial Markets. In *World Bank Annual Bank Conference on Development Economics 1993*, ed. Michael Bruno and Boris Pleskovic, 19–52.

Stock, J., and M. Watson (2003). Has the Business Cycle Changed and Why? *NBER Macroeconomics Annual 2002 (17)*, 159–218.

Taleb, Nassim Nicholas (2007). *The Black Swan: The Impact of the Highly Improbable* (Random House, New York).

Temin, Peter (1989). *Lessons from the Great Depression* (MIT Press, Cambridge MA).

Temin, Peter (2002). The Golden Age of European Growth Reconsidered, *European Review of Economic History 6*, 3–22.

Temin, Peter, and Barrie Wigmore (1990). The End of One Big Deflation, *Explorations in Economic History 27(4)*, 483–502.

Timmins, Nicholas (1996). *The Five Giants: A Biography of the Welfare State* (HarperCollins, London).

Tooze, Adam (2006). *The Wages of Destruction: The Making and Breaking of the Nazi Economy* (Allen Lane, London).

von Hayek, Friedrich (1931). *Prices and Production* (George Routledge and Sons, London).

von Hayek, Friedrich (1937). Economics and Knowledge, *Economica 4*, 33–54.

Wade, Robert (1990). *Governing the Market: Economic Theory and the Role of Government in East Asian Industrialization* (Princeton University Press, Princeton, NJ).

Wall, Richard, and Jay Winter, eds. (1988). *The Upheaval of War: Family, Work, and Welfare in Europe, 1914–1918* (Cambridge University Press, Cambridge, UK).

Wheatcroft, Stephen, and R. W. Davies (1994). Population. In *The Economic Transformation of the Soviet Union, 1913–1945*, ed. R. W. Davies, M. Harrison, and S. Wheatcroft (Cambridge University Press, Cambridge, UK), 57–80.

Williams, Eric (1944). *Capitalism and Slavery* (University of North Carolina Press, Chapel Hill, NC).

Williamson, Jeffrey (1995). The Evolution of Global Labor Markets since 1830: Background Evidence and Hypotheses, *Explorations in Economic History 32*, 141–196.

Williamson, Jeffrey (2006). *Globalization and the Poor Periphery before 1950* (MIT Press, Cambridge, MA).

Williamson, Oliver, and Scott Masten, eds. (1995). *Transaction Cost Economics*, vol. 2 (Edward Elgar, Brookfield, VT).

Woodford, Michael (2009). Convergence in Macroeconomics: Elements of the New Synthesis, *American Economic Journal: Macroeconomics 1(1)*, 267–279.

World Bank (1981). *Accelerated Development in Sub-Saharan Africa* (also known as the Berg Report) (Oxford University Press, New York).

World Bank (1993). *The East Asian Miracle* (Oxford University Press, New York).

World Bank (2002). *Transition: The First Ten Years* (World Bank, Washington, DC).

Young, Allyn (1928). Increasing Returns and Economic Progress, *The Economic Journal 38*, 527–542.

Young, Alwyn (1994). Lessons from the East Asian NICs: A Contrarian View, *European Economic Review 38*, 964–973.

Young, Alwyn (1995). The Tyranny of Numbers: Confronting the Statistical Realities of the East Asian Growth Experience, *Quarterly Journal of Economics 110*, 641–679.

Zagorsky, Jay (1998). Was Depression Era Unemployment Really Less in Canada Than the U.S.? *Economics Letters 61(1)*, 125–131.

Index